The Structure of Evidential Categories in Wanka Quechua

Summer Institute of Linguistics and
The University of Texas at Arlington
Publications in Linguistics

Publication 131

Publications in Linguistics is a series published jointly by the Summer Institute of Linguistics and the University of Texas at Arlington. The series is a venue for works covering a broad range of topics in linguistics, especially the analytical treatment of minority languages from all parts of the world. While most volumes are authored by members of the Institute, suitable works by others will also form part of the series.

Series Editor

Mildred L. Larson
Summer Institute of Linguistics

Volume Editor

Bonnie Brown

Production Staff

Bonnie Brown, Managing Editor
Laurie Nelson, Production Manager
Karoline Fisher, Compositor
Hazel Shorey, Graphic Artist

The Structure of Evidential Categories in Wanka Quechua

Rick Floyd

A Publication of
The Summer Institute of Linguistics
and
The University of Texas at Arlington

©1999 by the Summer Institute of Linguistics, Inc.
Library of Congress Catalog No: 99-60306
ISBN: 1-55671-066-6
ISSN: 1040-0850

Printed in the United States of America
All Rights Reserved

08 07 06 05 04 03 02 01 00 99   10 9 8 7 6 5 4 3 2 1

No part of this publication may be reproduced, stored in a retrieval system, or transmitted in any form or by any means—electronic, mechanical, photocopy, recording, or otherwise—without the express permission of the Summer Institute of Linguistics, with the exception of brief excerpts in journal articles or reviews.

Copies of this and other publications of the Summer Institute of Linguistics may be obtained from the International Academic Bookstore

Summer Institute of Linguistics
7500 W. Camp Wisdom Rd.
Dallas, TX 75236-5699

Voice: 972-708-7404
Fax: 972-708-7433
Email: academic_books@sil.org
Internet: http://www.sil.org

Contents

Abbreviations ix

1 Introduction 1
   1.1 Organization. 2
   1.2 A general perspective on evidentiality 3
      1.2.1 The data base. 6
      1.2.2 Introduction to the Wanka Quechua language. 8

2 Toward a Definition of Evidentiality. 13
   2.1 Introduction 13
   2.2 Evidentiality: core notions 14
      2.2.1 Information source distinctions. 16
      2.2.2 Validation. 21
   2.3 Some formal issues 27
      2.3.1 Evidentiality and grammaticalization. 27
      2.3.2 Grammatical aspects of the Wanka Quechua
           evidential system 30
      2.3.3 Interaction of evidentials with other grammatical
           systems 35
   2.4 Diachronic development of evidentials 37
   2.5 Summary. 39

3 Theory, Deixis, and Evidentiality 41
   3.1 Theoretical assumptions 41
      3.1.1 Domains, base, and profile. 42
      3.1.2 Category structure and categorizing relationships. . 43

    3.1.3 Construal. 45
    3.1.4 The subjectivity-objectivity distinction 46
3.2 Deixis 47
3.3 The prototypical relationships between speaker
    and proposition 52
    3.3.1 The direct evidential prototype. 52
    3.3.2 The reportative prototype 53
    3.3.3 The conjecture prototype 54

4 -m(i): Direct Evidence and Commitment 57
4.1 Introduction 57
4.2 Previous descriptions of the Quechua direct evidential
    versus schemas and prototypes. 58
4.3 An overview of the semantic network for -m(i). 60
4.4 The direct evidential prototype. 60
    4.4.1 External versus internal experience 61
    4.4.2 Certainty. 67
4.5 Certainty without direct evidence. 68
    4.5.1 Control and certainty: first person future 75
    4.5.2 Directives and second person past/present. 78
    4.5.3 The subjectification of control and second
        person future. 81
    4.5.4 Review. 84
4.6 The direct evidential in Wanka questions 85
    4.6.1 WH questions. 85
    4.6.2 Yes/no questions 89
4.7 Summary 92

5 -chr(a): Inference and Attenuation. 93
5.1 Introduction 93
5.2 Conjecture markers in Quechuan languages 94
5.3 -chr(a)'s range of meanings 95
5.4 The inferencing process 96
5.5 Inference versus speculation. 100
5.6 Likelihood. 101
5.7 Discussion of examples 104
5.8 Nonprototypical uses 106
    5.8.1 Mild exhortation. 106
    5.8.2 Acquiescence 108
    5.8.3 Interrogative -chr(a) 111
    5.8.4 Irony 114
    5.8.5 First person inferences 118

Contents

    5.9 Summary 122
6 *-sh(i)*: Hearsay and Revelation 123
    6.1 Introduction 123
    6.2 Reportatives in the literature 124
    6.3 Uses of *-sh(i)* 126
        6.3.1 Hearsay 127
        6.3.2 Folktales, myths, and legends 133
        6.3.3 Riddles 141
        6.3.4 Mirativity 143
    6.4 The relevance of validation 152
    6.5 Summary 158
7 On Directness, Proximity, Ground Domains, and Evidentials . . 161
    7.1 Introduction 161
    7.2 Directness 162
    7.3 Proximity 164
    7.4 Ground domains 168
    7.5 Subdomain proximity 172
        7.5.1 Reality/irreality and proximity 173
        7.5.2 Space and proximity 174
        7.5.3 Time and proximity 175
        7.5.4 Participants and proximity 178
    7.6 Evidentiality, directness, and proximity 181
    7.7 Conceptual proximity and subdomain alignment 188
    7.8 Areas for further study 193
    7.9 Conclusion 193
References 195

Abbreviations

1	first person subject	ABL	ablative
1>2	first person subject, second, person object	ACC	accusative
		AFAR	translocative (at a distance)
1>2FUT	first subject, second object, future	AG	agentive
12	first person inclusive	ASP	aspect
12FUT	first person inclusive, future	ATTRIB	attributive
		BCM	become
12P	first inclusive, possessive	BEN	benefactive
		CAUS	causative
12POT	first inclusive, potential	COM	comitative
12PURP	first inclusive, purpose	CONJ	conjecture
1FUT	first person future	DEF	definite
1OBJ	first person object	DIR	direct
1P	first person possessor	DUB	dubitative
2	second person subject	DS	different subject
2OBJ	second person object	EMPH	emphatic
2P	second person possessive	EXCL	exclamation
		FPI	first person inference
3	third person subject	FURTH	furthermore
3>2	third person subject, second person object	GEN	genitive
		GOAL	goal
3FUT	third person future	HAVE	having
3P	third person possessor	HSY	hearsay

ix

HYP?	hypothetical question	POL	polite
IMP	imperative	POT	potential
IMPV	imperfective	PROP	propensity
INDEF	indefinite	PST	simple past
INF	infinitive	PSV	passive
ITER	iterative	PURP	purposive
KJV	King James Version	REF	reflexive
LIM	limitative (just)	REP	reportative
LOC	locative	RPST	recent past
NEG	negative	RQ	rhetorical question
NOM	nominalizer	SIM	similarity
NPST	narrative past	SS	same subject
PART	participle	TOP	topic
PARTIC	particle	VOC	vocative
PL	plural	VRB	verbalizer
PLIMPV	plural imperfective	Y/N?	yes/no question
PMOT	purpose motion		

1
Introduction

> *I know you believe you understand what you*
> *think I said, but I am not sure that you realize*
> *that what you heard is not what I meant.*
> -anonymous

This study concerns how speakers of the Wanka dialect of Quechua encode the source and reliability of their knowledge. Descriptions of evidential systems—particularly in Quechuan languages—have tended to focus on information source and speaker commitment concepts, to the neglect of interesting and theoretically significant extended meanings that shed light on the nature of linguistic category structure.

Based on a corpus of conversations, the analysis of the Wanka Quechua evidential system is couched in terms of a cognitive view of grammar (Langacker 1987a, 1991 in particular). I will show that the unity as well as the diversity among the uses of the three evidential suffixes can be explained in terms of principles of cognition and categorization that find their roots primarily in the work of Wittgenstein (1953) and have been subsequently elaborated by Zadeh (1965), Berlin and Kay (1969), Rosch (1978), Lakoff (1987) and Langacker (1987a, 1991) *inter alia.*

Evidentials are polysemous in nature and are analyzed as complex network categories. Each evidential has a prototypical meaning that is characterized primarily in terms of information source notions. The prototype provides the principal basis for extended meanings, which may have nothing to do with information source per se and which may, in turn, motivate other extended senses. In addition, each evidential has an abstract schematic meaning that can be characterized in terms of some aspect of epistemic modality. The schemas for two of the evidentials concern the degree of commitment that the speaker has towards the proposition marked by the evidential, whereas the schema for the third concerns the proposition's "mirative" status, i.e. the potential for surprise attached to a proposition originating from beyond the bounds of the speaker's knowledge structure.

The investigation of this relatively unexplored domain of linguistic structure is partially motivated from the observation that evidentials in Wanka exhibit obvious co-occurrence tendencies with person and tense marking. Based on the assumption that conceptualization motivates and affects linguistic structure, I explore this phenomenon in the latter part of the book.

My principal aim is to provide a unified account of the Wanka Quechua evidential system within a conceptualist approach to grammatical structure. More broadly, I hope to refine and expand our general understanding of what evidentiality entails and to broaden the range of grammatical categories for which an appeal to cognitive principles may provide an insightful analysis.

1.1 Organization

The study is organized as follows. In the remainder of this chapter I provide a general overview to the topic of evidential study, followed by some comments on the nature of the data that was used as well as a brief introduction to the structure of the Wanka Quechua language.

After outlining the broad cross-linguistic context for evidential study in this chapter, in chapter 2 I consider in a bit more detail the core notions which have been associated with the study of evidentiality. Information source encoding and the speaker's degree of commitment to a proposition are the two elements typically identified as central to the characterization of evidentiality. But other aspects of epistemic modality may be involved as well. I will adopt a view of evidentiality in which information source notions are associated with prototypes and epistemic modal meanings with schemas.

Deixis and the deictic nature of evidentials are the main topics of chapter 3. Evidentials are shown to be a particular kind of deictic expression, viz., grounding predications which are characterized by a radical kind of "subjectivity."

Introduction

The core of the analysis is found in chapters 4, 5, and 6 which deal with the direct, conjecture, and reportative evidentials respectively. Each evidential has a network category structure organized around prototypical meanings which concern information source notions. Extensions are motivated on the basis of some facet of the prototype or from another extended meaning. A type of subjectification is suggested as a contributing factor in the extension of category boundaries. The schematic values for each evidential pertain to the domain of epistemic modality.

Chapter 7 once again takes a pan-systemic perspective and draws together a number of threads woven throughout the fabric of the preceding chapters. Here I discuss abstract directness and proximity, and how these concepts serve as organizing principles for our conceptualization of the evidential system as a whole and for the domains to which deictic elements typically refer. It is suggested that abstract proximity motivates the co-occurrence tendencies between evidentials and markers for specific "ground domains." I conclude chapter 7, noting areas which have surfaced in the course of the investigation which merit further research.

1.2 A general perspective on evidentiality

Evidentiality, particularly as it concerns the grammatical marking of information source, has come to be recognized as a linguistic category only in this century. Early (pre-twentieth century) grammatical descriptions show that what we now know to be the marking of information source distinctions was often not recognized as such. For example, Ludovico Bertonio (1603:326, [cited in Hardman 1986]) considered the data source markers of Aymara to be merely "ornate particles" since "without them the sentence is perfectly fine." Likewise, for Torres Rubio (1619:244 [cited in Hardman 1986:113]), they were particles "which serve no other function than to adorn the sentence." In his work on Wanka Quechua, Ráez (1917) described the suffix -mi as a substitute for the copula in the present indicative tense (1917:64f.). The function of these affixes as indicators of the source of the speaker's knowledge went unnoticed.

In the linguistic tradition of the day there was a tendency to assume that the categories found in Indo-European languages were to be discovered in every language (cf. Boas 1911:35). Since the classical Indo-European languages did not mark information source by means of grammatical devices, it is not entirely surprising that the phenomenon would escape the notice of these early analysts.

In contrast, Boas chose to describe the languages and cultures of North America in their own terms (cf. Haas 1976), not with a predetermined idea of what the relevant categories should be. Certain categories so fundamental to expression in classical Indo-European languages like gender and case did not seem to be necessarily crucial for Amerindian languages, whereas other categories irrelevant for Indo-European languages were obligatorily invoked. Of particular relevance to the present study was Boas' observation for Kwakiutl that unless a speaker was an eyewitness to some event, he had to specify the basis for his statement, i.e., whether his knowledge was based on hearsay, a dream, or some other kind of evidence (1911:43).

Grammaticalized indicators of information source were likewise observed in other Amerindian languages. References to markers specifying "source of information," "source or nature of speaker's knowledge," and "modes of evidence" appear in numerous grammatical descriptions from the first half of this century (cf. Goddard 1911:124; Sapir 1922:157-9; Swadesh 1939:82; Haas 1941:117f. *inter alia*).

The term "evidential" appears in Swadesh (1939) and in Boas (1947), but it refers specifically to only one kind of information source, that of "inference," and not to information source marking in general. With Jakobson's work on Slavic (1971 [1957]) came two important contributions: he introduced the term as a tentative label for a grammatical category distinguished from mood that concerned the marking of information source in general, and he also suggested that the category existed in Bulgarian, introducing the notion that grammaticalized information source marking might be a relevant concept for the description of languages outside the Americas. Since then, the term "evidential" has been applied to a broad range of syntactic and semantic structures.

The grammatical marking of information source is certainly more widespread than was once believed. Information source distinctions seem to be quite a prevalent feature of the languages throughout North America. In his areal survey of languages north of Mexico, Sherzer (1976) lists grammaticalized information source markers as a characteristic of Wakashan, Salishan, Siouan, Nadene, Athabaskan, Chemakuan, Uto-Aztecan, Algonquian, Hokan, and Penutian language families.

Unfortunately, no survey comparable to Sherzer's exists that covers the rest of the Americas.[1] Even so, a cursory survey of individual grammars shows that languages with "hearsay" particles or "quotatives" are ubiquitous, e.g., Cora (Uto-Aztecan [Mexico], Casad 1992); Otomí

---

[1] Granted, this would be a formidable undertaking; Derbyshire and Pullum (1986, 1990) do, however, provide much information for languages covering an extensive area from a wide variety of families in South America.

Introduction

(Otomanguean [Mexico], Hess 1968); Tzotil (Mayan [Mexico], Cowan 1969, Haviland 1987); Urubu-Kaapor (Tupí-Guaraní [Brazil], Kakumasu 1986); Sanuma (Yanomami [Venezuela, Brazil], Borgman 1990); Apalai (Carib [Brazil], Koehn and Koehn 1986); Hixkaryana (Carib [Brazil], Derbyshire 1979); Pirahã (Mura [Brazil], Everett 1986); Guaraní (Tupí-Guaraní [Paraguay], Gregores and Suárez 1967); Bora (Huitotoan [Peru], Wes Thiessen, p.c.); and Piro (Preandine Arawakan [Peru], Matteson 1965 and Wise 1986).

Languages having only one marker of data source exhibit some kind of "minimal" evidential system. A more complex system differentiating three kinds of evidence is found in Quechuan languages (cf. Levinsohn 1975; Jake and Chuquin 1979; Weber 1986 *inter alia*), as well as in Aymara and Jaqaru (Jaqi [Bolivia and Peru], Hardman 1986).

Evidential systems of still greater complexity are found in Tuyuca (Tucanoan [Colombia], Barnes 1984); Kogi (Chibchan [Colombia], Hensarling 1982); Nambiquara (unclassified [Brazil], Lowe 1972); and Jamamadí (Arauan Arawakan [Brazil], cf. Derbyshire 1986). These may distinguish different subtypes of direct, reported, and inferred evidence. Along with information source, the markers in some cases may also signal tense, aspect, person, and even gender distinctions.

Outside the Americas, evidential systems with different characters and varying degrees of complexity have been reported in Basque (Jacobsen 1986:7fn); Turkish (Slobin and Aksu 1982); Sissala (Voltaic [Burkina Faso], Blass 1990); several Philippine languages (Ballard 1974); Warlpiri (Haviland 1987, Laughren 1981); Tibetan (DeLancey 1986); Akha (Thurgood 1986); Korean (H. Lee 1985); and Japanese (Akatsuka 1985; Aoki 1986; Inoue 1978; Kuroda 1973; Shinzato 1991) to name just a few. Some of these works elaborate the nature and origins of the particular system with a fair amount of detail, while in others there is insufficient investigation to provide more than a superficial characterization of the system. The irregularity of descriptive depth makes cross-linguistic studies of the phenomenon difficult. In comparison to the large number of analysts that report evidential distinctions in individual languages, those undertaking a general investigation among typologically diverse languages are markedly few in number. To my knowledge, only Anderson (1986) and Willett (1988) have attempted to approach the topic from a more global perspective. But in spite of the difficulty, the contributions provided by Anderson's "evidential space" mappings and Willett's "evidential typology" are highly valuable and much welcomed to this area of study which still finds itself in relative infancy.

1.2.1 The data base. The analysis presented here is based on studies of conversational discourse in the Wanka dialect of Quechua, collected on two extended stays in Peru between 1981 and 1986 and between 1989 and 1991 under the auspices of the Summer Institute of Linguistics and the Peruvian Ministry of Education.

Following Levinson (1983), I consider conversation to be prototypical language use. It is the form of language to which we are first exposed —"the matrix for language acquisition." As Longacre has stated:

> We must not understimate the importance of dialogue to the structure of language...we must view dialogue as a basic function of language: viz., conversational interchange between people, communication. Seen from this point of view it is monologue that is the special development. Prolonged self expression in which one person speaks to a group of people who take the passive role of hearers is clearly a secondary development. (1976:165)

In addition to its prototypical status, conversation provides a kind of analytical "self-check." According to Levinson:

> Conversation, as opposed to monologue, offers the analyst an invaluable analytical resource: as each turn is responded to by a second, we find displayed in that second an analysis of the first by its recipient...A good case can therefore be made for the methodological priority of the study of conversation over the study of other kinds of talk or other kinds of text. (1983:321)

Levinson points out the relevance of conversation to our understanding of deictic domains when he states that the "unmarked usages of grammatical encodings of temporal, spatial, social and discourse parameters are organized around an assumption of co-present conversational participants" (1983:284). This has obvious import for the study of evidentiality, whose deictic nature will be discussed in chapter 3.

Normal speech, then, assumes a listener. From the point of view of the speaker, the indication of an information source or his degree of commitment to a proposition makes sense primarily in a conversational context. Any study of evidentiality must therefore assume the potential for an interactive dynamic between speaker and addressee.

For Stubbs, one of the issues central to linguistic investigation is "How do speakers show that they understand one another?" (1983:30). Haviland (1987) observes that markers of evidence and validation serve to convince and persuade the interlocutor of the speaker's point of view,

Introduction

and therefore aid in the goal of achieving a "one mind" status with the interlocutor. I agree, and maintain that evidentials are part of the speaker's inventory of devices that are brought to bear precisely in his attempt to provide an interlocutor who cannot know his mind fully with a bridge to mutual comprehension.

Although my data base consists primarily of conversational material, the purpose behind the study is not directed toward the discovery of principles that govern the structure of conversation per se, such as is commonly associated with conversation analysis (cf. Taylor and Cameron 1987). My intent is rather to examine evidentials in their most naturally-occurring context of face-to-face conversational interaction.

The study is based primarily on a corpus of spontaneous conversations which qualifies them as "unplanned discourse" (cf. Ochs 1979). In some instances, I have incorporated nonspontaneous or "planned discourse"—evidentially-marked structures were elicited and contrasted with the naturally-occurring forms in the same conversational contexts. In many cases this provided information regarding certain subtle semantic nuances associated with an evidential form that did not otherwise emerge with any degree of salience elsewhere in the conversational corpus. In addition, I have found it necessary to augment the data base with examples from nonconversational genres, such as folktales or riddles, in order to address the full range of uses of a particular evidential. All told I considered a total of 1,344 utterances coming mostly from the following conversational texts:

ABSENT: A man and his wife argue over his unexplained disappearance for several days.
CHULIK: A woman accuses a man of fathering her child.
DREAMS: Two people relate frightening dreams they have had.
KID: Parents discuss the fact that their child has reportedly been asking for money from one of the neighbors.
KUCHI: A woman complains to her neighbor about his pigs who have just destroyed her potato field.
LIMA: Two people discuss their personal experiences in the capital city of Lima.
MUSEUM: A man tells his wife about his recent visit to a museum.
PREWED: A man and woman discuss preparations for their upcoming wedding.
RETURN: Two people speculate about what villagers might say when they return home from a trip to a town far away.
SCHOOL: A father tries to convince his daughter to go to school. She resists and explains why.

SUWA 1 and SUWA 2: Two texts where one individual accuses another of stealing.
THOUGHTS: A man questions his in-laws concerning their thoughts about their children leaving on long trip.

1.2.2 Introduction to the Wanka Quechua language. Before moving on, it is convenient at this point to offer a brief introduction to the general nature and structure of the Wanka Quechua language. Wanka Quechua (or Huanca Quechua) is spoken by some 250,000 people in and around the city of Huancayo in the central Andean highlands of Peru. In Parker's (1963) classification it is one of many central Peruvian dialects collectively known as Quechua B, as Quechua I (Torero 1964), or as Central Peruvian in Landerman's (1991) classification. It has been the focus of numerous studies, particularly by Cerrón-Palomino (1973, 1975, 1976a, 1976b, 1977). Unless otherwise stated the data utilized in this study are representative of the Wanka dialect as it is spoken in the district of Cullhuas, in the Department of Junín.

The phonemes of Wanka Quechua are given in figures (1) and (2). Phonemes in parentheses are from loans.

(1) Consonant phonemes of Wanka Quechua

	labial	alveolar	palatal	retroflexed	velar	glottal
occlusives	p (b)	t (d)	tʃ	tʂ	k (g)	ʔ
fricative	(f)	s	ʃ	ʂ		h
nasal	m	n	ñ			
lateral		l	ʎ			
vibrant		R (r)				
semivowel	w		j			

(2) Vowel phonemes of Wanka Quechua

	anterior	central	posterior
high	i i:		u u:
low		a a:	

The orthography used in the present work follows a number of regional orthography resolutions that differ in several respects from the 1975 Orthography Resolution from the Peruvian Ministry of Education, which is

Introduction

used by many of the works cited here. A comparison of the two orthographies shows that they agree in the majority of the representations chosen. For simplicity, I have indicated only where the orthography of the 1975 Resolution differs from that used in this work.

(3) | Phoneme | This work | 1975 Resolution |
| --- | --- | --- |
| /p/ | p | |
| /b/ | b | |
| /t/ | t | |
| /d/ | d | |
| /tʃ/ | ch | |
| /tʂ/ | chr | tr |
| /k/ | k | |
| /g/ | g | |
| /ʔ/ | ' | q |
| /f/ | f | |
| /s/ | s | |
| /ʃ/ | sh | [not recognized] |
| /ʂ/ | shr | sh |
| /h/ | j | h |
| /m/ | m | |
| /n/ | n | |
| /ñ/ | ñ | |
| /l/ | l | |
| /ʎ/ | ll | |
| /r/ | r | |
| /w/ | w | |
| /j/ | y | |
| /i/ | i | |
| /iː/ | ii | |
| /a/ | a | |
| /aː/ | aa | |
| /u/ | u | |
| /uː/ | uu | |

Wanka Quechua has two major lexical classes: verbs (which are classified on the basis of their transitivity) and substantives (including pronouns, quantifiers and a large, open class of noun-adjectives). Wanka, like other Quechuan languages, is an agglutinative, exclusively suffixing language. A rather extreme example of suffixation is given in (4).

(4)   yana-taa-ykachra-yaa-lpa-chi-wshi-lla-k-man
      black-BCM-ITER-IMPV-ASP²-CAUS-aid-LIM-12-POT-

   -laa-tak-chuchr   ka-n-si
   still-FURTH-NEG = CONJ be-3-even
   Furthermore, I don't know that I will still be able to be helping you turn it completely black or not (politely spoken).

Information conveyed by Wanka suffixes includes (but is not limited to) the following:

SUBJECT and OBJECT: *taka-**ma**-**nki*** 'You (will) hit me (present/future)', where -*ma* indicates first person object, and -*nki* second person subject;
TENSE: *taka-maa-**la**-nki* 'You hit me' (past), where -*la* indicates past tense;
ASPECT: *taka-**ykachra**-maa-la-nki* 'You were hitting me repeatedly', where -*ykachra* indicates iteration;
GRAMMATICAL CASE RELATIONS: *wallpa-**p** luntun-**ta**-m mikun* 'he eats hen's eggs', where -*p* indicates genitive case and -*ta* indicates accusative case;
EPISTEMIC MODALITY: *wankayuuchruu-**chra** yachran* 'He probably lives in Huancayo', where -*chra* indicates the speaker's lack of certainty.

Wanka is considered to have a basic SOV word order (cf. Greenberg 1966), but like many SOV languages substantial flexibility in the sequencing of these elements is found. Cerrón-Palomino (1976a:80f.) provides the examples in (5) as equivalents of *The hen ate corn*; (5a) is the unmarked word order, the other variants being due to numerous discourse factors which will not be considered here. (The examples are given in the orthography used in this work.)

(5)   a. *wallpa-ka jala-kta miku-ulu-n*
         hen-DEF   corn-ACC ate-RPST-3

      b. *Wallpaka mikuulun jalakta.*
      c. *Jalakta wallpaka mikuulun.*
      d. *Jalakta mikuulun wallpaka.*

---

²The directional suffixes (-*lku* 'up, -*yku* 'in', and -:*lu* 'out') also have aspectual meanings whose precise senses are still under investigation. Therefore for the present time I have chosen simply to gloss them as ASP without further distinguishing their semantics. In the Wanka dialect, the directional -*lpu* 'down' does not appear to have evolved an aspectual sense.

I reserve discussion of details of the grammar that pertain more directly to the formal apsects of the evidential system for chapter 2.

2
Toward a Definition of Evidentiality

2.1 Introduction

The purpose of this chapter is to examine relevant semantic and structural parameters in order to establish a framework that will adequately accommodate the Wanka evidential system.

I begin in section 2.2 by discussing the semantic notions typically associated with evidentiality. A central concept is the encoding of the information source on which a speaker bases a proposition. After elaborating on the nature of the principal information source distinctions encoded cross-linguistically, I take up the issue of validation, which I will define as the varying degrees of certainty the speaker has toward his knowledge. I then consider the relationship between information source and validation.

While evidential concepts per se can probably be expressed in any language, it is important to consider the kinds of structures that are used to express these notions. I do this in section 2.3 which deals specifically with the grammaticalized status of the evidential encodings, and some of their interactions with other grammatical systems. Ultimately, for the analysis of Wanka Quechua I will be concerned only with evidential notions that are expressed by means of a paradigmatic set of highly grammaticalized markers.

In section 2.4 I will propose that the Wanka evidential system be considered in terms of a model of categorization that relies on notions of both schematicity and prototypicality. Information source notions are found to be particularly relevant with respect to an evidential's prototype, whereas an evidential's schematic characterization is best described in terms of validational concepts.

2.2 Evidentiality: core notions

Anderson 1986 provides a useful characterization of archetypal evidentials in terms of a number of semantic criteria. First of all, an evidential involves a source of evidence interacting with the speaker's cognition.

> Evidentials show the kind of justification for a factual claim which is available to the person making that claim, whether direct evidence plus observation (no inference needed), evidence plus inference, inference (evidence unspecified), reasoned expectation from logic and other facts, and whether the evidence is auditory, or visual, etc. (1986:274)

According to this view, a speaker's claim is supported on the basis of evidence obtained through the various sensory modalities, sight, hearing, or otherwise, or through some other reasoned process of inference which may or may not have its roots in physical evidence.

Furthermore, according to Anderson, the designation of evidence is the primary function of an evidential and cannot be merely the result of pragmatic inferencing (Anderson 1986:274). For example, the fact that I may interpret a statement in the present tense to imply that the speaker was on the scene as an eyewitness does not qualify present tense as evidential marking, since typically the primary function of tense markers is to locate the time of an event with respect to the moment of speech and not to indicate information source notions.

Evidentials function crucially as metacomments on a proposition. "Evidentials are not themselves the main predication of the clause, but are rather a specification added to a factual claim ABOUT SOMETHING ELSE [emphasis in the original]" (Anderson 1986:274).

Anderson (1986:276) provides the English sentences in (6) to illustrate the difference between metacomment and main predication. The capitalized words receive the strongest stress.

(6)   a. [I hear] Mary won the PRIZE.
          b. [I heard] (that) Mary won the PRIZE.
          c. I HEARD that Mary won the prize.
          d. I HEARD she won it, but nobody told me what the prize WAS.
          e. I already HEARD that, you don't need to tell me AGAIN.

In (8a) and (b), *I hear/I heard* function as metacomments on the source of the information contained in the proposition, whereas in (8c–e) *heard* constitutes the main predication itself. (Note that although English has no grammaticalized information source markers, *I hear* in (a) comes close; tense marking has been eliminated even though the information was received in the past. Cf. Thompson and Mulac 1991 on the encoding of epistemics in English.)

As noted above, evidential marking indicates the *justification* for a claim. That is, evidentiality involves not just notions of information source but also what those markings indicate about the speaker's attitudes and beliefs concerning his knowledge. Such attitudes and beliefs belong to the domain of epistemic modality and also have the status of metacomments rather than as main predications. Typically, what is communicated is the speaker's attitude of *reliability* or *certainty* with respect to the information, concepts to which I will refer generally as *validation*.

That evidentiality is concerned at some level with speaker attitudes is generally accepted; what is more difficult is deciding what attitudes should properly fall within the domain of evidential study and which pertain to a broader domain of epistemicity, if indeed such a distinction is even possible to make. For Chafe and Nichols (1986:vii), English sentences in (7b)–(h) are all pertinent to evidential study since in each case the speaker expresses an attitude about the proposition in (7a), *it's raining*.

(7) a. It's raining.
     b. It's probably raining.
     c. Maybe it's raining.
     d. It might be raining.
     e. It must be raining.
     f. It sounds like it's raining.
     g. It's sort of raining.
     h. Actually, it's raining.

Examples (7b)–(e) reflect the speaker's diminished commitment in terms of likelihood judgments. In (7f) and (g) the speaker indicates that the phenomenon in question deviates from what he considers to be a prototypical manifestation of raining. And (7h) reflects the notion that it is raining contrary to the speaker's expectations. Furthermore, the devices used to indicate these attitudes range from adverbs, auxiliary verbs, to larger phrases, etc. The semantics and the devices that are used to convey the semantics must be considered independently. What we will see is that although a particular evidential marker may tap into multiple regions of semantic space, we will not consider all markings associated with those "same semantics" as evidentials. While these epistemic notions in (6) and (7) are certainly relevant to the semantics of evidential study, as hopefully will become more apparent, I do not consider these particular grammatical devices to be "evidentials." Rather, the definition of evidential that I will adopt considers semantics alongside certain formal criteria, namely, the grammatical status of the marker in particular—criteria that will be elaborated in more detail later.

2.2.1 Information source distinctions. The primary information source contrast signalled grammatically in human languages is that of direct versus indirect evidence (Givón 1982; Akatsuka 1985; Bybee 1985a). In his invaluable study on evidentiality, Willett refers to direct evidence as "attested" and subdivides indirect evidence into two kinds: reported and inferred. There are further subdivisions beyond these, yielding the possibilities indicated in (8) below (taken from Willett 1988:57):

(8)   Willett's classification of evidentials

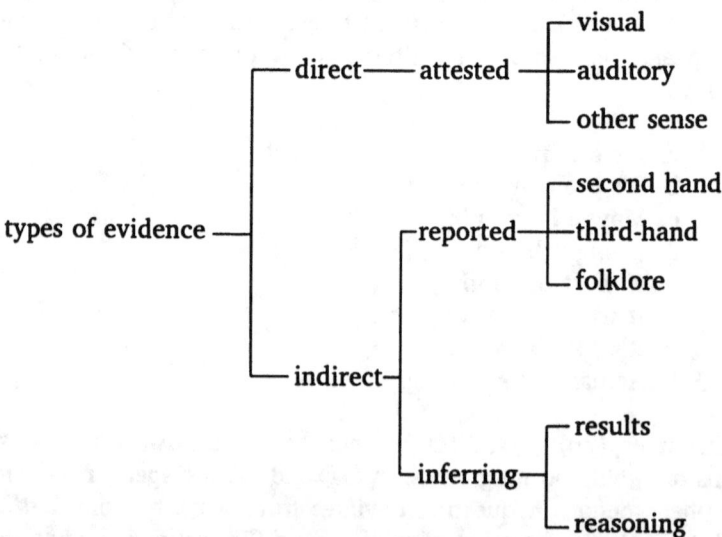

Figure (8) should not be understood to imply that a language will necessarily distinguish all of these possibilities. It is more often the case that a language will make a major distinction, say between direct and indirect, or between attested, reported, and inferring, and simply not bother to further specify the nature of the evidence in that category.

Let us consider the character of the evidential distinctions individually. Direct evidence is that which the speaker directly perceives through his own senses. In the Wanka sentence (9), the suffix -*m(i)* indicates that the speaker was an *eyewitness* of the event she is reporting.

(9) kuchiki-*m*   akshrullaata   lliw chraklantinta kamakaña
     your^pig-DIR my^potato^ACC all its^field^ACC finished^off
     Your pigs completely destroyed my potato field. (I saw it happen.)

Internal states, emotions, etc., also fall into the category of direct evidence. In Japanese, Sherpa, and Jaqaru, for instance, statements about the speaker's happiness, hunger, or other conditions of an intrinsically personal nature are expressed with direct evidential marking. Predictably, in these languages the internal bodily states of someone other than the speaker cannot be marked as direct knowledge, but must be coded instead with some other marker.

Most languages do not distinguish between the various sensory modalities. However, some languages like Tuyuca do make a distinction between visual evidence and evidence obtained through other senses. A marker of direct but nonvisual evidence indicates that the situation was perceived through some other sense besides vision. For example, in such a language, the statement *An ambulance just went by* marked with a nonvisual sensory marker would probably indicate that the speaker has heard a siren, but has not actually witnessed the passing of the ambulance. In other words, the speaker is directly involved in perceiving the actual event encoded by the statement, but not through the sense of vision.[3] The following examples from Barnes (1984:275) illustrate the distinction in Tuyuca, where -*wi* and -*ti* indicate visual and nonvisual direct evidence, respectively.

(10) a. *díiga apé-wi*[4]
        He played soccer. (I saw him play.)

---

[3]Direct auditory evidence is different from reported evidence which does involve an auditory channel but differs in ways which will be discussed. The distinction between direct auditory evidence and an inference based of some kind of evidence can be appreciated by considering the difference between a. An ambulance just went by and b. There's just been an accident. The sentence in (a) pertains much more directly to the auditory perception than does the sentence in (b), which reflects a conclusion based upon evidence.

[4]Barnes does not give morpheme-by-morpheme glosses for her examples.

b. *dīiga apé-ti*
He played soccer. (I heard the game and him, but didn't see the game or him.)

Barnes (1984:259) notes a number of extensions of the basic direct evidential sense. For example, in addition to reporting eyewitness events, Tuyuca uses the direct-visual marker for encoding what she terms "timeless" expressions, i.e., circumstances that are within the realm of the speaker's general experience, illustrated by example (11):

(11) *īsã kõnẽa hĩi-a.*[5]
We call them woodpeckers.[6]

The nonvisual sensory evidential also has extended uses in some languages. In Wintu, in addition to direct auditory evidence, the nonvisual sensory evidential may mark a statement as being based on "any kind of intellectual experience or 'sixth sense'," for talking about the supernatural and for predicting events which are felt to be imminent (Schlichter 1986:47).

Willett notes that there appear to be "implicational orderings of the physical senses" cross-linguistically (1988:59), with visual evidence predictably emerging as prominent. "When only one sensory mode is uniquely specified by an evidential morpheme, it is always the visual sense; and when two sensory modes are uniquely specified by separate morphemes, they are always the visual and auditory senses." The priority of vision is evidenced in Tuyuca where if more than one sensory modality is involved in the perception of some event, one of which is visual, the visual marker will always be used to mark the event. Secondly, Willett finds that if a language distinguishes more than one kind of sensory evidence, visual evidence will have its own unique marker and auditory evidence will be grouped with other senses. No language was found in Willett's study to specify three distinct sensory modes, e.g., vision, hearing, and taste.

Indirect evidence markers indicate that the situation being described is based on something other than the speaker's direct sensory perception. A report from another individual or an inference drawn on the basis of some other kind of evidence are typical of what is usually included in this category.

---

[5]-a is the non-third person present direct visual evidence marker.
[6]It is not clear how knowledge of the kind in example (13) is different from the "assumed knowledge" category which Tuyuca also expresses, which will be discussed.

Reported evidence may be general, indicating simply that the speaker has received his information through the words of another person. For example in Sissala (cf. Blass 1990:99):

(12) nánásuse ba kaa konni yo ta ré
some died they took cut throw leave HSY[7]
Some died and were untied and left there (it is said).

Some languages encode subtypes of reported evidence as well. For example, Cora distinguishes second- and third-hand reports. A second-hand report is one which comes to the speaker from a direct witness of some event; a third-hand report is removed one more step and comes to the speaker from someone who was not a direct witness of the event. Not surprisingly Cora's third-hand report marker is also used to mark folklore or traditional history. Jaqaru, on the other hand, marks both second- and third-hand reports with the same form, but distinguishes these from the marking of folklore. In addition Willett notes that S. E. Tepehuan uses the same marking for second-hand reports and folklore, but that these are distinguished from third-hand reports (Willett 1988:97). None of the languages in Willett's survey distinguished all three kinds of reported evidence.

It should be noted that, in addition to these reportative types, Anderson (1986) adds a fourth, "quotative," i.e., an independent verb form indicating "This is what X said." Anderson considers quotatives to be only marginally evidential. Presumably, this is because independent verbs can be construed as main predications and, therefore, do not fit his characterization of an archetypal evidential.

The other major category of indirect evidence concerns inference, which can be understood as a conclusion the speaker draws on the basis of some kind of evidence. Consider the following examples from Wintu (Schlichter 1986:51):

(13) heke ma:n hara:ki-re:m
somewhere EXCL go-COM^DUB
He must have gone somewhere. (I don't see him.)

(14) hadi winthu:h minelbi-re:m
why person die-IMPV^DUB
Why, a person must have died. (I see or hear someone cry!)

---

[7] I have supplied HSY (hearsay) as the gloss, which Blass lists as only one of the functions of the 'I(nterpretive-use) M(arker).

Note that the statement in (13) is not about "not seeing someone," nor is (14) about "hearing someone crying." The sensory phenomena merely constitute the basis for the speaker's conclusion about something else.

Most languages do not further differentiate inferences as to subtype. In some languages, however, e.g., Wintu (cf. Schlichter 1986) and Tuyuca (cf. Barnes 1984), an inference may be particularly specified as being either based on the observable results of some event, as in the previous examples, or on an intuition, logic, dream, or what Willett refers to as some other "mental construct" of an unspecified nature.

Barnes (1984:262) refers to this second type of inference as "assumed evidence," which concerns "prior knowledge about the state of things or about habitual or general behavior patterns." The following examples illustrate the distinction (annotations in parentheses are those of Barnes):

(15) a. *díiga apé-yi*
He played soccer. (I have seen evidence that he played: his distinctive shoe print on the playing fields. But I did not see him play.)

b. *díiga apé-hĩyi*
He played soccer. (It is reasonable to assume that he did...he usually does in these circumstances.)

An interesting extension within this second subtype of inference occurs in Wintu; Schlichter (1986:53) notes several instances where the suffix normally used to mark an inference based on previous experiences or regular patterns, is used as a kind of "hearsay" marker.

We may consider information source space as being comprised of three major categories, subcategories and then these extended cases where a particular use of one evidential seems to extend into the semantic territory normally encompassed by a distinct marker. What does not seem to occur is direct and reported marked the same with inference marked distinctly. or direct and inference marked the same with reported marked distinctly.

"Information source space," then, can be viewed as being composed of basic "direct," "reported," and "inferred" regions, as indicated in figure (16). What I take to be prototypical for these categories is shown in bold circles, the reasons for which will be elaborated in following chapters.

Toward a Definition of Evidentiality

(16) Information source space

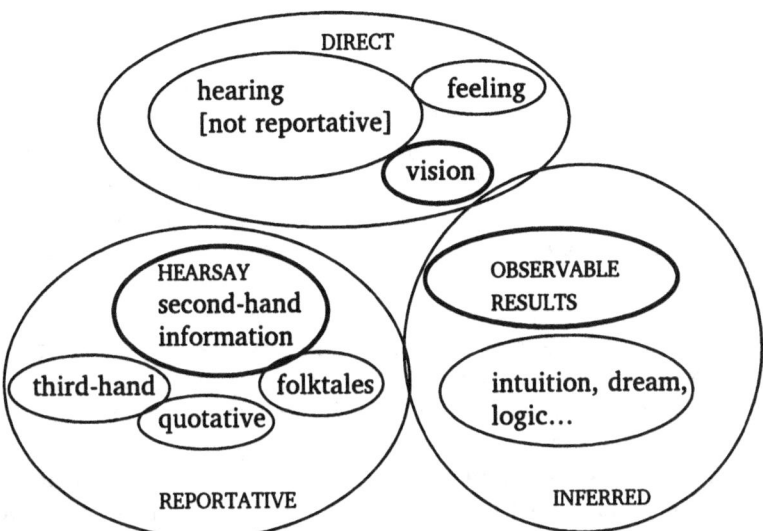

Up to this point I have considered evidentiality solely from the perspective of information source concepts. In the next section I consider the relationship between information source and the concept of validation.

2.2.2 Validation. Validation, or speaker commitment, is the other major core notion generally associated with evidential phenomena. I view validation as a specification of the degree to which a speaker incorporates a proposition into his view of reality. A proposition considered as true, i.e., having factual status, has been accepted by the speaker as comprising part of his personal view of reality. Of course, a speaker does not regard all propositions as being true, and those that are not may differ as to how likely they are to be true. (Validation can thus be viewed as involving some kind of scalarity, which will be explicated more fully below.) Assessments of the truth or factuality of a proposition traditionally fall into the domain of modality.

Even though Willett's study (1988) is concerned mainly with information source distinctions (1988:56), he recognizes the overall modal character of evidential phenomena.

> There is little doubt that evidentiality as a semantic domain is primarily modal. It participates in the expression of the speaker's attitude toward the situation his/her utterance

describes, rather than relating strictly orientational information about the temporal setting of the situation, as do tense and aspect... (Willett 1988:52)

It seems appropriate, then, to consider briefly the general nature and scope of modality in order to situate the study of evidentiality in its proper place. According to Palmer (1986:16), "modality could...be defined as the grammaticalization of speakers' (subjective) attitudes and opinions." Notions such as reality, irreality, commitment to truth, probability, possibility, certainty, obligation, and permission among others lie within its purview.

Modality is fairly standardly divided into epistemic and deontic subtypes (cf. Bybee 1985a). Deontic modality specifies conditions of obligation and permission specifically on the grammatical subject; the scope of a deontic modal is therefore limited to that subject. Epistemic modality, on the other hand, indicates the degree of personal commitment the speaker has to the truth of the proposition as a whole, and consequently functions as a metacomment on the status of the speaker's knowledge. Thus, the scope of an epistemic modal is over the entire proposition, not just the subject.[8] Examples are given in (17a) and (b).

(17) a. [Deontic]
Erik must leave as soon as possible.
[His life depends on it.]
b. [Epistemic]
Erik must have already left.
[His car is gone.]

In (17a) deontic *must* points to an obligation placed on the grammatical subject *Erik* by some unspecified set of circumstances, whereas in (17b) epistemic *must* reflects a strong degree of commitment that *the speaker* has with respect to the proposition *Erik has already left*. It should be noted, however, that *must* endows the proposition with a different status from that of the assertion: although the speaker may be fairly certain of the conclusion he has drawn, he does not consider it to have fully factual status.

---

[8]There is a parallel between the sentential scope of epistemic modality and the "sentential" nature of the evidential suffixes, in that, in Wanka at least, the latter are not specifically verbal morphology—they may attach to other lexical classes as well—whereas markers of deontic modality are typically associated with verbal morphology. Sentential scope is also related to the notion developed in chapter 3, where I will characterize the Wanka evidentials as grounding predications that schematically designate a proposition.

Chung and Timberlake (1985) make a further distinction between epistemic and "epistemological" modalities. In their view, epistemic modality is concerned with the actuality of an event from the perspective of actual or possible worlds. This is not exactly the same view of epistemic modality already presented, since for Chung and Timberlake sentential modality is judged in terms of "objective truth" and not on the basis of "speaker opinion" which is subjective. (See Givón 1982 for a critique of this view.) The point, however, is that their 'epistemological' category involves a "source" which encodes whether or not the event is "experiential," "inferential," "quotative," or based on "thought, belief, or fantasy." Their epistemological category thus correlates most closely with information source marking.

Palmer includes evidentials—specifically information source marking—within the domain of epistemic modality on the grounds that they indicate "the status of the speaker's knowledge or understanding" (Palmer 1986:51). Within epistemic modality also falls what he refers to as "judgments." In his view, by qualifying a statement as a judgment, a speaker indicates how committed he is to what he is saying vis-à-vis a scale of commitment values ranging from strong to weak. A strong epistemic judgment—"the only possible judgment" (Palmer 1986:62)—is associated with inferences or deductions that are conclusions drawn from known facts. In English, strong epistemic judgments are indicated by the modal verb *must*, as in example (17b) or *You must be the murderer; you were the last one to see her alive.* Weaker "assumptive" judgments fall in the middle of his scale. Like deductive judgments, these also are based on known fact, but particularly on facts that are considered to be "what is usually the case." These can be characterized as "reasonable judgments" (Palmer 1986:62) and may be expressed in English by the modal *will*, as in *That will be the postman.* At the other end of the scale come "speculative" judgments, which simply present a proposition as a possibility[9] and are indicated in English by *may* as in *He may be there by now.*

---

[9]Palmer goes on to note that epistemic judgments in English can be further qualified or modified by means of either past tense marking (*may* > *might*, *will* > *would*) as well as by "harmonic combinations," such as *I'm sure, certainly,* etc., and hedges which serve to either reinforce or attenuate the modality along the certainty scale. However, it does not appear to me, nor to others I have asked, that this is always the effect of the "harmonic combinations." Consider the difference between:
  a. That's Melanie at the door.
versus
  b. I'm sure that's Melanie at the door.
The second, with the overt "reinforcer" appears to be less certain than the one with no special marking. Sentence (b) calls attention to the possibility of doubt, where this is not an aspect of (a).

Palmer's epistemic judgments comprise a scale such as that given in example (18).

(18) Epistemic judgments

    Strong   deductive (inferred from known fact; the only possible judgment)
    | assumptive (based on the usual case; reasonable judgment)
    Weak   speculative (presented only as a possibility)

A comparison of Willett (1988) and Palmer (1986) points out the ambiguous nature of these inference-type phenomena. While for both authors, epistemic modality encompasses a domain of information source, they differ regarding the status of inferences. Willett considers inferences alongside direct and reported evidence as a kind of information source. For Palmer, the information source domain includes only reports and evidence obtained directly through the senses (Palmer 1986:51). Deductions, i.e., inferences from evidence, fall into the category of judgments.

Palmer's strong-weak commitment values associated with judgments largely correlate with what I refer to as validation. But I do not equate them fully for the following reason. It seems that in Palmer's view judgment concerns levels of noncommitment and pertains primarily to inference-type phenomena, to the exclusion of direct evidence. Validation, as I use the term, also incorporates the level of full commitment that inherently attaches to a proposition based on direct evidence.

Figure (19) depicts a rough picture of what I perceive to be involved in evidential space. Evidentiality in this view involves a relatively clearly-identifiable domain of information source notions, along with an associated range of commitment values.

Toward a Definition of Evidentiality

(19)   Basic evidential space[10]

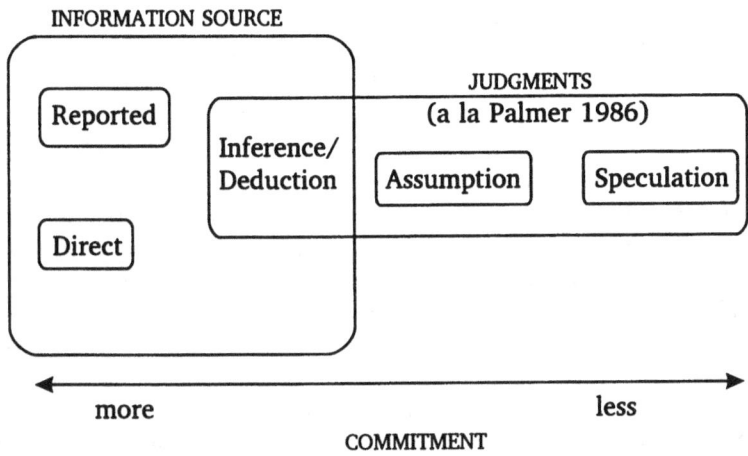

The association of evidence with the speaker's degree of commitment to a proposition's truth is an oft-noted characteristic of evidential systems. Boas (1947) refers to the evidentials in Kwakiutl as a group of suffixes that "expresses source *and certainty* of knowledge" (italics mine). Patwin's information source markers also indicate degrees of reliability (Whistler 1986:69ff.). Payne and Payne (1990:424ff.) note a clitic in Yagua that may be related to the verb for 'say' and indicates 'belief but with lack of certainty' or 'apparently so'. Weber's (1986) discussion of the Huallaga Quechua evidential system shows the same kinds of intimate links between these two semantic domains.

A fairly straightforward relationship between information source and validation typically obtains. According to Givón, certainty judgments are "an inferential by-product of the evidentiary, experiential aspect of knowledge" (1982:25). In other words, one is much more likely to believe what he has seen than what he has heard from others or is simply speculating about. The implication in Givón is that validation follows from evidence. In his analysis of Balkan Slavic, Friedman holds the opposite view and considers information source to be derived from speaker commitment (Friedman 1986:168f.). The point remains that there is a strong connection between validation and information source that is

---

[10]Figure (21) may be taken to imply that reportatives are generally associated with the same level of commitment as is direct evidence. The view I take is that reportatives (at least in Wanka Quechua) are only indirectly associated with validation, but inherently associated with another aspect of epistemic modality: mirativity. The status of reportatives with respect to validation will be taken up in detail in chapter 6.

attested cross-linguistically. In principle, of course, validation and evidence are independent of each other. It is certainly possible, for instance, for someone to see something, but not believe it or accept it strictly on the basis of its appearance. But the prototypical associations—direct evidence with strong commitment and indirect evidence with weak commitment—are what become encoded grammatically in languages.

Validation is certainly a prime example of an epistemic concept. But many languages encode other speaker attitudes with markers that contrast paradigmatically with those for information source and validation, showing that epistemic modality extends beyond mere validation. In Pirahã, for example, particles for 'observation', 'hearsay', and 'deduction'—clearly information source concepts—contrast with others for 'intensive', 'emphatic', and 'frustrated initiation and termination of action' (Everett 1986:297ff.). In Terena, information source and validation suffixes for 'hearsay', 'supposition', and 'certainty' contrast with those meaning 'poor thing', 'as their custom is', 'ineffectual, frustrated', and 'lapse of memory' (Derbyshire 1986:526). In Waurá, the 'hearsay' marker contrasts with others indicating two degrees of certainty, two degrees of uncertainty, as well as with 'urgency, impatience' and 'displeasure' (Derbyshire 1986:526f.). In Apalai particles for 'eyewitness', 'deduction, assumption', and 'speaker's claim to knowledge' contrast with validational particles 'certainty', 'possibly' and 'uncertainty, doubt', as well as with particles for 'impatience', 'polite', 'immediacy', 'irritation', 'pity for person in trouble', and 'emphatic and without regard for the opinion of the recipient of the order' (Koehn and Koehn 1986:117ff.). Finally, Mithun notes that in Cayuga, for example, the particle indicating 'it seems', besides being used to hedge precision and certainty can also serve as a marker of courtesy (Mithun 1986:90f.). Similar relationships are seen in other Northern Iroquoian languages.

The point is this: given the range of epistemic speaker attitudes found in languages it should not be unexpected if a language, like Cayuga, utilizes any one of its limited set of markers for more than one aspect of epistemic modality simultaneously. One marker may be associated with information source and a validational value, whereas another marker may be associated with information source and some other, perhaps nonvalidational, aspect of epistemic modality. This is particularly important for the analysis of the Wanka reportative, which, as I will argue in chapter 6, schematically is essentially nonvalidational, having more to do with the concept of mirativity—surprise (cf. DeLancey 1990).

To recap this section, I consider the main information source notions elaborated in Willett (1988), i.e., perceptually attested, reported, and inferred, as constituting the central core of "evidential space." Information source notions such as these stand out as being clearly and easily compared cross-linguistically. Validation notions bear strong and obvious connections to information source notions but are conceptually independent. Information source and valication markers often contrast with other grammatical markers for a wide range of noninformation source and nonvalidational speaker attitudes such pity, irritation, and politeness; but in some cases, a validation marker may be co-opted to express meanings in this other area of epistemic space. This suggests that a study of the semantics of evidential markers may extend beyond its traditional bounds.

2.3 Some formal issues

In this section I briefly present two issues relating to the formal manifestations of information source/validation notions: the degree to which these markers are grammaticalized, i.e., as indicated by their syntactic independence and their obligatoriness, and their interaction with other grammatical subsystems. I will restrict the term evidential or evidential marker to indicators of information source/validation notions that have grammatical status in a language.

2.3.1 Evidentiality and grammaticalization. Willett notes that most languages do not have a grammatical category of evidential (1988:64). Rather, the marking of the semantic domain of information source/validation is usually spread over various facets of a language's tense/aspect/modality system, as in Tibetan (DeLancey 1986) or Sherpa (Woodbury 1986).

All types of linguistic devices have been described as encoding information source/validation concepts. Grammaticalized information source/validation markers are usually bound up with verbal inflectional morphology (cf. Bybee 1985a) such as the bound verbal affixes in Tuyuca (although Jacobsen [1986:20f.] identifies a nominalizer in Makah as having evidential properties). In addition, Willett (1988:64) points out that due to the universal tendency of languages to prefer suffixes over prefixes (cf. Greenberg 1966), evidentials almost always appear as the former. In the Jaqi languages (Aymara, Jacaru and Kawki), on the other hand, evidentiality is expressed by means of "sentential particles," bound morphemes whose distribution is not restricted to occurrence on verbs, but may occur on any lexical category. This is also the case for Quechuan languages.

And we have already seen that, at the other end of the spectrum, independent lexical items (verbs, adverbs, etc.) and phrasal constructions have been cited as expressing evidential notions for English (Chafe 1986). I summarize these points in figure (20) below.

(20) Evidential devices

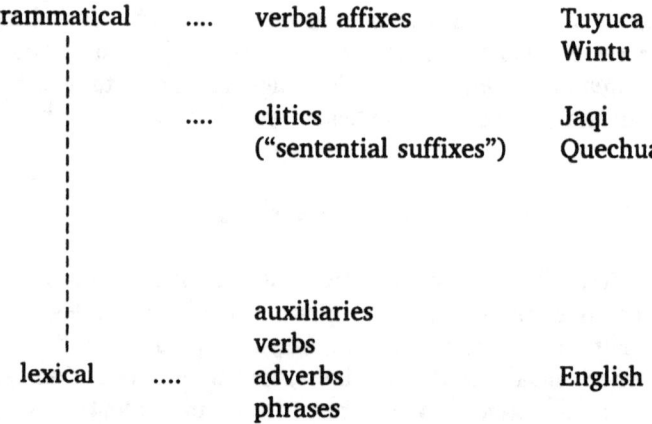

The mere use of a structure to indicate information source or validation concepts does not automatically determine that structure's status as an evidential. A crucial issue for the present study, then, is obviously not whether information source and validation notions can be expressed linguistically—the evidence is that they can—but rather, the grammatical status of the markings.

Whether or not the range of phenomena under consideration is restricted has serious consequences for typological comparison. As Dahl points out:

> Findings from the study of related categories such as tense and aspect suggest that the range of meanings expressed by grammaticalized categories is rather narrow. If this is true also with regard to evidentiality, it is to be expected that the picture will be much more homogeneous cross-linguistically if only grammaticalized evidentials are considered. (1990:684)

This has been the tack of Sherzer; although he states that evidential concepts can probably be encoded in any language, he considers only evidential markers in the verb in identifying a language as one that exhibits evidential contrasts (1976:17, 13). Similarly, Willett (1988:90, footnote 6) restricts the vast range of syntactic phenomena that have been referred to under the rubric "evidential" and considers only grammaticalized markers of information source.

Without considering the issue of grammaticalization, the marking of information sources and validation in a language like English is potentially open-ended. Visual evidentials would include *see, perceive, observe, notice, visualize, behold, note, discern,* and possibly *appear* and *seem.* Add to this nonvisual sensory evidence: *hearing, smelling, tasting,* and *sensing,* and markers indicating inferences, hypotheses, and speculations, in their respective verbal, adverbial, adjectival, and paraphrased forms. In addition to the encodings of information source, any morphological element that qualifies RELIABILITY OF INFORMATION would be a potential candidate for evidential status: *very [sure], almost [certain], really [true], maybe [right],* etc.; the number of evidentials becomes enormous.

English stands in stark contrast to a language like Tuyuca where information source distinctions, limited to five in number, are signalled by means of a paradigmatic, closed class of verbal suffixes, and are not differentiated, for example, for multiple kinds of visual perception. There may be lexical items or other devices in Tuyuca of which the language avails itself to make some of the same kinds of semantic distinctions as those indicated for English; but since they are not grammaticalized, Barnes (1984) does not list them as evidentials.

The grammaticalization issue also affects our understanding of the relationship between validation and evidence. In a language like English the overt use of an evidential phrase may carry semantic nuances that are absent in languages with more grammaticalized systems. Compare the English sentences:

(21) a. My grandmother's father's name was John.
  b. It is said that my grandmother's father's name was John.

Compared to (a), sentence (b) with an explicit reportative phrase connotes a degree of lack of commitment on the part of the speaker that the equivalent sentence in Wanka Quechua would not necessarily have. Dahl observes:

> This nuance...[in the English sentences] is clearly due to a Gricean conversational implicature: the listener assumes that the speaker would not supply the evidential qualifier if there were not a good reason for doing so. But notice that if the use of an evidential marker is obligatory, this implicature is bound to weaken or disappear—the speaker needs no good reason for the use except that the grammar requires it. (1990:685)

In spite of the range of phenomena that have been referred to as "evidential" in one form or another, there is a principled basis for restricting the range of phenomena that should ultimately be considered for this study. Therefore, I will be concerned only with highly grammaticalized structures that communicate information source/validation as metacomments on a proposition.

2.3.2 Grammatical aspects of the Wanka Quechua evidential system. Like other central Peruvian Quechuan languages, Wanka Quechua has a paradigmatic set of three evidential markers: -*m(i)* 'direct evidence', -*sh(i)* 'reported evidence', and -*chr(a)* 'conjecture', illustrated by examples (22)–(25).

(22) ya'a-lla-kta-ña-***m*** suma-a ima-yki-yupay-ta-si
I-LIM-ACC-now-DIR really-TOP what-2P-SIM-ACC-even

jita-yka-a-ma-nki
throw-ASP-ASP-1OBJ-2
You just throw me away like one of your possessions.

(23) marya-si llaki-***sh***-ari ka-ya-n
Mary-also sad-REP-EMPH be-IMPV-3
Mary is sad as well (I hear).

(24) walmi ima-wan-si puli-n-***chra***
woman what-with-INDEF walk-3-CONJ
He's probably running around with some other woman.

Only one evidential is allowed per sentence, unless the sentence embeds a direct quote, in which case the matrix sentence may itself contain an evidential as shown in (25).

(25) chay-***shi*** jampi-ku-u-ka jintil-kaa-***mi*** daaña-shra
then-REP heal-REF-NOM-DEF ANCIENT^ONES-DEF-DIR damage-PART

ni-la
say-PST
Then the healer said, "He's been damaged by the ancient ones."

Unlike many languages where evidential marking is restricted to the verb, Wanka allows evidentials to appear on almost all lexical classes.

There are some restrictions, however. Evidentials do not appear on imperative forms. For example,

(26) *shramu-y*
      come-IMP
      Come!

(27) **shramu-y-mi*

Nor do evidentials appear on certain particles borrowed from Spanish with discourse functions, such as *bwinu* 'well...', *intunsi* 'then', or *piru* 'but', although the conjecture marker *-chr(a)* does appear with *simpri*.[11]

Interestingly, when occurring as single-word responses to a yes/no question, *aw* 'yes' and *mana* 'no' differ in their ability to take evidential marking. The direct evidential may appear only on *mana* (as *manam*), never on *aw* (**awmi*). In this respect Wanka contrasts with several other central Peruvian dialects, e.g., Dos de Mayo, where the direct evidential regularly appears on both.

The syntactic distribution of Quechua evidentials has been discussed by Levinsohn (1975) for the Inga (Colombia) dialect and by Weber (1986) for Huallaga Quechua. In Wanka it is highly complex and entails investigation that is beyond the scope of the present study. There are, however, a number of broad generalizations that can be made in order to provide an overall picture of what is involved.

As modals, the evidentials are sentential in scope, tending to occur preverbally in "second position" (i.e., at the end of the first major syntactic constituent), consistent with cross-linguistic tendencies of modal clitic placement observed by Steele (1973). Consider the following:

(28) *chay-piita-m mancha-shra   lumi-p   jana-n-kuna-kta*
      that-ABL-DIR fear-PART   stone-GEN   top-3-PL-ACC

      pasa-chi-ku-ya-a   jatuchra lumi-p jana-n-kuna-p
      happen-CAUS-REF-IMPV-1   big stone-GEN   top-3-PL-GEN
      Then, scared, I made it go over the rocks, over the tops of the big rocks.

---

[11]Coombs et al. (1976:150) note that simpri does not occur with evidential marking in San Martin Quechua. Apparently, in Wanka simpri has undergone a semantic shift and does not mean 'always', as does its Spanish counterpart, but rather has taken on a more adverbial concessive-like meaning of 'in any case' or 'at any rate', as seen in the following:
  Simpri-chr   iglisya-kuna-chruu-si ni-ma-n'a
  anyway-CONJ church-PL-LOC-ALSO say-1OBJ-3FUT
  The ladies from the church will ask me anyway.

(29) kay walashr-ninchik-**shi** juk bisinu-nchik   eugenio-pi
      this boy-12P-REP   one neighbor-12P eugenio-ABL

   prista-ka-mu-ña   illay-ta
   borrow-REF-AFAR-NPST money-ACC
I hear that our boy borrowed money from one of our neighbors, Eugenio.

(30) paaga-llaa-ma-nki-**chr**
      pay-POL-1OBJ-2-CONJ
      You will pay me.

Evidential positioning is affected, however, by the appearance of other markers such as -'a 'topic' and -pis (or -si) 'also'. Evidentials cannot appear on the same word with any of these markers, so they are consequently "bumped" back to a position later in the sentence:

(31) chay-piita-'a   mas-ta-'a   pin'a-ku-shra-nilaa-tak-**mi**
      that-ABL-TOP   more-ACC-TOP   be^ashamed-REF-PART-SIM-FURTH-DIR

   ka-ya-a
   be-IMPV-1
   Then I'll be more ashamed.

(32) burrachu-ku-yku-l-'a   falsiya-shrunki-man-**si**   ka-n-tak-**chra**
      drunk-REF-ASP-SS-TOP   pick^fight-32-COND-EVEN   be-3-FURTH-CONJ
      If he's drunk he might even pick a fight with you.

In a complex sentence, structure, only one evidential may occur, usually at the end of the subordinate clause, which precedes the main clause:

(33) pero upya-pti-ki-**m** rabya-ku-u ya'a
      but drink-DS-2-DIR   anger-REF-1 I
      But when you drink I get mad.

In cases where there are multiple subordinate clauses (indicated in (34) by the same subject marker -l), the evidential will appear on the last one:

(34) lula-chi-ku-l-pis   mas-ya-tya-l   mas-ya-tya-lku-l-**chra**
      do-CAUS-REF-SS-even   more-BCM-PROP-SS   more-BCM-PROP-ASP-SS-CONJ

Toward a Definition of Evidentiality

    pay-kuna-kta u-yku-u-man
    s/he-PL-ACC give-ASP-1-POT
    Even if I gave them work, I would give them more and more. (Lit.: Even giving them work, increasing it, I would give it to them.)

While the occurrence of the evidential in second position prior to the main verb is a tendency, it is anything but a hard and fast rule. Evidentials are sentential clitics and may appear in other places as well, e.g., the evidential marking follows the subordinate clause in (35), and in (36) and (37) it marking appears postverbally.

(35) *kay-chru ka-pti-n suma-a sumaa-mi ima-nuy-si*
      this-LOC be-DS-3 very-TOP very-DIR what-SIM-INDEF

      ima-kta-si lula-alu-u-man chay ayapa-yki-ta
      what-ACC-INDEF do-ASP-1-POT that man-2P-ACC
      If he's here, who knows what I'll do to your husband. (Lit.: He being here, I might really truly do anyway, anything to your husband.)

(36) *tapa-chi-mu-llaa-shra kiki-n daañiru-ku-u-kaa-ta-chr*
      SOW-CAUS-AFAR-POL-1FUT SELF-3 damage-REF-NOM-DEF-ACC-CONJ
      I'll sow seed right where the damage was.

(37) *ya'a illay-nii-ta mana ancha-p gasta-na-a-pa*
      I money-1-ACC not too^much-GEN spend-NOM-1-PURP

      chrula-a-man banku-u-man-chra parti-kta-a ash-lla
      put-1-POT bank-DEF-GOAL-CONJ part-ACC-TOP bit-LIM

      ash-lla-kta-pis
      bit-LIM-ACC-also
      I might also put a bit of my money in the bank so I wouldn't spend too much of it.

There is some indication that the evidential's position in a complex sentence may actually affect the meaning of a sentence. Consider the following which occurs in the context of an accusation of theft.

(38) *bwinu am-si limataali-pti-ki bwinu pues*
      well you-ALSO contradict-ASP-DS-2P well then

*arregla-shrun chawraa fis-chruu-**chra***
fix-12FUT   then   judge-LOC-CONJ
Well, since you're contradicting [me] like that yourself, well then we'll settle this with the judge.

My language consultant informs me that if the evidential appears at the end of the subordinate clause as it does in (38) (i.e., *limataaaliptiki-chr*), the sentence would indicate that the speaker was threatening to take the addressee to court precisely because of his manner of speaking and not because the speaker thinks he is a thief. More investigation of this phenomenon is needed.

Interaction between particles with discourse functions like those mentioned may be what prompts Levinsohn (1975) and Weber (1986) to explain evidential positioning within a sentence by appealing to notions like theme/rheme (or topic/comment). (See, e.g., Firbas 1971.) Weber (1986:146) views a sentence as "a crescendo of communication-advancing material" which builds on elements that relate old information (i.e., theme) to new information (rheme). In Huallaga Quechua sentences, the topic marker, the evidential, and verb occur in the aforementioned sequence in a relatively predictable pattern and together form an "information profile": "one can tell what parts [of the sentence] are thematic and what parts are rhematic simply from the pattern of -*qa(s)* [the Huallaga topic marker], the evidential, and the verb" (Weber 1986:147).

Weber is careful to state, however, that the evidential does not mark any particular element as being specifically "the first rhematic" or the "last thematic" one. Instead he makes the generalization that in "ordinary" sentences, "the thematic material occurs to the left of the evidential suffix and the rhematic material follows the last preverbal -*qa*" (1986:147). A deviation from the general pattern usually marks a crucial point in a narrative—such as the conclusion of an episode among others—and could therefore be viewed as a rhetorical device. It remains to be seen to what extent these generalizations hold for Wanka; I leave such investigation for future research.

An examination of Wanka conversational texts shows that not all sentences are marked for evidentiality. For example, in one conversation containing approximately 125 sentences, excluding those structures which are never marked for evidentiality (e.g., imperatives), only 66% of those remaining actually appear with an evidential. Zero-marking also tends to occur in clusters. Consider the following excerpt from a text where a man is complaining to his wife about her behavior:

(39) mana taashra-ku-nki-chu
      not   wash^clothes-REF-2-NEG
      You don't wash clothes.

   mana yanu-ku-nki-chu
   not   cook-REF-2-NEG
   You don't cook.

   mana ima-si   lula-nki-chu
   not   what-INDEF do-2-NEG
   You don't do anything.

These sentences unmarked for evidentiality reflect the husband's view of his wife in terms of general characteristics and not specific events. They may be interpreted as the aspects of the way he conceives the structure of the world in general. This is in line with Weber's observations that the Huallaga Quechua direct evidential is not used for " 'non-events', i.e., happenings not somehow embedded in time" (1986:141). It does not appear in "how to make" texts, such as how to make a basket or weave a poncho, nor does it appear in descriptions of static objects or descriptions of cultural practices, etc. Wanka shows the same tendency for generic sentences to be unmarked for evidentiality, even though there are exceptions.[12] This also is an area for further research.

2.3.3 Interaction of evidentials with other grammatical systems.

As has already been mentioned, it is usually the case that evidentials interact with other grammatical systems on a number of levels. The interactions take numerous forms. For example, evidentials may be interwoven with the agreement system. In Jamamadí several of the validation/information source suffixes are marked for gender agreement with either the subject or object of the clause (cf. Derbyshire 1986). Tuyuca evidentials indicate not only information source and person (including gender and number) but also tense.

Interestingly, the interpretation of information source/validation markers may be affected by co-occurrence with other grammatical

---

[12]It is not my intent here to account for zero-evidential marking—much more investigation remains to be done. However, I do believe that its explanation lies in the semantic characterization of evidentials as "grounding predications" (cf. chapter 3) in conjunction with the distinction between "type" and "instance" as developed in Langacker (1991). Grounding predications enable the speech-act participants to establish contact with a conceived situation and relate it to their own knowledge and circumstances (Langacker 1991:90). Crucially, "a grounding predication presupposes that an instance of some entity has been established" (Langacker 1991:58).

elements. In Maricopa, interpretation of an information source/validation marker is partially dependent on grammatical person. Gordon (1986) notes that direct evidence marking is typically redundant with first person subjects—it is uncommon for a speaker not to be present in events in which he is a participant. With first person subjects—then, the direct evidence suffix marks an event as emphatically true (i.e., a validational notion) and sets it unambiguously in the past (Gordon 1986:77). In Sherpa "the morphemes signalling evidential categories are peculiarly skewed: what marks a particular category in one tense takes on a different meaning in another tense; there, a different morpheme expresses the meaning of the first category" (Woodbury 1986:189).[13]

Finally, in Chinese Pidgin Russian, with third person subjects the sole "evidential" marker contributes a meaning of inference (evidence). But with first person subjects of past punctual verbs, what is conveyed is the notion of "immediacy", which Nichols describes as "a spontaneous reaction to a new, salient, often surprising event just as it happens" (1986:248). As mentioned above, surprise is neither an information source nor a validational notion; it pertains to a distinct portion of epistemic modality. Nichols goes on to note that "a generalization holds for a number of languages...something the linguist could call 'perfective' is associated with inferential meaning, and something that could be called 'imperfective' is associated with immediate meaning" (p. 254).

While, in principle, information source and validation are independent of tense and aspect, the facts of the matter show strong co-occurrence tendencies and restrictions: all evidentials do not necessarily occur in all tenses. In Tibetan, for instance, inference is marked only in the perfective system (DeLancey 1986). Barnes notes that the "apparent evidence" marker (i.e., that which indicates an inference drawn indirectly from some kind of physical evidence) is very rare in the present tense and is nonexistent for first person present for clearly conceptual reasons: "A speaker either states what he considers to be facts about himself, which requires the visual evidential, or he reports how he feels, which requires the nonvisual evidential" (Barnes 1984:261). There is no present tense paradigm at all for the second-hand information marker; it is used only for legends and recent reports.

Interactions of the kind Barnes notes for Tuyuca should not be unexpected, and, in fact, are observed for Wanka as well. I will address the co-occurrence tendencies between Wanka evidentials and other grammatical markers, particularly person and tense, in chapter 7, where I suggest possible motivating factors.

---

[13]See Kuroda (1973), Inoue (1978), Akatsuka (1985), Aoki (1986), and Shinzato (1991) in connection with the overlap of evidentials with other areas of Japanese grammar.

2.4 Diachronic development of evidentials

Although this study focuses on the synchronic aspects of Wanka Quechua evidentiality, in the interest of completeness it is worth mentioning a few issues related to the diachronic development of evidential systems. It will be sufficient here to provide a cursory overview of the most frequently observed diachronic sources for the marking of the three major types of evidence—direct, reported, and inferred. I will end with a few speculations about how the three evidential markers may have come to appear in Quechua.

Markers of evidentiality are quite often transparently derived from verbs with particular semantic qualities. Markers of direct evidence frequently arise from verbs of perception, as has been noted for Wintu (Schlichter 1986), Maricopa (Gordon 1986), Makah (Jacobsen 1986), and others. Anderson specifically proposes that "nonvisual sensory evidentials often arise by weakening and generalization of an auditory evidential ['I hear...'], which (always?) [sic] arises from a verb 'to hear'" (1986:286).

Reportative markers can frequently be traced back to verbs of speaking. This again has been evidenced in Makah, as well as in Akha (Thurgood 1986), Aymara (Hardman 1986), and Yagua (Payne and Payne 1990).

Finally, inference markers often develop from perfect constructions, which typically point to past events with present relevance. In Turkish, the development of one of the evidential senses of the past tense morpheme from a perfect gives testimony to this. "The Bulgarian and Macedonian indefinite pasts, and the Chinese Pidgin Russian inflectional auxiliary all come from, and still reflect the meaning of, perfects that developed from auxiliary verbs" (Willett 1988:79).

Other less transparent sources for evidential phenomena have also been noted. For Sherpa, it appears that the direct and indirect evidentials derive from uninflectable linking verbs whose semantic source is not clear (Woodbury 1986:192). In Tibetan the marker for first-hand knowledge of an event which does not involve the speaker as an active participant is etymologically a perfective of the verb meaning "go." Conversely, the first-hand nonvolitional evidence marker derives from a perfective form of a verb meaning "to arrive, appear, come into view" (DeLancey 1986:210f.). Akha has four visual evidential particles, all of which indicate that the event was witnessed first hand, but are distinguished as to tense and whether or not the event is a surprise to the speaker. They descend historically from the first person singular pronoun. Thurgood suggests that the evidential sense most plausibly arose out of the semantics of a construction "I" plus a cognition or perception verb. The "nonvisual expected" evidentials are derived from a concessive particle "although, in spite of," and the "nonvisual nonexpected" evidentials from the verb "be able" (Thurgood 1986:217f.).

The Guaraní reportative *-je* may possibly come from the verb *jeko* 'to lean on' (Maura Velazquez, p.c.). Its development into a marker of information source can be understood in terms of an extension from a concrete domain into an abstract domain. As one may lean on some object for physical support, so one may also "lean" on the report of another as support for a particular claim. Along somewhat similar lines, the marker in Pirahã for visual evidence/strongest certainty comes from a phrase meaning "strong arm" (literally "arm thickness") (Dan Everett, p.c.).

There is no evidence that evidentials in Quechua arose from sources like those described above. Synchronically, the verbs that would be the most likely candidates from a semantic point of view bear no phonological similarity to the present day evidentials in any of the dialects. Consider the following data from the Tarma dialect:

(40) Perception Verbs   Evidentials

rika-   'see'   -mi   'direct'
uyari-   'hear'   -shi   'reportative'
musya-   'feel, sense'   -chri 'inference'

There are, of course, no written records of any dialect of Quechua prior to the Conquest. And cross-dialectal comparative data reveal only miniscule variations in the forms of the evidentials; reconstructed forms hardly differ from their present ones.

According to Landerman (p.c.), an argument can be constructed in favor of Quechua borrowing its evidentials from Aymara to the south.[14] The reportative in Quechuan languages is virtually identical to the Aymara quotative verb *si* 'to say'. This is the form the reportative has in the southern dialects, with the exception that it is phonologically bound. (Cf. Landerman 1979 for a discussion of the phonological changes in sibilants that would make this account plausible.)

With respect to the conjecture marker *-chi*, borrowing again suggests itself. According to Hardman (1986) the suffix *-chim* in Aymara, although not considered one of the main devices for indicating information source, is, however, used to relinquish all responsibility for the contents of a statement, marking the "extreme of nonpersonal knowledge. Not only does the speaker have no direct knowledge, but direct knowledge is, in fact, unobtainable" (Hardman 1986:126). This suffix

---

[14]The possible genetic relationship between Quechua and Aymara has been explored by Orr and Longacre (1968); and Cerrón-Palomino (1987); *inter alia.*

bears roughly the same form as the conjecture marker in the southern Quechua dialects, although there are problems in accounting for a retroflexed affricate in the central dialects. The semantic parallels are obvious and need no elaboration.

Finally, Landerman (1991) has also suggested that the evidential *-mi* might stem from proto-Jaqi **mi* 'go-3d person'. Recall that the Tibetan direct evidential has similar origins.

2.5 Summary

In this chapter I have sketched the semantic space relevant to evidential study in terms of epistemic modality, with information source and validation as central notions. Links between these domains and a domain of other speaker attitudes such as surprise and pity has also been observed.

With respect to their formal manifestations, only markers that are highly grammaticized will be considered as relevant to the present study, i.e., particularly those found in a paradigmatic set of bound morphemes such as affixes and clitics. Furthermore, some measure of interaction of evidentiality with other grammatical systems is expected. Specifically, the co-occurrence of evidential morphemes with other grammatical markers such as tense or person is likely to have bearing on how the evidential markers are interpreted.

3
Theory, Deixis, and Evidentiality

In this chapter I discuss the theoretical assumptions which underlie the discussion of the Wanka evidential system. Crucial to the analysis is the nature of deixis; I maintain that evidentials belong to the class of deictics called GROUNDING PREDICATIONS, the defining feature of which is a kind of "radical subjectivity" (Langacker 1985:116).

3.1 Theoretical assumptions

I assume a nonmodular, cognitive view of grammar as articulated primarily in the works of Langacker (1987a, 1991 *inter alia*) and Lakoff (1987), in which the analysis of grammatical structure is not independent of semantics. In fact, cognitive grammar considers any firm divisions between syntax, semantics and pragmatics to be only arbitrarily determined and ultimately untenable. Although proponents of cognitive approaches to grammar maintain divergent views on many issues, there are certain tenets that characterize them in general. The following points, based principally on Geeraerts (1988b), are particularly germain to the discussion.

1. Lexical concepts have vague boundaries; they contain clearly identifiable conceptual centers surrounded by peripheral areas. This contrasts with the view that categories are discrete, well-defined entities.

2. Lexical concepts are viewed as polysemous clusters of overlapping semantic nuances, in contrast to the view that the various senses of a lexical item can always be strictly separated from each other.
3. There is not necessarily any one set of attributes that defines all the members of a category.
4. Category membership may be based on similarity rather than on the possession of some supposed "essential" attribute.
5. Attributes within (or exemplars of) a category do not all have the same degree of salience. Those attributes which are not shared by all or the majority of the members of a category are less important than those shared by the majority. The more frequent attributes are more salient and are therefore more important definitionally. Similarly, certain members of the category will emerge as being better exemplars because they possess more of the salient attributes.
6. Because lexical concepts can be defined in terms of similarity rather than identity, conceptual categories are extremely flexible. This increases their usage potential and makes for a much more economic system by maximizing the amount of information that can be provided by the least cognitive effort (cf. Geeraerts 1988a:208).
7. Lexical concepts must be studied against the background of human cognition in general. This contrasts with the view that lexical concepts must be studied as part of an autonomous linguistic structure.
8. And finally, a cognitive approach rejects a firm distinction between semantic and encyclopedic knowledge (cf. Haiman 1980). Consequently, semantic studies cannot ignore the experiential and cultural background of the language user.

3.1.1 Domains, base, and profile. Linguistic expressions are categorized relative to COGNITIVE DOMAINS which may involve any level of complexity. Time, space, and emotive domains, for example, are relatively simple or "cognitively irreducible" in some sense (Langacker 1985:110); other domains may be much more elaborate in their structure, e.g., the human body, politics, the rules for a game of chess, etc. It is assumed that multiple domains typically figure into the conventional meaning of a linguistic expression, blurring the distinction between "linguistic" and "nonlinguistic" knowledge.

The set of domains (or portions thereof) that a term invokes is referred to as its SCOPE OF PREDICATION or its BASE. We can think of the base as the context necessary for the characterization of the entity designated by the lexical item and may include conceptual structures of immense complexity. The portion of the base that is raised to a distinctive level of prominence and is designated by a linguistic expression is referred to as the expression's PROFILE. It serves as the focal point of the base. Meaning does not reside in either the base or the profile alone; both are crucial for the characterization of an expression's meaning.

To illustrate briefly, consider an example borrowed from Langacker (1988b). An adequate characterization of HYPOTENUSE necessarily requires the conceptualization of a right triangle which serves as the base figure (41a). Hypotenuse specifically designates the side that lies opposite the 90 degree angle, shown by the bold line in figure (41b). The term evokes both profile and base as distinct but conjoined aspects of an overall gestalt. It is clear that apart from the conceptualization of a right triangle there is no basis on which to identify a diagonal line as a hypotenuse (figure (41c)).

(41)   Hypotenuse

a   b   c

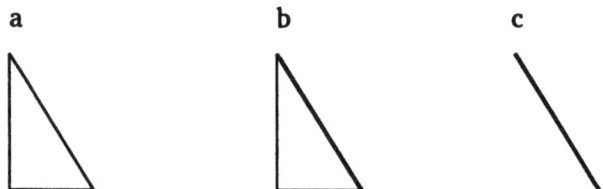

3.1.2 Category structure and categorizing relationships. As stated earlier, it is assumed that linguistic units are normally polysemous. The various conventional senses of a lexical item can be thought of as nodes within a network. The nodes themselves are linked by relationships of either ELABORATION or EXTENSION to form categories that have a "network" structure (cf. Langacker 1987a:378 and Lakoff 1987). Such categories are typically organized around best examples, or prototypes. I will elaborate the concept of a prototype more fully in following chapters, but for the present it may be thought of as the sense that will most likely be activated by the use of a particular term in a "neutral" environment.

Elaboration involves two entities in a relationship such that one exemplifies the other in greater detail. The relationship [A] → [B] (with the solid arrow indicating elaboration) can be read either as [A] is elaborated by [B] or as [A] is schematic for [B]. In other words, [B] has a character that is fully consistent with all the specifications of [A], but is expressed in finer-grained detail. On the other hand, a relationship of extension, [A]-→[B], indicates that [B] is an extension of [A], i.e., there is a perceived similarity between [A] and [B], but that there is also a degree of conflict between the specifications of the two entities.

As a simple example of how these principles are brought to bear in an analysis of a polysemous lexical item, consider example (42), taken from Langacker (1988b:52), which illustrates a portion of the semantic network for *ring*.

(42) Ring

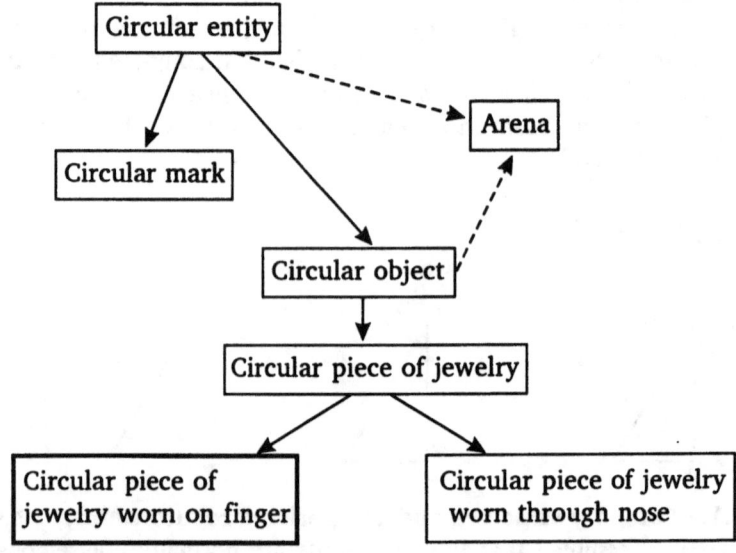

The figure shows that "circular entity" is schematic with respect to both "circular mark" (e.g., *Draw a ring around the correct answer*) and "circular object." "Circular object" is itself schematic for "circular piece of jewelry," which, in turn, is elaborated further by concepts that specify in greater detail where the jewelery is worn. *Ring* is also used to refer to the concept of an arena, which may be circular as in a bullfighting ring, but does not have to be: wrestling and boxing rings are rectangular. "Arena," therefore, incorporates the notion of an enclosure, but may conflict in terms of the specification of circularity. The "arena" sense of ring, then, is an extension of "circular entity" or "circular object." The most salient sense of *ring*—the one that is most likely activated in a "neutral" context and could be considered the prototype—is probably "circular piece of jewelery worn on the finger" and is indicated in the figure by the bold outline.

Networks of this type have been elaborated for lexical structures of various kinds, as seen in the works of Lindner (1981) on verb-particle constructions in English, Brugman (1989) on the preposition *over*;

Rudzka-Ostyn (1989) on *ask,* and Maldonado (1992) on the Spanish reflexive *se,* among others. It is my intent to detail similar networks for each of Wanka Quechua's three evidential markers.

3.1.3 Construal. Langacker (1987a:488) defines construal as "the relationship between a speaker (or hearer) and a situation that he conceptualizes and portrays, involving focal adjustments and imagery." The speaker's ability to construe a situation from a host of perspectives, regardless of what his actual vantage point may be, has its effect not only on linguistic structure (Langacker 1987a:138ff.), but also on the addressee's understanding of an utterance. Consider how adopting a particular construal affects the use and comprehension of deictic expressions in the following illustration. Several years ago my son who was around the age of four, was explaining to me a drawing of a boat and some fish that he had made. With his paper on the floor in front of him he drew lines from each fish to the boat and said, "That one comes up, and that one comes up, and this one comes up." What struck me as curious was that, from the perspective of his location in the room where he made the statement, Ryan's use of the deictic expressions seemed peculiar at best. "This" and "that" are deictic expressions typically designating entities located at different degrees of proximity to the speaker. And the expression "come up" implies vertical movement toward the speaker. But in Ryan's drawing, the three fish were on the same page, within two inches of each other, so there was no appreciable difference in distance between him and any of the fish to warrant a strong distinction between "this" and "that." More importantly, the use of "come up" was anomalous in a couple of respects: Ryan drew the lines away from himself *toward* the boat rather than toward himself as *come* would normally imply. And there was no sense in which any vertical movement took place; the lines were drawn *across* the page, not *off* the page *toward* the speaker.

Nevertheless, the statement is perfectly intelligible once one recognizes that "this," "that," and "come up" were not grounded to Ryan's location in the room where the utterance was spoken, but rather to a location within the conceptualized world of the drawing itself. If the conceptualizer displaces himself and construes the scene from a "surrogate" ground on the boat, one fish would appear to be nearer than another. Furthermore, from this displaced perspective, the fish would indeed "come up" out of the water "toward" the speaker. It seems clear, then, that the construal adopted by the speaker affects how deictic expressions are both used and understood, and therefore needs to be considered as an important element in the analysis of any such expressions.

3.1.4 The subjectivity-objectivity distinction.

The subjectivity-objectivity distinction highlights the importance of construal for the characterization of deixis, and ultimately of evidentiality. It concerns the fundamental asymmetry that exists between the observer in a perceptual situation and the particular entity that is observed. The "optimal viewing arrangement" (Langacker 1985:121) is one in which the differentiation of observer/observed roles is maximized, and may be understood as being somewhat analogous to the situation of an audience observing a performance on a stage. This configuration, given in figure (43), shows the Self (S) observing a distinct object (O) situated such that it is distinguished sharply from its surroundings and within a region that is close to the observer but does not include him or the area immediately surrounding him. This "on-stage" region (OS) is indicated as the area encompassed by the broken line. Crucially, the viewer's attention is focussed exclusively on his object, and not on himself in any way (Langacker 1987a:129). To the extent that this situation obtains, we may speak of S's role as maximally subjective and of O's as maximally objective. Put in other terms, S is subjectively construed, O is objectively construed.

(43) Optimal viewing arrangement

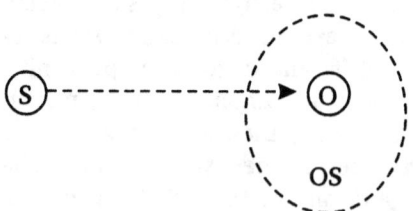

However, this distinction may be blurred to the extent that S is aware of himself in the observer role. In this case the locus of viewing attention—OS—is expanded to incorporate S's own perspective, as shown in the egocentric viewing arrangement in (44). Here S is no longer simply an observer but is, to some degree, also an object of observation. S may in some sense be thought of as having the status of an "on-stage" entity, albeit not the entity that receives the focus of his attention.

(44) Egocentric viewing arrangement

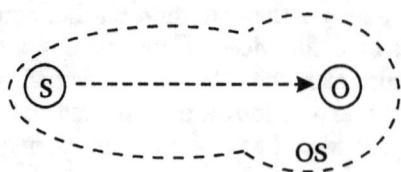

An analogy can be drawn between construal relationships such as these and certain elements in the communication of a proposition. The conceptualizer in the construal relationship is equated with the speaker; the maximal region of perceptual access in the construal relationship, with the *maximal* scope of predication; the objective scene (general locus of viewing attention), with the *immediate* scope of predication; and the primary object of observation (i.e., the focal point within the objective scene) with the entity/proposition designated by a predication (Langacker 1987a:130).

If the subjectivity-objectivity distinction involves the role the speaker plays within a conceptualization as either an off-stage or on-stage conceptualizer, then it enters into the characterization of all expressions as being either deictic or nondeictic. A nondeictic expression is one for which the subjectivity-objectivity distinction is maximized: *the scope of predication*—those elements that provide the necessary context for the characterization of the expression—does not include the speaker, nor by extension any aspect of his location in time or space. On the other hand, a deictic expression is one that requires reference to the speaker in some capacity (Langacker 1985:113).

3.2 Deixis

We need to consider in a bit more detail what deixis involves. Deictic expressions necessarily make some reference to what Langacker (1987a:126) refers to as the GROUND, i.e., the speech event and by extension the participants and their location in space and time. (Cf. Anderson and Keenan 1985 for a general discussion of deixis.) Spatial deictics, such as *this* or *that*, make reference to the ground by locating some object in terms of its relative proximity to the speaker. Temporal deixis situates the time of an event with respect to the moment of speaking, and is exemplified by tense markings, or particular senses of certain lexical items such as *yesterday*. Personal deixis would include the identification of speech event participants (speaker or addressee) as with the pronouns *I* or *you*, but it often involves more, e.g., the indication of the sex of the speaker, as in Spanish *nosotras* 'we (fem.)', or of the addressee in Hebrew *ata* 'you (sg. masc.)' versus *at* 'you (sg. fem)'. A deictic expression may also identify the social status of speaker and addressee, as do the honorific affixes found in languages such as Tamil (cf. Levinson 1979).

Although Anderson and Keenan have not mentioned them in this context, evidentials are clearly deictic expressions since they reflect information specifically about the experiential justification a speaker has for making a particular statement. The Wanka evidential system, for example, in the most prototypical uses of the markers, identifies the basis of an utterance either as the speaker's direct experience, the speaker's conjecture, or a report that has come to him from another individual, as illustrated by the following examples:

(45) chay-chruu-**mi** achka wamla-pis walashr-pis
that-LOC-DIR many girl^also boy^also

   alma-ku-lkaa-ña
   bath-REF-PLIMPV-NPST
   (I saw) Many girls and boys were swimming.

(46) daañu pawa-shra-si ka-ya-n-**chr**-ari
field finish-PART-EVEN be-IMPF-3-CONJ-EMPH
(I guess) the field might be completely destroyed.

(47) ancha-p-**shi** wa'a-chi-nki wamla-a-ta ni-mu-shra
too^much-GEN-REP cry-CAUS-2 girl-1P-ACC say-AFAR-1FUT
I'll tell her, "(I hear) you make my daughter cry too much."

As we will see, evidentials, and particularly the direct and conjecture evidentials, may also reflect the degree to which the speaker is committed to what he is saying.

It is insufficient, however, to simply classify an expression as deictic or nondeictic as there is a subtle level of complexity that needs to be explored. Consider a couple of specific examples. We observe both nondeictic and deictic senses for *Tuesday* in the following.

(48) a. **Tuesday** is the second day of the week.
b. **Tuesday** is going to be difficult.

In (48a) a conventionally-determined set of time frames (days in a week falling in a particular order) is evoked as the overall base with *Tuesday* profiling one of these periods in particular (see figure (49)). Significantly, the conceptualizer is in a maximally subjective relationship to the designated entity and is, therefore, irrelevant as a reference point in the characterization of the term. The ground is thus excluded from the scope of predication, indicated in the figure by the solid box surrounding the days of the week. Construed in this way, *Tuesday* in (48a) has an indefinite number of potential referents; there are as many possible *Tuesdays* as there are possible weeks.

Theory, Deixis, and Evidentiality

(49) Nondeictic *Tuesday*

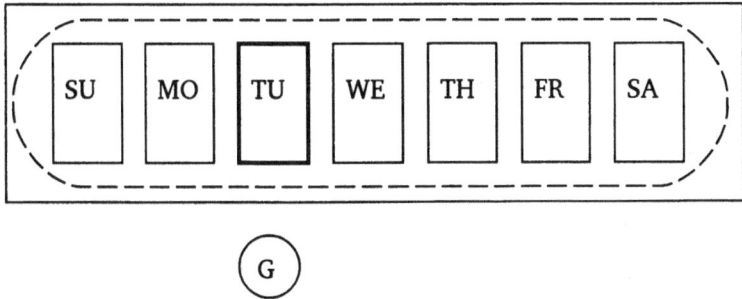

However, in (48b) *Tuesday* is used deictically; we understand that it is not just any *Tuesday* that is being referred to, but one that is future and proximal to the day on which the utterance is spoken. Although the same conventional time frame organization used for (48a) is also evoked here as the base, a ground element—the moment of speech—serves as an important reference point which limits the potential referents to a specific *Tuesday*. The ground must therefore be included within the maximal scope of predication for the characterization of *Tuesday*'s deictic sense, even though the moment of speech itself necessarily remains unprofiled; nowhere in the sentence is the moment of speech actually referred to. In other words, for the deictic sense of *Tuesday*, the ground is maximally subjectively-construed, yet is within the scope of predication, as indicated in figure (50).

(50) Deictic *Tuesday*

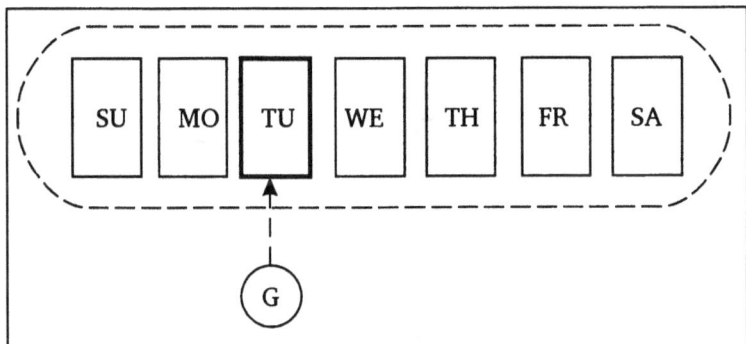

Consider another example. The second person pronoun *you* is usually thought of as a clear case of a deictic expression. But Anderson and

Keenan (1985:260) note that in the sentence *When you're hot, you're hot,* the second person pronoun is nondeictic, i.e., it is an abstract personage whose actual referent is not dependent on the context of the utterance. Since there is no reference to any aspect of the speech event, the ground does not figure among those elements necessary for the designation of this sense of *you;* hence, the ground clearly lies outside the scope of predication (see figure 51).

(51)   Nondeictic *you*

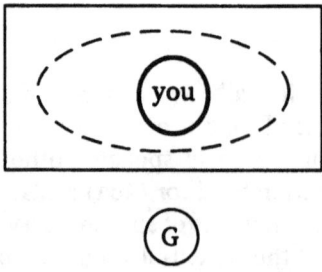

The deictic sense of *you* is evident in *You are now reading this sentence.* Although a ground element is profiled, the speaker—or in this case, writer—of the sentence serves as the subjectively-construed reference point for the identification of the addressee; the identity of *you*, of course, changes depending on who the addressee/reader is. Figure (52) depicts this by showing the addressee as the designated profiled entity within the immediate scope of predication. The speaker figures as an off-stage reference point, i.e., outside the immediate scope of predication, but within the maximal scope, i.e., among those elements necessary to describe this sense of *you.*

(52)   Deictic *you*

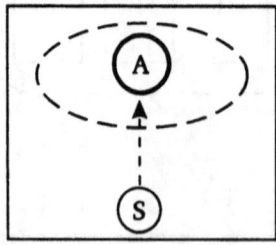

Theory, Deixis, and Evidentiality

Note then that deictic expressions may differ as to how subjectively or objectively the ground element is construed. The crucial issue is the degree of salience or profiling that is accorded to the ground. Maximal objectification (and salience) of a ground element is exemplified by the first person pronoun *I* or the deictic use of *you*; not only is reference to the speech event participant required, but the reference point is itself placed on stage and profiled as the designated object of conceptualization.

On the other hand, the deictic sense of *Tuesday* allows for a ground element to be within the scope of predication, but remain unprofiled; it simply serves as an off-stage reference point. This latter configuration involving an unprofiled, radically subjectively-construed ground within the scope of predication is characteristic of the class of what we may refer to as grounding predications (Langacker 1985:116).

If prototypically the Wanka evidentials specify the speaker's experiential basis for an utterance as I mentioned earlier, then an evidential's deictic character is apparent. Furthermore, it functions specifically as a metacomment on a proposition, and does not constitute the main proposition itself. In other words, the speaker's experience serves as a subjectively-construed reference point for the interpretation of the main proposition in a way that precisely parallels that of grounding predications. In this aspect at least, evidentials fit the semantic characterization of other grounding predications[15] and might be represented in highly schematic fashion as indicated in figure (53):

(53)   Evidential schema

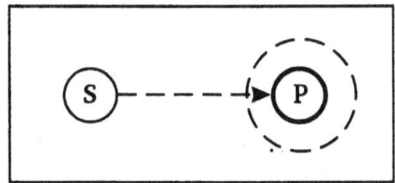

This shows that a speaker S construes proposition P in a particular fashion. The profiled entity is the proposition indicated by the circle in boldface, and the speaker is included within the maximal scope of predication as a reference point crucial to the interpretation of the main proposition, but is subjective and therefore excluded from the immediate scope of predication.

---

[15]I refer the reader to Floyd 1993:73ff. for a discussion of the grammatical behavior that evidentials display, which is also characteristic of grounding predications. (Cf. Langacker 1985:116ff.)

The detailed array of the relationships between speaker and proposition is, of course, the focus of the present study and will be fleshed out fully in subsequent chapters. However, it is convenient at this point to at least sketch briefly the prototypes for each evidential so that their respective "flavors" can be appreciated.

3.3 The prototypical relationships between speaker and proposition

3.3.1 The direct evidential prototype. The direct evidential -*m(i)* (chapter 4) prototypically indicates that an utterance is based on the conceptualizer/speaker's direct sensory perception (usually visual) of some scenario. If I say, for example, the Quechua equivalent of *Lucas*-DIR *is bludgeoning his brothers again* (where DIR represents the direct evidence marker), the addressee will most likely interpret my utterance as indicating that I personally witnessed my youngest son attacking the other two; the direct evidential reflects the speaker's personal sensory experience.

Conceptually then, the direct evidential involves a base which consists in part of a conceptualizer (C) directly perceiving some event or object (O). This is indicated in figure (54) where the dashed arrow represents the perceptual relationship between *C* and *O*.

(54)   Direct evidence—perception event

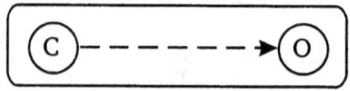

In the subsequent communicative event, the speaker conveys this construal of his perception, as indicated in figure (55) by the dashed arrow between *S* (Speaker) and *P* (Proposition); the dotted line indicates co-identity or correspondence between the speaker of the communication event and the conceptualizer of the perception event. The proposition designated and profiled by the utterance (indicated in boldface) corresponds to the object or circumstance originally perceived.

Theory, Deixis, and Evidentiality

(55) Direct evidence—communication event

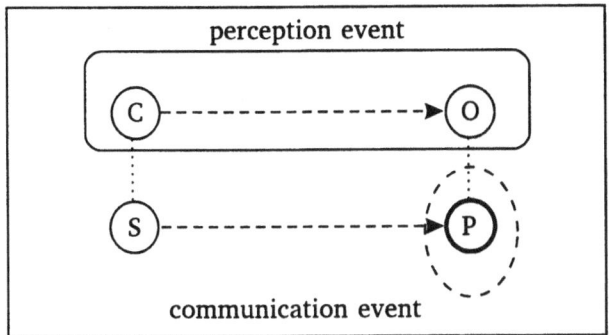

3.3.2 The reportative prototype. Reportative situations (chapter 6) prototypically involve hearsay; the speaker communicates some propositional content to the addressee, and additionally that he himself is not a direct witness of the designated scenario, but has merely been the recipient of a verbal report about it from some other individual.

Therefore, in order to characterize a reportative situation, we have here the complication of additional conceptual embedding in that the base necessarily subsumes a direct evidence scenario such as that discussed above. Returning to the previous example, suppose Lucas whacks his brother Ryan with a plastic bat. Ryan, who consequently has been involved in a direct perception scenario par excellence, may then come to me and shriek the Wanka equivalent of *Lucas*-DIR *is hitting me with a bat.* I may then inform my wife what the commotion is all about with *Lucas*-REP *is bludgeoning his brother again* and mark my utterance as a reportative. The marking indicates that my statement is based purely on the report of another unspecified individual.

The nested configuration in figure (56) abstractly captures the nature of hearsay. The base involves a direct perception scenario along with its subsequent communication event in which some propositional content (P) is communicated to an addressee (A), as laid out in section 3.3.1. We can think of the addressee as the perceiver of that communication event, indicated in the figure by the dashed arrow from *A* to the "direct perception—prior speech event" scenario. In addition hearsay's conceptual base involves (1) *A* in the direct evidence scenario assuming the role of speaker (S) in the subsequent "current" communicative event and (2) his conveying essentially the same propositional content to a distinct addressee. Note the correspondence lines between *A* and *S* and the correspondence lines between the two *P*'s. In contrast to direct evidence, the original conceptualizer in the prior speech event and the speaker of the current speech event are *distinct* individuals. As with the direct evidential, the above characterization is consonant with the nature of other grounding predications since the speaker—indeed, multiple speakers—are included within the scope of predication but remain unprofiled, serving only as reference points for the interpretation of the designated proposition.

(56)   Hearsay

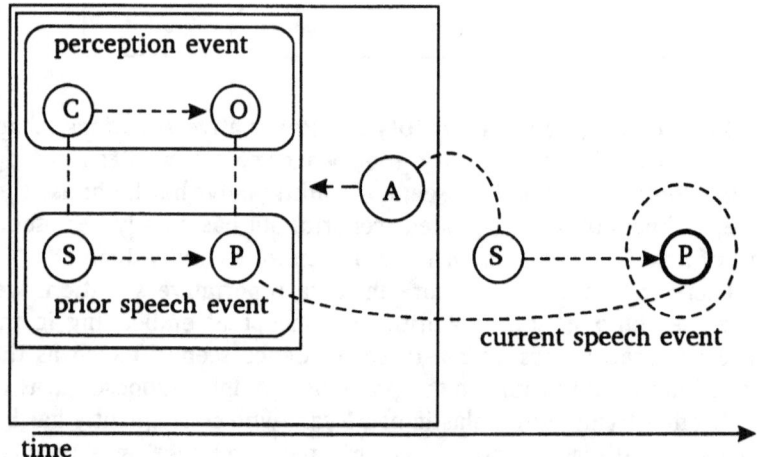

3.3.3 The conjecture prototype. A conjecture (chapter 5) involves a conceptualization that has been extrapolated from the speaker's experience or knowledge, but whose content is distinct from it. Returning to the squabbling siblings example, suppose after I hear thuds and groans my son Ryan comes running into the house crying loudly and holding his head. I look out the window and see Lucas holding a bat. I might make a statement like *Lucas-CONJ is bludgeoning his brother again*, and mark it as an inference. Note, however, that the utterance itself does not reflect what actually serves as the stimulus for the statement; it is not about one child crying or the other holding a bat. Statements concerning those things would be based on direct evidence, and would bear the appropriate evidential marker. Rather, the conjecture is an attempt to relate observed effects to a plausible cause; it is a stimulus-induced hypothesis.

Here as well, the base for a conjecture nests layers of conceptual content as illustrated in figure (57). For the sake of simplicity we will say

Theory, Deixis, and Evidentiality

that, as with a reportative scenario, the base subsumes a direct perception situation wherein a conceptualizer C directly perceives some objective content O. But based on O, C extrapolates a distinct but related conceptualization O'. When C/S speaks, what is communicated to the addressee is the content of O', not O. The original perception O which underlies O' is not encoded at all. Here as well, the characteristics of grounding predications surface in that a ground element serves as a necessary but unprofiled reference point for the interpretation of the designated proposition.

(57) Inference

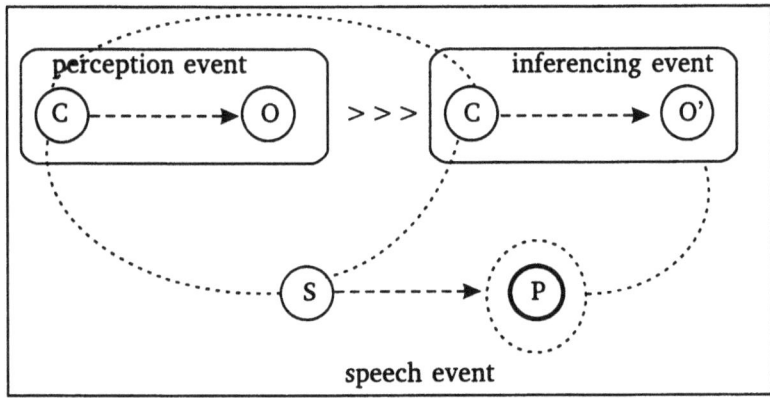

With this as an overview I now turn to the detailed analysis of the Wanka direct evidential.

4
-m(i): Direct Evidence and Commitment

4.1 Introduction

In this chapter[16] I focus attention specifically on the direct evidential in Wanka Quechua. In Quechua languages the direct evidential is usually characterized as indicating that a speaker's statement is based on personal experience with the concomitant conviction that what he is saying is true. While this may suffice for a good portion of the Wanka data, it fails to explain a range of data where neither personal experience nor conviction figure as prominent notions. Nor does it address the anomalous appearance of the direct evidential in questions.

Evidential categories are best understood by considering the interplay of both schema and prototype. Validational notions-convictions concerning the truth of a statement-are particularly relevant with respect to the schema, whereas matters of evidence pertain primarily to the prototype. The direct evidential -m(i) indicates the speaker's strong personal conviction concerning the veracity of the circumstance expressed in the sentence, which is most strongly justified on the basis of his direct personal experience. However, the speaker may also justify his commitment to the extent to which he construes a situation as subject to his control (§4.5.1). In §4.5.2 and §4.5.3 I discuss

---

[16]Portions of this chapter appeared in *Experience, Certainty and Control, and the Direct Evidential in Wanka Quechua Questions,* Foundations of Language 3:69-94 (1996) and are reprinted with the permission of John Benjamins.

how the various rhetorical effects observed in conjunction with the direct evidential can be explained as arising through a type of subjectification of the notion of control. And finally, in §4.6 I will show how the subjectification process relates the curious use of the direct evidential as a question marker to the rest of the category.

4.2 Previous descriptions of the Quechua direct evidential versus schemas and prototypes

In most Quechua dialects the direct evidential suffix has the form *-mi* (or *-m* if it follows an open syllable). These are the forms it has in Wanka (with one arguable exception which will be treated later in the discussion of questions). In the Cuzco dialect, the direct evidential appears as *-mi* and *-n* (Cusihuamán 1976:240). Some dialects, however, do not delete the final vowel, and allow only the full form *-mi*.

Characterizations of the direct evidential across Quechua dialects cluster around two concepts. Some authors describe the suffix primarily in terms of evidence source. For example, Carpenter (1982:314) glosses *-m(i)* in Ecuadorian Quichua simply as 'witness'. Levinsohn (1975:14) describes *-m(i)* in Inga (a Quechuan language of Colombia) as indicating 'action witnessed-affirmative'. Jake and Chuquin are somewhat more explicit: they consider *-m(i)* (and its emphatic counterpart *-mari*) as "factive predicates" that "convey that the speaker has first-hand knowledge or experience of the truth of what he is saying" (Jake and Chuquin 1979:173).

Adelaar, on the other hand, describes Tarma Quechua *-m(i)* primarily in validational terms as indicating that "the speaker is convinced about what he is saying" (1977:79). Along the same lines, Coombs, Coombs, and Weber (1976:149) state that for San Martín Quechua "*-mi* indica que el hablante está seguro de lo que afirma en la oración o el discurso que lo contiene."

Others, however, note both evidence source and speaker commitment in the meaning of the direct evidential. Although Weber (1989) considers *-m(i)* in Huallaga Quechua to have a "basically evidential" meaning of 'learned by direct experience', he clearly recognizes its legitimate

-m(i): Direct Evidence and Commitment

validational interpretation, "because of the axiom that direct experience is reliable (and thus one is convinced about it)" (Weber 1989:421).[17]

Information source and validation are both relevant parameters; however, I maintain that their primary relevance is found within different domains of category structure: validation pertains to the schema, whereas information source notions are seen most clearly in the prototype. By considering the evidential categories simultaneously from these two perspectives we are afforded a framework within which we can achieve a more coherent understanding of what evidentiality actually involves. Figure (58) sketches out in broad strokes the relevant concepts for the direct evidential.

(58) Direct evidential schema and prototype

	Schema	Prototype
Persona	some speech event participant	current actual speaker
Proximity relation	certainty	certainty corroborated by direct visual experience
Ground	any mental space	current reality

Schematically, the direct evidential involves a sense of certainty, one of numerous proximity relationships (cf. chapter 7), between a speech event participant and a circumstance in some mental space. Prototypically, the direct evidential indicates certainty that is justified on the basis of the current speaker's direct experience (and particularly on his visual involvement) within present reality.

---

[17]In addition to deictic characterizations such as these which appeal to various aspects of the speech event itself, the direct evidential has also been associated with certain discourse functions. In his description of the Wanka dialect, Ráez (1917:65) notes that in certain cases "se sobreentiende que se ha de hablar con énfasis ó se hace para dar propiedad á la dicción ó se habla en sentido enérgico [sic]." Others (e.g., Quesada (1976:157) or Cerrón-Palomino (1976a:100ff.)) mention similar associations of the direct evidential with some notion of "emphasis" or "focus," but what is actually meant by such terms is usually left unexplicated. Although I will not explore this view here, I refer the reader to Levinsohn (1975), who has provided a more detailed analysis along these lines for the evidentials in Inga.

4.3 An overview of the semantic network for -m(i)

The semantic network for the direct evidential is given in figure (59):

(59)   Basic network for -m(i)

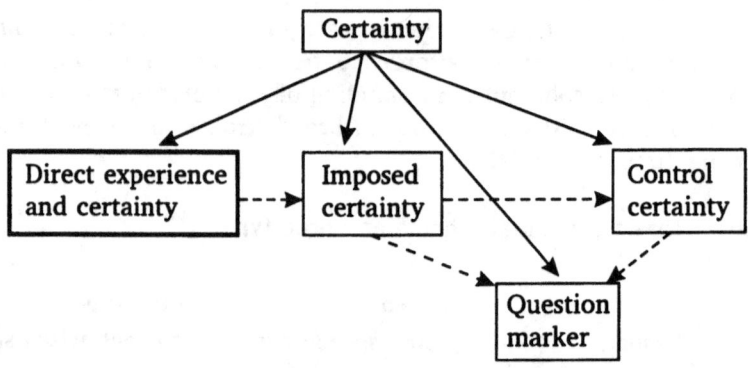

The figure shows that the direct evidential has four interrelated uses, all of which involve some sense of commitment. In the prototype, indicated by the bold face box, -m(i) indicates the speaker's commitment that is based on his direct experience of a state or event. In a second use (which could be considered an extension of the first) -m(i) is used in cases where there is no direct personal experience involved, and a certainty construal is simply imposed on the scene. A third use is similar to the second in its lack of personal experience, but in addition, it involves some situation which is construed as coming under the speaker's control in some way. Both the second and third uses extend to a fourth use in which -m(i) marks questions. It is this latter use that presents a particular problem for an analysis of the direct evidential couched simply in terms of direct experience or commitment to some propositional content. It can, however, be understood as an extension motivated by other elements found elsewhere in the semantic network. Let us consider each of these uses in a bit more detail.

4.4 The direct evidential prototype

Prototypically, the direct evidential indicates a complex relationship between the speaker and a proposition, which involves a merger of both validational and evidential parameters: the speaker indicates his firm

-m(i): Direct Evidence and Commitment   61

conviction concerning the truth of a proposition, his conviction being best supported when he is personally involved in the designated event.

4.4.1 External versus internal experience. Although the nature of direct personal experience may at first seem obvious, it is nevertheless profitable to consider it in some detail. Whorf (1956:163ff.) suggests that human conceptualization universally distinguishes between the external field of visual observation and the "egoic field," a domain in which the processing of introjected, nonvisual experience occurs. Experiences in the egoic field are "felt as immediate to the experiencer" as opposed to those entities that "take up space" in the external world. The distinction between internal and external experience is important, since many languages do not allow direct evidential marking on statements about the internal experience of nonspeakers (cf. Aoki 1986 on Japanese as an example). Although it does occur in Wanka, it has a slightly different sense.

External experience involves the speaker as a participant in some "external" event, i.e., one that is also potentially perceivable by others. As is to be expected, the direct evidential appears on those events in which the speaker figures as an "on-stage" (i.e., clausal) participant, as in (60)-(63):

(60) ya'a ya'a-si juk-kuna-man-**m**-aa   shra-ka-mu-u
      I   I-also other-PL-GOAL-DIR-EMPH come-REF-AFAR-1

      mana-**m** am-lla-man-chu
      not-DIR you-LIM-GOAL-NEG
      I, I even go to others, not just to you.

(61) ñawi-i-wan-**mi** lika-la-a
      eye-1P-with-DIR see-PST-1
      I saw [them] with my own eyes.

(62) ya'a-lla-kta-ña-**m** suma-a   ima-yki-yupay-ta-si
      I-LIM-ACC-now-DIR really-TOP what-2P-SIM-ACC-even

      jita-yka-a-ma-nki
      throw-ASP-ASP-1OBJ-2
      You just throw me away like one of your possessions.

(63) fastidiyaa-ma-nki-**m** kada bis
      irritate-1OBJ-2-DIR   each time
      You bug me every time.

But even if the speaker is not morphologically marked as a clausal participant, the direct evidential still implies the speaker's personal participation in an event as an observer, as in (64), (65), and (66):

(64) juk-nin juk-nin-**mi** ma'a-la-ali-ku-n iskuyla-a-chru
one-3P one-3P-DIR hit-ASP-PL-REF-3 school-DEF-LOC
Each one of them [the teachers] beat everyone at school. (I've seen them do it.)

(65) trabaja-a-ña-**m** li-ku-n
work-PMOT-now-DIR go-REF-3
He's gone to work. (I saw him go.)

(66) lishi kanan wala-alu-n-ña-**m**
Lishi now dawn-RPST-3-now-DIR
Lishi, it's morning now. / The sun is already up. It has dawned. (I see the sun.)

Unlike some languages, e.g., Tuyuca (cf. Barnes 1984), Wanka does not distinguish different kinds of direct evidence. Although visual evidence is typically indicated, the direct evidential may also be used in statements based on evidence obtained through other sensory modalities as well, such as hearing (67) and (68) or taste (69):

(67) chay-pii-**mi** kiki-n-man chra-alu-pti-i mana
that-ABL-DIR self-3P-GOAL arrive-ASP-DS-1 not

    lima-shra-a-ta-pis uyali-i-chu
    say-NOM-ACC-EVEN hear-1-NEG
When we arrived at the water itself, I couldn't even hear myself speak.

(68) ancha-p ancha-p-ña-**m** buulla-kta lula-n
too^much-GEN too^much-GEN-now-DIR noise-ACC make-3

    kada tuta-**m**
    each night-DIR
He really makes too much noise...every night. (I hear it.)

(69) chay-chru lurin yaku-kuna-si llalla-ku-n-**mi**
that-LOC Lurin water-PL-also be^salty-REF-3-DIR
Even the water around Lurin is salty.

-m(i): Direct Evidence and Commitment

Internal experience, on the other hand, involves the speaker's sensations, emotions, thoughts, etc., which are not directly outwardly apparent to the rest of the world. These also are typically marked with -m(i):

(70) ya'a wanuku-kta li-sha ni-pti-ki llaki-sha-m ka-la-a
I Huanuco-ACC go-1FUT say-DS-2 sad-ATTRIB-DIR be-PST-1
When you said you were going to Huanuco I was sad.

(71) kushi-ku-lka-a-ña-m-ari kuti-ila-ali-mu-pti-ki-a
glad-REF-IMPF-1-NOW-DIR-EMPH return-ASP-PL-AFAR-DS-2-TOP
When you came back, we were happy.

(72) pata-yuu-ña-m-ari ka-ya-a ya'a
stomach-HAVE-NOW-DIR-EMPH be-IMPF-1 I
I sure AM pregnant.

While it is true that emotional states may be perceived by others via some outward manifestation, e.g., tears or laughter, pregnancy, likewise, is a state that will ultimately be patently obvious to everyone. The statements in (70)-(72) are based not on external signs, but on the speaker's own internal sensations or experience that may not be apparent to others at all.

The direct evidential also appears in statements about the speaker's knowledge and awareness of his own thoughts.

(73) ima-ni-shaa-la ni-ya-a-mi
what-say-1FUT-HYP? say-IMPF-1-DIR
I'm wondering about what I'll say.

(74) rasun-pa chay-nuu-ta pala-ma-pti-ki abista juk
really-GEN that-SIM-ACC insult-1OBJ-DS-2 sometimes another
walmi-k-si ashi-ilu-y-si pinsa-ña-a-mi
woman-ACC-INDEF seek-ASP-IMP-EVEN think-PST-1-DIR
Really, when you insult me like that I find myself thinking of trying to look for another wife.

In addition, -m(i) occurs in statements of self-assessment or opinion and limitations of his knowledge and abilities.

(75) bwinu ya'a pushra-na-k-pa   mana-**m** upa-chu   ka-a
      well I   lead-NOM-1>2-PURP not-DIR   stupid-NEG be-1
      I'm not so dumb as to marry you.

(76) mana-**m** ya'a suma-a yachra-a-chu ima-nuy
      not-DIR   I   really know-1-NEG   what-SIM

   kiida-paaku-shra-yki-ta
   stay-PL-NOM-2P-ACC
   I don't really know how you were left.

(77) ya'a mana-**m** lima-pa-y-ta   yachra-a-chu
      I   not-DIR   talk-BEN-IMP-ACC know-1-NEG
      I don't know how to advise them.

Before leaving the issue of what is encompassed under the rubric of personal experience we need to consider the status of dreams, which present us with an interesting situation. I do not consider dream events to be prototypical personal experiences; if one were to ask someone to relate a personal experience to them, it is doubtful that they would recount a dream over an event in the conscious world. However, dreams are not unrelated to the discussion of the direct evidential prototype. They are like other kinds of internal psychological experiences in that dream events are purely mental, and as such are not obvious to others. However, within the world of the dream itself, the dreamer holds the status of an objective observer of some unfolding scenario, also potentially observable by others in the dream world. And if the dreamer, himself, appears in the dream, he is in the curious position of one who has internal knowledge of the participant he objectively observes on stage. So dreams constitute a sort of intermediate or cross-cutting category between internal and external experience.

The evidential marking for dreams is relevant because in some languages, e.g., Turkish, dreams may appear with marking that distinguishes them from what might otherwise be used for the recounting of normal everyday experienced reality (cf. Aksu-Koc and Slobin 1986). In Wanka the evidential marking on dream events is no different from any we have seen up to this point, as shown by (78) and (79):

(78) ya'a suyñu-ñaa ka-a anyan   tuta katarpillar
      I   dream-PST be-1 yesterday night tractor

-m(i): Direct Evidence and Commitment

karritiira-a-ta trabaja-shra-nchik-kaa-ta-**m**
road-DEF-ACC work-NOM-12-DEF-ACC-DIR
Last night I dreamed about when we worked on the road with the tractor.

(79) chay-piita-**m** papaa-nii amachu-ka am ayuda-paa-ma-nki
that-ABL-DIR father-1P Amador-DEF you help-PL-1OBJ-2

chrula-y-ta
place-IMP-ACC
Then my dad, Amador and you helped me put it (back) on.

However, the evidential marking on dreams introduces an important element into our understanding of the overall picture, namely that events marked with the direct evidential can be grounded to realms other than the speaker's current or conscious reality. Adopting notions from Fauconnier (1985), we may understand dreams as involving multiple mental realms or surrogate grounds from which a scene may be construed.

Figure (80) shows a conceptualizer c in the root space of current waking reality R, corresponding to a counterpart dreamer d in a dream world DW. Dream events e are relevant to the "reality" of DW regardless of what their status (i.e., actual or not) might be vis-à-vis the root space or moment of speech. The construal relationship evoked by -m(i) obtains between d, who serves as the objective observer of the dream, and the dream event e, not the events of the root space.

(80) Dreams-1

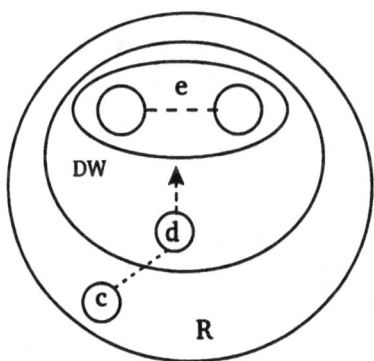

If *d* also appears as a participant in the dream, he has internal knowledge of an on-stage participant in *e*, evoking the configuration in figure (81).

(81)　Dreams-2

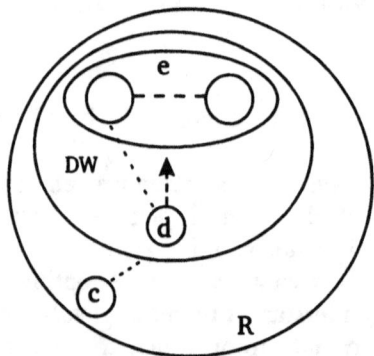

So even though the event in (78) is technically irrealis from the perspective of the time and reality in which the speaker made the statement, he nevertheless marks it like any other actualized event because from the perspective of the dream world it did occur.

I stated earlier that in the prototype we find the speaker's commitment to the truth of a proposition based on his direct personal involvement in the event. But given the importance of the distinction between internal and external experience we might well ask the question as to whether the prototype is more strongly associated with one or the other.

Geeraerts (1988a) observes that semantic nuances may appear in conjunction with the core uses of a lexical item that are absent in more peripheral ones. As we saw above, as an "insider" the speaker can convey certain subtleties about his own intrinsically subjectively-oriented domains, such as emotional states, that he cannot convey when these same semantic domains pertain to nonspeakers. This could constitute an argument for the special status of internal experience.

However, for a variety of reasons I would like to suggest that externally-directed experience in general, and the visual sensory modality in particular, is more prototypically associated with *-m(i)* than other kinds of direct experience (cf. example (82)). First of all, the special status of vision in evidential systems is observed cross-linguisitically. Willett (1988) points out that if the marking for evidence obtained through different sensory modalities is distinguished in a language, it will be vision that will

-m(i): Direct Evidence and Commitment

have a marking distinct from the others. The prototypicality of vision is further bolstered by the fact that, unless the context indicates otherwise, examples such as (64) in which the speaker does not figure as an on-stage participant, are understood by native speakers to imply that he has been an eyewitness of the situation in question.

(82) Direct experiences

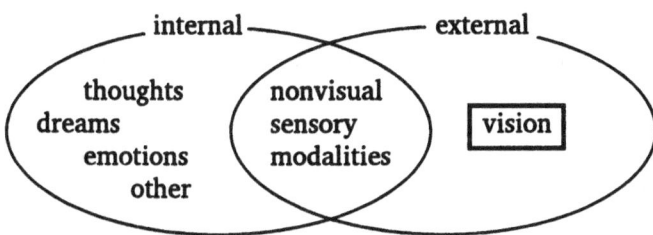

In addition, vision's uniqueness is appreciated in that external experiences can be independently corroborated by others, a fact echoed in a folk model of vision being "outwardly directed" towards some other entity in a way in which the other, more corpo-centric sensory modalities are not (cf. Talmy 1991). This has ramifications for validation as we will see.

4.4.2 Certainty. It has already been stated that in conjunction with personal experience, the direct evidential also typically communicates the speaker's conviction that what he says is true. This is hardly surprising; the natural association between personal experience and strong commitment reflects a folk model that the best justification for one's belief is provided by one's own personal involvement in the event in focus. In the examples considered thus far, it is the fact of direct perceptual experience that sanctions the speaker's certainty about his statement. Naturally, this commitment must be understood within the context of the event's relevant mental space.

Linked as they may be, commitment and direct experience are, of course, independent notions since departures from the canonical clustering may occur. For example, I imagine it would be possible in any language to communicate something along the lines of "I saw it, but I don't believe it!" However, I suspect that this would be accomplished through lexical means; no language that I am aware of has a grammaticalized marker of "disbelief of personal experience." Furthermore, as we will see, instead of marking propositions exhibiting a merger of direct experience and commitment, we observe cases where the speaker simply chooses to express his strong personal commitment regarding an event clearly in the absence of any supporting evidentiary justification.

4.5 Certainty without direct evidence

The independence of direct experience and commitment brings us to the issue of the encoding of the internal states of nonspeakers. It is clear that distinguishing between internal and external experience helps explain evidential marking tendencies vis-à-vis certain conceptual domains. Obviously, a speaker has less knowledge about nonspeakers than he does about himself. This suggests that the internal experience of nonspeakers would be excluded from direct evidential marking, as is the case in Japanese (Aoki 1986); naturally, the speaker cannot directly perceive a feeling or emotion in another like he can in himself. The tendency in Wanka is toward the nonoccurrence of direct evidential marking on the internal states of others; such states are usually marked with either the conjecture evidential *(-chra)* or the reportative *(-shi)*.

(83) kay-lla-man-pis   tayku-ku-y pishipaa-shra-*chr*   ka-ya-nki
here-LIM-GOAL-even sit-REF-IMP be^tired-ATTRIB-CONJ be-IMPV-2
Sit here; you must be tired.

(84) marya-si   llaki-sh-ari   ka-ya-n
Marya-also sad-REP-well be-IMPF-3
Marya (said she) was sad too.

But this is not a hard and fast rule since occasionally the internal states of nonspeakers may appear with the direct evidential.

(85) llaki-ku-n-*mi*
sad-REF-3-DIR
He's sad.

In cases like these, however, the evidential does not indicate the speaker's direct experientially-based knowledge as it does when the speaker refers to his own experience, since, again, the internal states of others are only indirectly perceptible. Native speakers judge statements like these as simply pointing to the speaker's conviction concerning the experiencer's emotional state. There is the implication that the experiencer of the emotion has told the speaker of his condition (which

-m(i): Direct Evidence and Commitment 69

technically amounts to hearsay), but that the speaker has accepted the report as a fact.

Or consider the following:

(86) *papaa-kaa-si mana-m atipa-n-chu lula-y-ta*
father-DEF-also not-DIR be^able-3-NEG do-IMP-ACC
Our parents can't do it either.

Taken by itself, this sentence could be interpreted as a comment made by the speaker while in the process of watching his parents failing at some task. In the context of this particular example, however, the speaker is merely declaring his belief that they are incapable of performing the job in question.

And only very rarely does the speaker express his certainty over something as inherently unobservable and cognitively distal as the addressee's thoughts, but it does occur.

(87) *mana-m ni ima-lla-si lula-na-a-chra ni-nki-chu*
not-DIR even what-LIM-INDEF do-NOM-1-CONJ say-2-NEG
You don't even think about doing anything. (Lit.: You don't even say "I have something to do.")[18]

So then, when internal experiences are marked for nonspeakers, the direct evidential has a slightly different sense: it indicates the speaker's certainty, but not on the basis of his direct experience.[19]

Much more common are examples of the direct evidential on nonintrojected, "external" events. Example (88) occurs in the context of a narrative where the speaker is explaining why her father has a deformed foot. She encodes almost each proposition with the reportative evidential *-sh(i)* (cf. chapter 6), but half-way through the story she makes the following comment:

(88) *chay-pii-mi papaa-nii-si chraki palta-n nana-y-ta*
that-ABL-DIR FATHER-1P-also foot palm-3P hurt-INF-ACC

---

[18]The two evidentials in this example of course reflect distinct mental spaces to which the propositions are grounded.

[19]It is unclear as to whether one can report nonvisual sensory evidence from the perspective of another person, e.g., *To him it is salty-m(i)*, or *He can't hear himself speak-m(i)*. Nor is it certain if a sentence such as *So and so had a dream-m(i)* is acceptable. Presumably, as with the expression of a nonspeaker's internal states, the direct evidential would indicate certainty on the part of the speaker with the implication that the experiencer has conveyed this information and the speaker has accepted it as true. However, this remains to be investigated more fully.

allayku-yku-la
begin-ASP-PAST
That's why/when the bottom of my father's foot began to hurt.

Two factors indicate that the use of *-m(i)* in (88) is not indicative of evidence obtained through the speaker's personal experience. Since all the events happened prior to the speaker's birth and were told to her presumably by her parents, the story is factually second-hand information. This is clearly indicated by the repeated use of *-sh(i)* throughout the narrative as a whole. Furthermore, as I have noted, the internal state of another being is inherently a conceptually distal domain which cannot be directly perceived. The speaker has no way of directly knowing the moment her father's foot began to hurt. The direct evidential reflects only that she considers the events she has been told as constituting a valid and true reason for the deformed foot. Rather than implying that she has directly perceived the events, example (88) achieves the effect of a personal corroboration.[20]

Similarly, in the following the speaker relates the story of the foundation of his home town. (Due to the length of the excerpt I have chosen not to include morpheme-by-morpheme translations.)

(89) [a]...*kay malkaka unay el año 1957 siparakamula wik Sapallanga malkapiita Retamaman.* [b]*Retamapi ishkay nuna shramula kay Piwasman istansachru yachraanu.* [c]*Istansapii-mi...chay ishkay nunapii-mi siparakamun Retamapi kimsa tawa picha chrunka nunalla juk un grupu nishan.* [d]*Chaypii-mi paykuna furmaalun kay malkachru ulay wayu Pampa Pukyu nishanchru...*

[a]...this town separated from Sapallanga and aligned itself with Retama long ago in 1957. [b]From Retama two men came here to Piwas to live in the pasture land. [c]After those from the *estancia-mi*...after those two men-*mi* three, four, five, ten others from Retama, a group. [d]Then-*mi* they formed this town down in what's called Pampa Pukyu.

Dates are included in the narrative which are prior to the speaker's birth, so we must conclude that he knows the story only through some other source besides direct experience. In this sense it bears similarity to the circumstances surrounding (88). However, almost all of the clauses in the text are marked by *-m(i)*.

---

[20]Dedenbach-Salazar (1991:7) explains a similar shift from *-sh(i)* to *-m(i)* in the Huarochirí texts as the author's personal comment on the content of the story itself.

Two possible analyses of this example come to mind. One may involve the fact that this information came to the speaker through a document he read in the town archives. One might view, the active, deliberate reading process as analogous to other modes of direct perception, particularly vision; accordingly, this would suggest that reading supersedes hearing, and that any information so obtained may be considered first hand even if it is technically hearsay.

My objection to this stems from the fact that evidential marking is reduced to the technicalities of how evidence is obtained and ignores the possibility of potential construal imposition. It is true that reading may in some sense be a more "active" or "deliberate" action than simply being the recipient of someone else's verbal report. However, this is not definitive. In one instance, my language consultant summarized a magazine article he had read about how a certain fiesta was celebrated by the systematic torture of a condor; all of the events were marked with -sh(i), not -m(i). So it is not the active nature of reading that determines the marking.

I think a more reasonable conclusion is that evidential encoding in general is determined only partially as a matter of the technicalities of how one receives information. In spite of the second-hand nature of the information the certainty construal that normally accompanies direct experience is clearly present. But I do not think that this is a case of the speaker merely considering a proposition as valid and encoding it as such, as we saw in (88). One thing that leads me to the conclusion that more is involved is the fact that the whole narrative is encoded with -m(i), not just selected comments. The effect is not one of mere corroboration of facts learned elsewhere, as a shift from -sh(i) to -m(i) might imply. Rather, the presentation of the entire narrative with -m(i) results in a construal that is pervasively personal. Consider Weber's comments in this regard:

> ...TCV [a language consultant] knows a man (referred to by his neighbors as "loko") who constantly uses -m(i). TCV reports that no one believes what he says because he "always speaks *as though he had witnessed what he is telling about*" [emphasis mine]. (1986:142fn)

This is not to imply that others consider my language consultant to be crazy because he encodes the history of his town with the direct evidential, but simply to highlight the nature of the overall construal that is achieved by doing so. It is as though the speaker is speaking from the perspective of an eyewitness, even though we know from other facts that this cannot be the case.

In Floyd (1989) I suggest that the community and its history are construed as metaphorical extensions of the speaker's own personal domain.

On this view, they could be conceptualized as having the same character on a par with personal experiences or any other element within his domain. The speaker's strong personal association with his community outweighs the fact that the story is technically second-hand information. In Slobin and Aksu's terminology, the facts have a great measure of "psychological proximity" to the speaker, being part of his store of cultural knowledge, and are therefore presented as part of his own personal "general mental set" that has been molded and developed through repeated exposure to particular facts, beliefs, etc. over a period of time (Slobin and Aksu 1982:196). This might also explain why the information about the condor fiesta was marked with -sh(i): the fiesta is no longer celebrated in this way and is consequently completely foreign to the speaker's experience. The -sh(i) capitalizes on the inherent "other-ness" of the reportative construal.

The original prompt for the narrative, given in (90), lends additional support to the view that a uniquely personal construal is involved. A question like *What is the history of your town?* (90) is quite different from *What do people say the history of your town is?* (91). While in English the two questions have very different structures, in Wanka the semantic difference may be signalled simply by the particular evidential used.

(90) *ima-nuy-mi piwas-pa mila-y-nin ka-la*
what-SIM-DIR Piwas-GEN increase-NOM-3P be-PAST
What is the history of your Piwas?

(91) *ima-nuy-shi piwas-pa mila-y-nin ka-la*
what-SIM-REP Piwas-GEN increase-NOM-3P be-PAST
What (do they say) is the history of Piwas?

We will consider in more detail the use of the direct evidential in questions in section 4.6. For the present, consider that in (90) the speaker presumes that the hearer's perspective on his town's history is that of an insider. But in (91) the speaker does not solicit the hearer's personal perspective, but rather the perspective of another individual.

This appears to be a clear case of what Sacks and Schegloff call "recipient design" (Kwong 1989 [quoting Sacks and Schegloff 1979]) or what Chafe calls "empathy" or "packaging." According to Chafe:

> [the] cognitive basis [of empathy] appears to lie in the fact that people are able to imagine themselves seeing the world through the eyes of others as well as from their own point of view, and that *this ability has an effect on the use of language* [emphasis mine]. (Chafe 1976:54)

-m(i): Direct Evidence and Commitment

By framing the question with -sh(i) the speaker of (91) invokes a secondhand information source in a prominent way, effectively construing the addressee as potentially distinct and somehow more psychologically detached from the community at large. I predict that if (91) had been asked instead of (90), reportative marking would have been used frequently in the response. It would open the hearer to construing himself as psychologically distant from his information source and that would overtly manifest itself in linguistic structure.[21] (See also Schiffrin (1987) for a discussion of how the linguistic form of the question shapes the answer.)

Consider a final example where the deliberate imposition of a certainty construal can be clearly seen. The circumstance involves an accusation of paternity: the woman informs the man that he is the one responsible for her pregnancy, and he denies it. A crucial element to his argument is that he claims to have seen the woman with lots of other men, and sees a potential way out of the predicament by claiming that the child could have been fathered by someone else. So in the course of the discussion the man declares:

(92) mana-**m** chay ya'a-pa-chu
      not-DIR that I-GEN-NEG
      That [the child] is not mine.

First, while the speaker most certainly at one point was enough of an active participant in circumstances to warrant his being accused as the father in the first place, -m(i) marks a proposition concerning the condition of fatherhood, not a denial of his previous sexual involvement. In essence the identity of the child's father is a matter of inference. Secondly, if other statements he makes in the larger conversational context have any validity whatsoever, the child could have been fathered by any number of men. The speaker has what he considers to be ample reason to not claim the child as his own.

Now speakers of the language also have the conjecture evidential -chr(a) at their disposal (cf. chapter 5). Since the identity of the child's father must be inferred, if evidential marking were strictly a matter of information source, the man should have said:

(93) mana-**chr** chay ya'a-pa-chu
      not-CONJ that I-GEN-NEG
      That [child] is probably not mine.

---

[21]This specific case remains to be investigated, as does the general issue of evidential marking between question-answer pairs.

But this leaves open the possibility that he actually could be the father, which is precisely what he does not want to do. Because the notion of certainty is available in the prototype, -*m(i)* is the most likely candidate to be pressed into service in a case like this one where the speaker is more interested in making a point than he is about the facts. So he deliberately imposes a certainty construal on the scene and couches what is technically a conjecture as a directly-observed fact. The suffix is essentially used as the "flip side" of a hedge (cf. Kay 1987).

So then, even in cases where it is clear either pragmatically or contextually that there is no direct experience involved, a speaker may nevertheless mark a statement with -*m(i)* and thus convey the certainty construal that is characteristic of directly perceived or experienced events.

The question is raised, What about evidential marking on future verbs? Here is a case where clearly the possibility of the speaker's direct experience is precluded. Just as there is a natural association between the speaker's personal experience (i.e., participation in "real" or "actual" events) and his subsequent commitment, there is also a natural association between nonreal events and noncommitment. That is why in Wanka, future events, which are by nature unreal and unactualized, are normally marked with the conjecture evidential -*chr(a)*.

(94) *paaga-llaa-shrayki-**chra**-a*
pay-POL-1 > 2FUT-CONJ-EMPH
I suppose I'll pay you, then.

(95) *pay-kuna-kta-a chay intiiru wanuku-kuna-chru puli-mu-la-a*
him-PL-ACC-TOP that entire Huánuco-PL-LOC WALK-AFAR-PST-1

*ni-shaa-**chra***
tell-1FUT-CONJ
I'll (probably) tell them that I travelled/walked over the whole department of Huanuco.

(96) *siguuru-si kanan-'a chraa-lu-pti-nchik*
sure-INDEF today-TOP arrive-ASP-DS-1 > 2P

*lika-paa-ka-yaa-maa-shrun suma sumaa-**chra***
see-BEN-REF-IMPF-1OBJ-1 > 2FUT VERY VERY-CONJ
Today when we arrive, they will (probably) be really staring at us.

-m(i): Direct Evidence and Commitment

In these examples the conjecture evidential reflects the speaker's appreciable lack of certainty concerning an event which has not yet taken place.

Not surprisingly, it is quite rare to find the direct evidential marking a third person future event. But it occasionally does occur, as in (97) where the speaker, worried about his daughter's trip to a town far away, is relating a neighbor's comments:

(97) kuti-mu-n'a-**m**   ni-n irmanu Luis chraa-mu-l
      return-AFAR-3FUT-DIR say-3 brother Luis arrive-AFAR-SS
      When brother Luis arrived he said [to me], "She will return."

The motivation for the direct evidential marking here cannot be Luis' personal experience. Quite apart from any identifiable evidentiary basis, Luis is clearly and deliberately imposing a certainty construal on an event that is unknown to him. But his purpose for doing this is obvious from the larger context: Luis is attempting to encourage the addressee not to worry about what the future holds. This precise effect could not be achieved with the typical evidential encoding for a third person future verb, the conjecture marker -chr(a), which instead would only imply that the speaker thought the return of the addressee's children was probable, but was ultimately uncertain-hardly a consolation for a worried parent.

Examples like (92) and (97) bring up the important issue of the motivation for using the direct evidential in a noncanonical context and its attendant effect within the communication event. With regards to (92) it was stated that when the speaker claims he is not the father of the child, he is more interested in defending himself against incurring unwanted responsibility than about accurately reflecting the evidentiary basis for his statement. Similarly, in (97), Luis is more concerned with achieving a particular co-lateral effect in his audience. We now take up the relation between co-lateral effects and evidential marking.

4.5.1 Control and certainty: first person future. While clear evidentiary motivation for marking a third person future event may be obscure, it is less opaque in cases like the following where the speaker is the subject.

(98) kiija-ka-mu-shraa-**mi** ka-n-si
      sue-REF-AFAR-1FUT-DIR be-3-even
      I'll sue.

(99) agulpis-si   ya'a ma'a-shrayki-**m**
     hitting-even I   beat-1 > 2FUT-DIR
     I'll even beat it [i.e., the truth] out of you.

Since the encoded events are as yet unrealized, the motivation for marking them with the direct evidential cannot be precisely the same as what we observed in the prototype where the speaker typically has at least the status of an observer to an actualized event, if not that of a full-fledged participant. Nevertheless, I take it as significant that in the data base used in this study in some 60% of the utterances where the direct evidential does mark a future event, the speaker is the clausal subject. Such sentences convey a sense of *intentionality* and *determination* on the part of the speaker with respect to the designated event that is not present when those same events are marked with the conjecture evidential *-chr(a)*. This suggests that (98) and (99) exemplify a type of extended internal experience.

Hargreaves' (1991a) insightful analysis of Kathmandu Newari is relevant to the analysis of Wanka at this point. Hargreaves shows that Newari grammar is sensitive to the (non)coreferentiality of the epistemic authority in a speech event, e.g., normally the speaker in declaratives and the actor in control type verbs, i.e., those "which describe intentional, or self-initiated behavior" (Hargreaves 1991a:27). Of particular interest here is his analysis of intentionality as involving a force dynamic of self-initiated action carried out in accordance with a mental plan. On this view, the construction of the plan and the efforts directed toward accomplishing it are both speaker-initiated and controlled.

The notion of control evokes the conceptualization of a "sphere of dominion," a region populated by entities over which the speaker potentially exerts authority or influence (cf. Langacker 1991:170ff.). Perhaps the clearest case of the control one entity may have over another is the physical manipulation of an object. Naturally, in order for any manipulation to take place the target entity must be located within the manipulator's general sphere of potential dominion so that physical contact is possible. Of course, not all control requires physical contact; metaphorical extensions of the prototypical association are possible. For example, in Psalm 32:8 "I will guide you with my eye" (KJV) *visual* "contact" results in influence over the object. The point is that prototypical control and manipulation of entities presupposes the concept of their being situated in some measure of physical or metaphorical proximity.

Past experiences then may be viewed as events that the conceptualizer has experientially "contacted." Any realis experience may be conceptualized as being located in the general domain of other realis entities, just like tangible objects that can be potentially contacted and manipulated. The paradigm case of a high-control, irrealis event would involve first person future tense, so we might understand the direct evidential marking of first person future events in Wanka along similar lines. In examples (98) and (99), the speaker envisions the direction of his efforts along a given line in order to actualize the conceptualization of a particular outcome that he already entertains. As shown in figure (100a), the path to this goal (events, actions, processes, etc.) is construed as being within his sphere of dominion, proximal and subject to his control and authority as any manipulable object would be. Any obstacles along the way (figure 100b) are similarly viewed as being subject to his influence and, therefore, can be potentially overcome.

(100) Intentionality

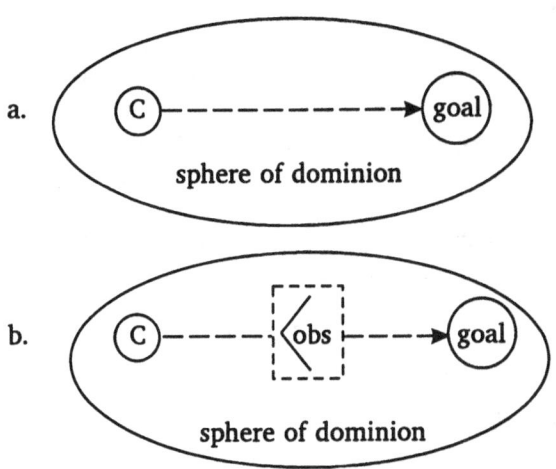

Since the speaker initiates and controls his own efforts and thereby serves as the proximal cause of a subsequent event his certainty is therefore justified. So then, the speaker's conceptualized influence over particular facets of an unactualized, unreal event (i.e., its conceptualization and initiation) constitutes a type of direct experience and also provides justification for his commitment to the truth of the encoded proposition.

If, as I suggest, the direct evidential imposes a construal of intentionality on a first person future event, then this may shed light on why my corpus has no examples of internal states or sensations encoded in the future tense with direct evidential marking. Indeed, in what sense can one "intend" to have a particular feeling or internal state? Feelings and emotions are typically reactive; they emerge as responses to the circumstances at hand rather than existing as projected goals within an overall plan of action.

Another interesting fact emerges as well. I already mentioned that sixty percent of the utterances where -m(i) appears on a future event are those where the speaker figures as the grammatical subject. Twenty-five percent are second person and only fourteen percent involve third person subjects. I take this to be nonarbitrary and significant. co-occurrence tendencies such as these will be considered in a general way in chapter 7. For the present, I conclude that, even though it may be possible, it is unusual to speak of future events with any degree of assurance, if those events do not concern the speaker himself. By doing so the speaker exposes himself to increased risk of being wrong, since he is making assertions about individuals and domains over which he inherently has little or no control.

Naturally, one's own actions are more subject to one's control than are the actions of others. But we may ask if the notion of speaker-influence or control is at all relevant when -m(i) marks events where a nonspeaker is the subject. I think it does, and, as was foreshadowed above, it emerges in the particular rhetorical effects that are frequently evident in such cases.

4.5.2 Directives and second person past/present. Consider the following second person past or present events.

(101) *ya'a-lla-kta-ña-m suma-a ima-yki-yupay-ta-si*
I-LIM-ACC-now-DIR really-TOP what-2P-SIM-ACC-INDEF

jita-yka-a-ma-nki
throw-ASP-ASP-1OBJ-2
You just leave (drop) me like one of your possessions.

(102) *am mana-m kaasu-ku-nki-chu llapa ni-sha-a-ta*
you not-DIR pay^attention-REF-2-NEG all say-NOM-1P-ACC
You don't pay attention to all that I say.

(103) *suma suwa-ku-la-nki raasun-pa-m*
really steal-REF-PST-2 true-GEN-DIR
You really did steal.

(104) *chakwashr-yaa-ku-ya-nki-ña-m mana liigi-y-si*
old^woman-become-REF-IMPF-2-now-DIR not read-INF-even

yachra-l
know-ss
You are turning into an old woman now without even knowing how to read.

What is the evidentiary basis for these statements? The fact that (102) through (104) are not future events might initially suggest that the comments are based on the speaker's personal observations. Indeed, as I have already stated, the default interpretation apart from any context tends to fall along these lines. However, this turns out not to be the case; an examination of the larger context of (103), for example, shows that the speaker is actually basing his statement on hearsay.

Based on the discussion in preceding sections it is safe—as well as completely correct—to say that at least part of what the direct evidential accomplishes here is the expression of the speaker's certainty concerning the designated proposition, i.e., the speaker is assured that the addressee stole certain goods, that the addressee is getting old without learning to read, etc. However, in spite of the fact that there seems to be no direct evidentiary motivation for the presence of *-m(i)*, I do not believe that its only function is to express the speaker's assurance. I suggest that in these examples, as well as others that will be examined, the direct evidential serves to achieve certain co-lateral effects within the domain of the speech situation itself that would not be present otherwise.

As a set of basic conversational postulates Grice's well-known Cooperative Principle and maxims provide us with what is in effect a schema or script of idealized conversational interchanges. Of particular interest here is the maxim of quantity which states "make your contributions as informative as is required for the current purposes of the exchange" (Grice 1975:45). Labov and Fanshel (1977:100) provide further detail in their discussion of general rules of discourse that operate according to the following classifications of shared knowledge:

(105) A-events: Known to A, but not to B.
      B-events: Known to B, but not to A.
      A-B events: Known to both A and B.
      O-events: Known to everyone present.
      D-events: Known to be disputable.

Now it seems intuitively obvious that when a speaker relates events in which he has participated (even if only as an observer of an event involving a third person), from the perspective of the addressee that information may be reasonably construed as being "new" or "informative" in some way: -*m(i)* indicates personal knowledge coming from one "in the know" (i.e., as the epistemic source) to one "not in the know," with the result of the utterance being informative as well as authoritative. But is there really any comparable informative value in sentences like (101) through (104)? Why should the addressee be informed about his own actions in the first place? After all, the addressee is normally a better evidentiary authority concerning his own affairs than the speaker would be. As Givón notes:

> The speaker cannot claim evidentiary authority over states/events in which the hearer was a conscious participant (and the speaker was not), since (a) the hearer's evidentiary support is stronger, and (b) there's no reason to inform the hearer of things he knows better than the speaker. (Givón 1984:308).

I suggest that the presence of -*m(i)* in a context that appears to flout the maxim of quantity results in a contextual effect or pragmatic inference. In these examples in particular the implicature is not unlike what typically results from an employer's remark to an employee: "You're late," i.e., criticism. The contexts surrounding these examples clearly support this; for example, in (103) the addressee is being reprimanded for stealing, and in (104) the father is expressing his displeasure at his daughter's refusal to attend school.

Note, I am not saying that the direct evidential encodes criticism, since the same second-person -*m(i)* morphological constellation may appear in the greater context of praise and gratitude. Consider the following excerpts from prayers.

(106) *an-mi   yachra-la-nki   ya'a-pa   shrun'u-lla-a-ta   taytáy*
you-DIR know-PST-2 I-GEN   heart-POL-1P-ACC father^VOC
You knew my heart, my father.

(107) *am tayta-a-mi   yachra-nki llapa llaki-ku-y-nin-ta*
you father-1P-DIR know-2   all be^sad-REF-INF-3P-ACC
You, my father, know all his sorrow.

Observe here that the speaker encodes the internal knowledge of another with the direct evidence marker even though, as stated earlier, such knowledge is inherently only indirectly available. In (106) and (107), by "informing" God of what God should already know the speaker paves the way for a petition.

-m(i): Direct Evidence and Commitment 81

The generalization here is that in almost every case where the speaker marks the present or past actions of the addressee with -m(i), in addition to expressing his own certainty regarding the propositional content, the speaker is also attempting to influence the addressee's behavior in some way and not merely inform.

4.5.3 The subjectification of control and second person future.

Note that the force dynamic notion of control or influence relevant to the sense of intentionality associated with first future events emerges here as well, but that its operative domain has shifted. Here the control relationship is not between the speaker and some event per se (as would be suggested with the first person future -m(i) combination), but rather between the speaker and another speech event participant. In other words, influence is relevant exclusively within the metapropositional domain of the speech event itself; it is the addressee, not the designated event, that the speaker construes as being under his (potential) control or influence.

We can understand this "proposition to metaproposition domain shift" as similar to what Traugott (1989) and Langacker (1990) have referred to as the process of subjectification. Traugott has pointed out that "meanings tend to become increasingly situated in the speaker's subjective belief state or attitude toward the proposition" (Traugott 1989:31). Langacker describes subjectification as a process in which some aspect of a relationship holding between objectively-construed entities becomes "realigned," such that an analogous relationship comes to obtain between the objective scene and the speech event itself (Langacker 1990:17).

Langacker exemplifies two different types of subjectification in the use of *across*. (108a) and (108b) exemplify the first in which spatial motion on the part of an objectively-construed participant is replaced by subjective motion on the part of the conceptualizer. Note in (108a) there is actual motion, whereas in (108b) there is none; instead the *speaker* subectively traces a line from Vanessa to Veronica across the table. The second kind of subjectification exemplified by (108c) and (108d) involves an originally objective reference point becoming identified with a facet of the ground, which retains its subjective construal. In (108c) *me* places a ground element on stage making it objective; in (108d) the same reference point is left entirely implicit.

(108) a. Vanessa jumped across the table.
    b. Vanessa is sitting across the table from Veronica.
    c. Vanessa is sitting across the table from me.
    d. Vanessa is sitting across the table.

For both kinds of subjectification, some aspect of a relationship (XY) that holds between entities in an objectively-construed scene (Tr and Lm)[22] becomes "realigned" such that an analogous relation (X') now holds between the objective scene and the ground, as illustrated in figure (109).

(109) Subjectification

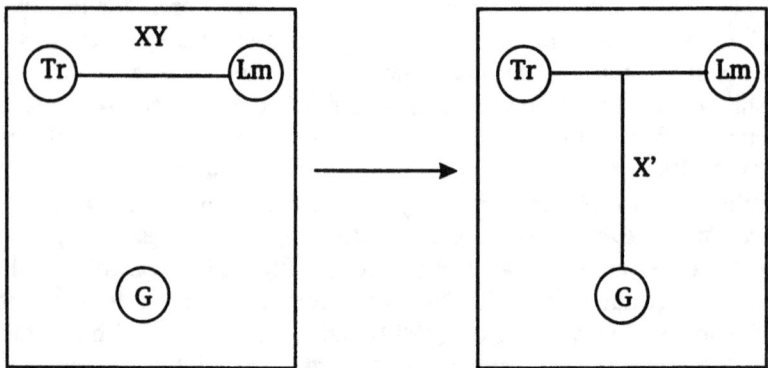

However, the shift we observe with the Wanka direct evidential use is best understood as an extension of subjectification in the following way. Langacker (personal communication) has noted that since evidentials prototypically specify aspects of the relationship between an objective scene and the speaker, this relationship is already subjective to begin with. Rather, as the force dynamic aspect of the direct evidential's semantics shifts from being relevant only to the designated proposition, to being directed towards the addressee within the domain of the speech event itself, subjectification is being taken one stage further-resulting in what we might consider as "metapropositional" or "intra-ground" subjectification.

The association of *-m(i)* with control or influence at this metapropositional speech event level becomes particularly clear in conjunction with second person future events. Consider the following:

(110) wik   punta punta muula-p   linli-n-ta-m   lika-nki
       yonder first   first   mule-GEN ear-3P-ACC-DIR see-2
       Look at the ears of that very first mule over there (Lit.: You will look at the ears...)

---

[22]Langacker characterizes landmark as "a salient substructure other than the trajector of a relational predication or the profile of a nominal predication" (1987a:490). Trajector is defined as "the figure within a relational profile" (1987a:494).

-m(i): Direct Evidence and Commitment

So what does -m(i) mean here? Like the first person future examples in section 4.5.1, it cannot indicate the speaker's direct observation of an actualized situation because the event of "looking" has not yet taken place; it is still future. The direct evidential might be viewed as indicating "the speaker's certainty that the event will take place." If there is a sense of certainty, it is not because the speaker is psychic and "knows" the future, a characterization that might be better attributed to a fortune teller who utters, "You will meet a tall, dark stranger." And it is certainly not because the speaker acts as some proximal cause for a subsequent event as we observed earlier where -m(i) in conjunction with a first person future event strongly suggested the speaker's intentionality. In (110) since the epistemic source and clausal agent are noncoreferential, the speaker simply does not have direct, intrinsic control or agency over the circumstance that would justify a full measure of certainty.

I maintain that by focusing on certainty here we miss the mark, since certainty is not the primary sense of what is communicated in such utterances. Second person future constructions marked with -m(i) are not generally interpreted as predictions. Rather, they are almost always understood as directives or as strong suggestions (cf. Lyons 1977:745ff.),[23] though not specifically imperative; imperative verbs are marked with -y, but are not marked for either person or evidentiality. Sadock and Zwicky (1985:178) point out that "most, if not all, languages have devices for distinguishing various degrees of emphasis, peremptoriness, politeness, and formality in imperative sentences." The distinction in the Wanka forms corresponds with precisely such a distinction in meaning: second person future forms marked with the direct evidential make strong suggestions to the addressee, but are not as restrictive, imposing, or authoritative as those marked as imperatives.

That this directive sense is associated specifically with the evidential, can be seen from the way -m(i) contrasts with the conjecture evidential -chr(a) in terms of directive strength. The examples in (111) show various forms of the verb *come*. The imperative form is given in (111a) and the second person future forms marked for evidentiality in (111b) and (111c):

(111) a. *shramu*-**y**
       come-IMP
       Come! (imperative)

---

[23]I have found only one or two cases where a directive interpretation is not applicable.

b. *shramu-nki-m*
   come-2-DIR
   You will come (directive)

c. *shramu-nki-chr*
   come-2-CONJ
   You might come (mild exhortation).come

The form in (111b) marked with *-m(i)* is understood to be much more like the imperative in (111a) (although again not as strong), whereas the *-chra*-marked form in (111c) is much milder in its potential manipulative effect.

I suggest that the rhetorical force clearly evident in second person future events marked with *-m(i)* is once again the result of a pragmatic inference. Since *-m(i)* appears in a grammatical constellation that does not inherently support its interpretation as a marker of direct evidence, the addressee is forced to deduce its relevance. The speaker's apparent certainty carries with it the expectation that the event will be carried out. The addressee is the main one in a position to effect the action, so, assuming some cooperative posture, complies. In a shorthand, abbreviated fashion, we can say that the speaker views the addressee as falling within his sphere of influence or control.

4.5.4 Review. Before proceeding, it is convenient to review the essential points made thus far. Prototypically, *-m(i)* indicates the speaker's certainty concerning a designated proposition based on some kind of direct, actualized experience. However, an event may be marked with the direct evidential even in the clear absence of such direct experience. In the case of first person future events, the speaker's commitment to a proposition may be justified to the extent that he construes his own subsequent actions as being particularly subject to his initiation and control. When *-m(i)* appears in contexts that clearly do not foster a prototypical interpretation, metapropositional contextual effects emerge that appear to be the result of an inferencing strategy. In these cases, while certainty may continue to be a relevant notion to the relationship between the speaker and the proposition, the force dynamic notion of control or influence becomes increasingly more significant in describing the relationship between the speaker and the addressee, with the latter as the controlled or influenced element.

-m(i): Direct Evidence and Commitment

The presence of evidentials in questions is explicable quite naturally as an extension of the processes discussed thus far. It is to this that I now turn.

4.6 The direct evidential in Wanka questions

Langacker states that subjectification is "often a central factor in the evolution leading from 'lexical' to 'grammatical' elements" (Langacker 1990:5). What we see with the direct evidential in a question is not so much a case of a move from lexical to grammatical, but of less grammatical to more grammatical.

4.6.1 WH questions. In Wanka *-m(i)* occurs as the default marker of content WH questions:[24, 25]

(112) *imay-**mi** wankayuu-pi kuti-mu-la*
when-DIR Huancayo-ABL return-AFAR-PST
When did he come back from Huancayo?

(113) *ima-pii-**mi** chay-ta lula-la-nki*
what-ABL-DIR that-ACC do-PST-2
Why did you do that?

Interrogative constructions may also appear with the conjecture and reportative evidentials as well:

(114) *ima-kta pinsa-l-**chra** chay-nuu-ta suyñu-ku-u-la-nki*
what-ACC think-SS-CONJ that-SIM-ACC dream-REF-ASP-PST-2
What do you suppose you were thinking about to dream that?

(115) *imay-**shi** yayku-n ya'a-pa umri-i*
when-REP enter-3 I-GEN man-1P
When did (they say) my husband entered [the house]?

---

[24]This statement goes contrary to what is implied by Cerrón-Palomino (1976a:108) where a question marked with the direct evidential is claimed to be "menos diplomática" than one marked with *-taq*. In my own investigation I have found precisely the opposite situation to be the case.

[25]It can also be shown that *-chun*, the marker for "yes-no" questions is derived historically from the negative *-chu* followed by the direct evidential. However, a full explanation of the semantic shift involved in the grammaticalization process in this instance is beyond the scope of the present study.

The interpretation of the conjecture and reportative evidentials in questions is not particularly problematic. But according to Adelaar, the appearance of the direct evidential on questions (in Tarma Quechua) is both "remarkable" and "virtually meaningless" (1977:255). This of course reflects the common understanding of evidentiality as a notion that applies principally (if not exclusively) to assertions as stated by Bybee:

> Imperatives and subjunctives occur in nonasserted clauses, while epistemics and evidentials, which occur in asserted clauses, serve to qualify the assertion in some way. (1985a:193)

and similarly Givón states:

> ...[evidentials] code the speaker's evaluation of the source of evidence of information processed in *declarative* sentences....Evidentiality is thus, ultimately, the source of the speaker's certainty and the hearer's willingness to challenge *asserted* information [emphasis mine]. (1984:307)

If we view the direct evidential strictly in terms of its prototypical manifestations, I would agree that it is difficult to make sense of its appearance on a question. In this view, a question, which is a request for information that the speaker presumably does not know, is marked by an element that prototypically marks information of precisely the opposite kind. Indeed, it seems that a question is the very place one would not expect direct evidential marking to occur.

The view I take, however, is that the direct evidential's appearance on a question is only superficially anomalous, and that it can be motivated straightforwardly on the basis of elements that have already been observed to be operative throughout the rest of the evidential's semantic network. Consequently, rather than being forced to posit a distinct but homophonous question-marking suffix, the view of category structure proposed here accommodates this sense quite readily as an extension.

I think it is fair to assume that prototypically questions are tools for problem solving (Goody 1978, Givón 1990:814), and that a speaker asks a question because he is seeking information that he does not already know. As Lyons (1977:754) points out, this is one of the felicity conditions that attaches to the appropriate utterance of questions (rhetorical questions notwithstanding). But although the speaker does not know the information he seeks, he assumes the addressee does. Otherwise, it would be pointless to ask the question. Again from Lyons, "What is at issue is whether, in uttering a question, the speaker necessarily assumes that his addressee knows the answer. If he does not make this assumption he can hardly impose upon the

-m(i): Direct Evidence and Commitment

addressee the obligation to supply the answer" (1977:754). (Cf. also Levinson 1983:240.) In terms of the present analysis, what this is actually saying is that in a question-asking circumstance, the speaker construes the addressee as being in a "direct relation" to some propositional content, which of course, precisely parallels the kind of relationship the speaker himself typically holds to a proposition in an assertion.[26]

Figures (116) and (117) show this state of affairs graphically. An assertion marked with -m(i) is illustrated in example (116). The speaker S and the proposition P are linked by a relation of commitment (indicated by the dashed arrow) that either stems from direct experience, or is imposed, or is based on the conceptualized control of some relevant element. When the role and perspective of the addressee A is considered, it is clear that he has a direct participant/observer relationship to the "scene" of the speaker speaking. But the addressee's relationship to the propositional content itself is indirect in that the addressee's only "access" to the proposition is mediated through the speaker.

(116) -m(i) in an assertion and A's construal of S

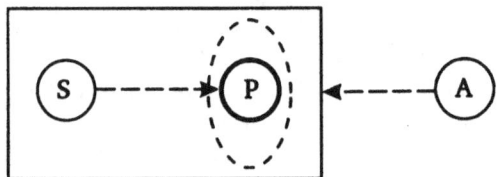

In the "inverted" configuration that holds in a question, the speaker construes the addressee as being the one in the direct relation to the proposition, while his own relation to the proposition remains indirect and mediated through the addressee, as shown in figure (117).

(117) -m(i) in a question and S's construal of A

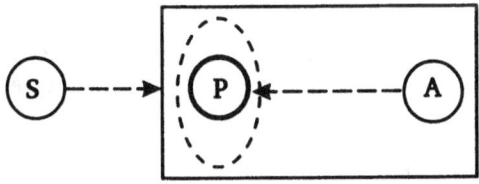

---

[26]This conceptual flip-flop again shows parallels with Kathmandu Newari. There, the set of suffixes that marks the coreference between speaker in the speech event and agent in control verbs in an assertion is the same set that marks second-person actor in questions (Hargreaves 1991b:380).

A couple of points are worth noting. First, by the speaker claiming "the addressee knows X," there is a conceptual parallel to other cases described previously where the direct evidential appears on something intrinsically only indirectly knowable, i.e., the knowledge or internal state of another individual. In addition, the analysis for questions resembles evidential already discussed involving contextual effects in that it also requires an appreciation of the speaker's construal of the addressee, not just the relationship between speaker and proposition.

It should be noted that in all previous cases certainty has figured as an element of the relationship between speaker and proposition. If the direct evidential in questions reflects the speaker's certainty that the addressee exists in such a relationship to a particular proposition, then, like control, certainty has become subjectified and is now a notion relevant primarily within the ground.

What about the force dynamic factor of influence or control that has elsewhere emerged as being relevant? It is generally true that questions place an obligation on the addressee to respond, and in that sense they may be considered as a type of directive. As Schiffrin notes, "Questions are among the linguistic means of enacting requests for information and actions, and thus impose—through their underlying appropriateness conditions...an expectation of fulfillment" (1987:333fn). Thus, as a commonly recognized adjacency pair (cf. Sacks, Schegloff, and Jefferson 1978), we expect questions to prompt answers. Therefore, a number of analysts treat questions as pertaining to the class of utterances including commands, demands, requests, and entreaties (cf. Lyons 1977:753 for discussion).

In Wanka, questions marked with the direct evidential do indeed place a strong obligation on the addressee to respond. If this analysis is correct, then its use here might be viewed as the conventionalization of an inference which takes roughly the following form: *You know X, I don't; so don't leave me in ignorance.* In marked contrast, questions marked with the conjecture evidential *-chr(a),* as in (118), do not put any such obligations on the addressee.

(118) *ima-lla-kta-chr   u-yku-shrun   llapa ayllu-kuna-kta-si*
     what-LIM-ACC-CONJ give-ASP-1 > 2FUT all family-PL-ACC-even

        chra-alu-l
        arrive-ASP-SS
     I wonder what we will give our families when we arrive.

Example (118) is much more like what Lyons (1977:55) describes as a "wondering" or "posed" question, rather than one that is verbalized for the purpose of actually soliciting information. (I will return to this in chapter 5.)

4.6.2 Yes/no questions. At this point we also consider the direct evidential in yes/no questions. Yes/no questions may be characterized as instructions to the addressee to assert one of the propositions of a disjunction (Lyons 1977:753).

Although it may not be immediately apparent, Wanka's yes/no question marker *-chun* is etymologically derived from the negative *-chu* followed by the direct evidential *-m(i)*. In most Quechuan languages the morpheme *-chu* serves as both yes/no question marker and the negative suffix[27] as shown in examples (119) and (120) from the Tarma dialect.

(119) *tarma-ta aywa-n-chu*
Tarma-ACC go-3-YN
Is he going to Tarma?

(120) *mana-m tarma-ta aywa-n-chu*
not-DIR Tarma-ACC go-3-NEG
He is not going to Tarma.

The question has only *-chu,* whereas the negative assertion involves discontinuous negative morphology (much like French *ne...pas*) consisting of the negator *mana-*to which the direct evidential attaches-and *-chu.* These elements bracket the relevant scope of negation.

In Wanka, however, the yes/no question marker and negative suffix have distinct forms, *-chun* and *-chu,* respectively. The above sentences would have the following forms in Wanka:

(121) *tarma-kta li-n-chun*
Tarma-ACC go-3-YN?
Is he going to Tarma?

(122) *mana-m tarma-kta li-n-chu*
not-DIR Tarma-ACC go-3-NEG
He is not going to Tarma.

---

[27]In a band of dialects extending from Ancash and into Dos de Mayo the yes/no question marker is *-ku.*

That negative polarity is not exclusively associated with *manam* is evident from casual speech, where often the negator-evidential combination is omitted. An utterance such as *Tarmakta linchu* will still be interpreted as negative.[28]

Evidence from neighboring dialects supports an analysis of the yes/no question marker *-chun* as deriving from the negator *-chu* followed by the direct evidential *-m(i)*. The yes/no question marker appears as *-chum* in Huancavelica and Ayacucho Quechua (cf. Soto Ruiz (1976:120), as well as in some dialects of Wanka (cf. Ráez 1917:67)). Recall that following open syllables an evidential loses its final vowel, i.e., *-chum* < *chu+mi*, and the morphophonemic alternation between *-m(i)* and *-n* is evidenced in at least two places. In Cuzco *-n* is the short form of the direct evidential (cf. Cusihuamán 1976:240f.), and in Ancash Parker (1976:147) suggests that one of the markers for content questions *-tan* may be a fusion of *-taq* and *-m(i)*.[29]

The derivation of *-chun* from the negative-direct evidential combination is further corroborated dialect internally. The negative has also fused with the other two evidentials to form the suffixes *-chuchr* and *-chushr*. The etymology of *-chuchr*, which indicates 'wonder' in example (123), is unambiguously seen as the fusion of *-chu* and the conjecture evidential *-chr(a)*. The negative has also merged with the reportative *-sh(i)* to form *-chushr* in (124), whose precise meaning is still under investigation, but does not seem to have any clearly identifiable reportative element.[30] In this way *-chun*, *-chuchr*, and *-chushr* form a regular paradigm, which is often a concomitant of grammaticalization (Lehmann 1985, cited in Hopper 1991:20).

---

[28]Adelaar (1977:78 fn 2) makes the same observation for Tarma Quechua. Likewise, Weber and Weber (1976:22f.) for Huayllas Quechua, adding that the form without manam is felt to be more discourteous.

[29]The grammaticalization process that the direct evidential has undergone in these instances is fairly typical, involving phonological erosion and semantic bleaching. An interesting twist on the grammaticalization process is reported by Carpenter (1982:316) where apparently in some Ecuadorian dialects the direct evidential has become an independent verb. The example he provides is the Salasaca equivalent of Imaburara *ali.mi* 'it's good':

alli.lladi mi.shka 'It's fine/okey [sic]'.

Although he provides no morpheme-by-morpheme glossing, dialectical comparison indicates that *alli* is 'good', *-lladi* is a variant of *-llataj*, an intensifier, and *-shka* is a verbal affix. According to Peter Landerman (p.c.) similar cases of suffix-to-verb reinterpretation have occurred in other northern Quechua languages.

[30]A previous stage would have exhibited the form *-chush*, with a nonretroflexed sibilant [ʃ]. Presumably, the loss of its reportative sense was followed by phonological erosion as the normal process applied that retroflexes [ʂ] to [ʃ] in the environment of a nonfront vowel.

-m(i): Direct Evidence and Commitment

(123) *iskuyla prufisura-kuna-man li-ilu-nki-man-chuchr*
school teacher-PL-GOAL go-ASP-2-POT-NEG=CONJ

tapu-mu-na-yki-pa
ask-AFAR-NOM-2P-PURP

I wonder if you should go to his teachers at school to ask them?

(124) *maa mana-chushr aani-ma-n'a*
let's^see no-NEG=REP agree-1OBJ-3FUT
Let's see if he'll agree. (or Hmm, will he agree?)

According to some (e.g., Schiffrin 1987:104) yes/no questions seek the confirmation or denial of a proposition. But I do not think that this can be said equally of all questions that seek yes/no answers. Compare (125a) and (125b) for example.

(125) a. Is Mike going?
b. Mike's going, isn't he?

The question in (125a) with auxiliary inversion solicits confirmation or denial of the "on-stage" propositional content, but in addition presents the speaker as having no firmly "formulated" notion of "Mike going"; the speaker is completely dependent on the addressee to supply that information. On the other hand, (125b) communicates something quite different. It shows the speaker already entertains a conceptualization of "Mike going" to which is naturally attached a particular level of speaker commitment. When followed by the negative tag, the effect that is achieved is quite distinct from that in (125a) in that the speaker begs, not the addressee's provision or elaboration of some kind of objective content, but rather his endorsement, reinforcement, or corroboration of the level of *subjective personal commitment* that the speaker *already* holds with respect to the conceptualization. In other words, the speaker attempts to construct between himself and the addressee a type of "auxiliary commitment"—a relationship within the ground that parallels what already exists between speaker and the on-stage proposition. And this is exactly what other instances of intra-ground subjectification have exhibited.

Therefore, far from being anomalous, the use of the direct evidential in questions is seen as a motivated extension evidenced by the numerous conceptual similarities it bears with its uses found in assertions.

4.7 Summary

The data presented in this chapter highlight two intertwining threads: the network structure of the direct evidential category and the role that a particular type of subjectification plays in the extension of category boundaries. I have shown that the direct evidential must be considered from the perspective of both schema and prototype. The schematic value of -*m(i)* is that it indicates the strong commitment a speech event participant has with respect to the truth of some predication. The prototypical semantic value of -*m(i)*, on the other hand, is as an information source marker; it points to the current speaker's direct experience which most strongly supports his validational commitment.

Justification of a speaker's commitment to a proposition is not limited to his direct experience. Certainty may be based on the extent to which the speaker conceptualizes a circumstance as potentially coming under his control. A number of rhetorical effects emerge through the speaker's imposition of a control construal on an event that does not inherently fall within his sphere of dominion, and these effects may actually be understood as a type of subjectified control. Finally, subjectification of commitment and control motivates the use of the direct evidential in questions. The analysis characterizes the direct evidential in both assertions and questions in the same terms, namely as involving a direct, unmediated construal relationship between some conceptualizer and a conceptualization, but in addition allows for that relationship to exist between the speech event participants themselves.

5
-chr(a): Inference and Attenuation

5.1 Introduction

In this chapter[31] I explore the semantics of the Wanka conjecture evidential *-chr(a)*. As with the direct evidential, I will consider both schema and prototype. Prototypically, *-chr(a)* functions as a marker of information source indicating that the utterance is an inference. Inferences and conjectures naturally suggest the speaker's noncommitment to the truth of an unexperienced or uncorroborated event, and in Wanka they are associated with assessments of probability, not factuality. Noncommitment to the truth of a proposition is one manifestation of the schematic nature of the suffix, which is attenuation in some domain. Its attenuative effect is evident in directives, for example, where those marked with *-chr(a)* are much weaker in their illocutionary force than those marked with the direct evidential *-m(i)*. And a number of other extensions show that *-chr(a)* contributes a sense of psychological distance or separation between the speaker and the proposition. Here we find "acquiescence", *-chr(a)*'s use in interrogative constructions, irony, and first person inferences (FPIs)-a kind of rhetorical "question." As with the direct evidential, intra-ground subjectification of some central aspect of the prototypical construal relation emerges as an important factor in category extension.

---

[31]Portions of this chapter appeared in Verspoor, Lee, and Sweetser (1997), and are reprinted by permission from John Benjamins.

5.2 Conjecture markers in Quechuan languages

The conjecture suffix in Quechua languages appears in various forms, *-ch(i), -ch(a), -chr(i),* or *-chr(a),* depending on the dialect area. As with the other suffixes of its class, the conjecture evidential may lose its final vowel if it follows an open syllable.

Descriptions of this suffix for the most part tend to be relatively brief, couched in terms of concepts such as speculation, lack of personal responsibility, probability, possibility, doubt, and uncertainty (cf. Coombs, Coombs, and Weber (1976:154); Cerrón-Palomino (1976a:239); Cusihuamán (1976:245ff.); and Soto Ruiz (1976:124) *inter alia*). Weber (1989:425ff.) is unique in noting some very intriguing facts about the conjecture suffix *-chi* in Huallaga Quechua, such as its inability to occur in certain cases that clearly seem to be semantically conjectural (cf. Weber 1989:425ff.). For example, in response to the question, *Why is your clock not working?* he notes that even though both (126a and b) are grammatical, only (126a) is acceptable as an appropriate answer.

(126) a. *mana musya-:-chu   kapas   pishi-n   millu-na-n*
          not know-1-NEG perhaps lack-3 wind-NOM-3

     b. *mana musya-:-chu   *pishi-n-chi   millu-na-n*
          not know-1-NEG lack-3-CONJ wind-NOM-3>2
     I don't know. Perhaps it needs to be wound.

He also mentions various "rhetorical effects" that may be associated with the suffix, e.g., that *-chi* may be used as a challenge/query or as a curt impolite negative (notations in brackets are his).

(127) *chay-ta musya-yka-:-chi*
     that-ACC know-IMPV-1-CONJ
     I know that. [but with rhetorical force of: 'So you think I know? I don't know a thing about it!']

(128) *noqa aywa-yka-:-chi qam-paq-qa*
     I go-IMPV-1-CONJ you-PURP-TOP
     I'm going on your behalf. [but with rhetorical force of: You might have thought I was going there, but I'm not.]

It may even be indicative of a flippant, sarcastic, or haughty attitude on the part of the speaker.

-chr(a): Inference and Attenuation

(129) *sapu-ta-chi   ima-chi   haru-riyku-: hahaa hahaha*
      frog-ACC-CONJ what-CONJ step-ASP-1   (laughs)
      It seems I've stepped on a frog, hahaha.

So, while the conjecture suffix in Quechua languages is typically characterized as indicating uncertainty, doubt, and possibility, the Huallaga data suggest the relevance of a broader range of semantic notions than what is usually noted.

5.3 *-chr(a)*'s range of meanings

The semantic network for the Wanka conjectural suffix *-chr(a)* is given in figure (130).

(130) The semantic network of *-chr(a)*[32]

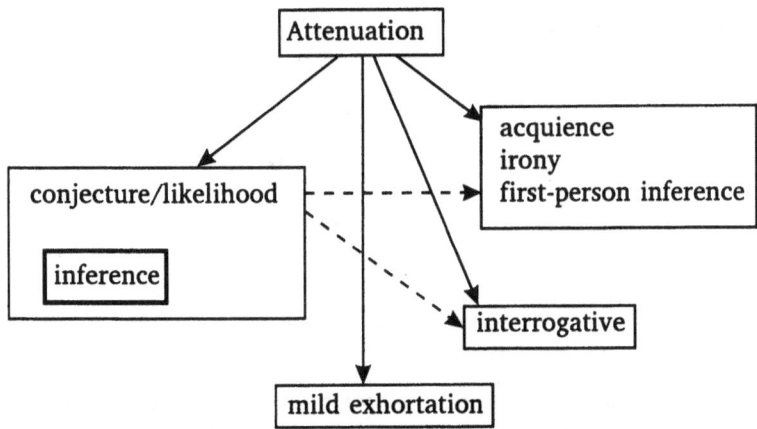

Schematically, *-chr(a)* conveys attenuation in some domain. In terms of information source, *-chr(a)* is one of two indirect evidentials, the

---

[32]The designation of semantic core and periphery can be supported by a consideration of the meaning frequencies found for *-chr(a)* across the database. The following percentages are based on 201 utterances marked by *-chr(a)*. Sixty-seven percent of these utterances are strongly associated with some value along the likelihood scale, which suggests this as the "neighborhood" of the semantic core. Most frequently, *-chr(a)* construes a circumstance in terms of either "possibility" or "probability" (64%). A particular token often occurs in a context that pushes its value closer to the "necessity" end of the scale than to "possibility." However, the precise likelihood assessment is in some cases indeterminate. The interrogative use accounts for 14% of the examples, exhortation for 10%, "acquiescence" for 6%, first-person inferences for 2%, and irony for 1%.

other being *-sh(i)*, the reportative (cf. chapter 6). I consider conjectures (which include both inferences and guesses) to be the prototype, indicated in the figure by the area outlined in boldface. As we saw with the direct evidential, there is a natural association between evidence type and validation. In this regard, *-chr(a)* conveys the speaker's noncommitment concerning the truth of the designated proposition, and couches it in terms of the speaker's assessment of a situation's likelihood as either possible, probable, or epistemically necessary. The attenuating effect of *-chr(a)* is evident in other domains as well. When marked with *-chr(a)* the force of a directive is diminished to that of a mild exhortation. Questions marked with *-chr(a)* do not obligate the addressee to an answer, as opposed to those marked with *-m(i)*, which do. In other senses such as acquiescence, irony, and first-person inferences (somewhat similar to rhetorical questions), the speaker presents himself as being somehow psychologically or emotionally distanced from owning the designated proposition. These latter three, in addition to interrogatives, can all be viewed as involving some kind of extension or intra-ground subjectification of a prominent notion found in the semantic core of conjectures and likelihood judgments.

5.4 The inferencing process

In his study of public land disputes among Trobriand Islanders, Hutchins talks about inference strategies in relation to conceptual schemas which the members of a culture share. A specific event may be construed as an instantiation of the abstract schema (cf. Schank and Abelson 1977). He states:

> Given a schema and a proposition within it, it is possible to infer the truth values of other propositions within the episode...Because of this feature it is possible for a speaker who shares the code with his listeners to omit from his verbal accounts statements which embody propositions, the truth values of which can be inferred from others in the discourse. The listener will be able to reconstruct the abbreviated discourse by applying the underlying schema and the inference routines. (1980:113f.)

Hutchins further observes:

> The conversational postulate (Grice 1975) that one should not say more than is needed to convey the meaning intended is

based in the ability of the hearer to use a knowledge structure such as the schema to fill in the discourse, and in the speaker's belief that the necessary knowledge structure is available to the hearer. (1980:114)

Although his discussion focusses primarily on the listener's perspective, it would seem that in principle any conceptualizer, on the basis of some prompt, verbal or otherwise, may "reconstruct" conceptual gaps in a scenario in order to make it conform to an abstract schema. The general claim is that an event structure schema makes inferencing possible.

One such schema that is particularly useful for our general understanding of inference is presented in Langacker (1991, chapter 6). According to the dynamic evolutionary model, reality is conceptualized as evolving and unfolding along a temporal path. Any given instantiation of reality is presumed to be related conceptually to its predecessors, inheriting its content largely from these prior instantiations and is additionally constrained by elements inherent in the world's structure. The conceptualizer is therefore not presented with a series of wholly distinct realities from one moment to the next, but rather with a continuity, which results in a kind of "evolutionary momentum." Combined, these elements quite naturally delimit the conceptualizer's expectations of the nature of unexperienced events.

The basic idea is illustrated in figure (131) which depicts any observed situation or event (E) as a slice out of the entire flow of reality as it evolves through time (t). Preceding events (E-n) have resulted in E (and perhaps states concurrent with it—E^0—of which the conceptualizer is unaware), and E itself contributes conceptual structure towards subsequent events (E+n). Even though a speaker may not have directly observed or experienced either E-n or $E+n$ (and thus they do not comprise part of his conceptualization of reality), he is nevertheless justified in advancing certain hypotheses on the nature of those events provided that they are not wholly distinct from each other and can be conceptualized as forming a relative continuity with E. Such hypotheses are, of course, constrained with respect to some set of assumptions, e.g., about the structure of the world, the propensities that certain entities may have, known history, other event schemas, etc.

(131) Event flow

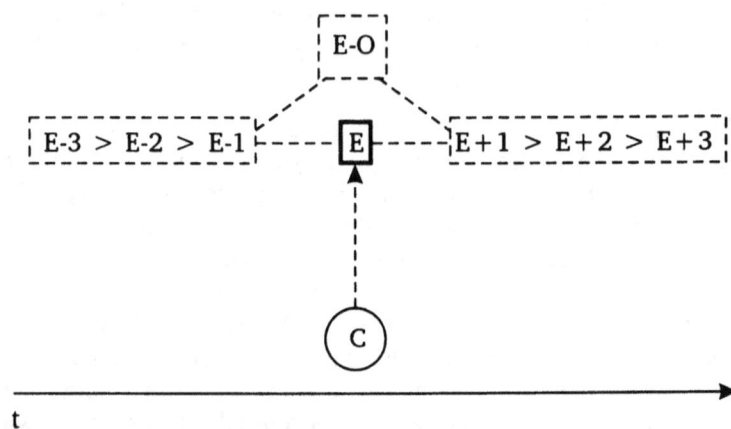

A proposal about the nature of an unobserverd or unexperienced $E\text{-}n$ or $E+n$ under these conditions amounts to an inference. Inferencing can be viewed as a sort of mental process where some perception (or belief) interacts with a set of assumptions to provide the impetus for the extrapolation of a conceptualization that is not directly perceived or experienced by the speaker. Put simply, an inference addresses the question, *What does the evidence at hand suggest or point to?*

To illustrate briefly, suppose that I hear the phone ring, I notice that the time on the clock is 1:00, and then remark, *Melanie must be home.* On the face of it, there is little inherent connection between a phone call, the time on the clock—which together would constitute the E of example (131)—and my conclusions about Melanie's location. However, if Melanie has told me she will call when she gets home from shopping, and I further know that she intended to be home around 1:00, then these circumstances quite naturally justify the inference about who is calling and where she is calling from. In this case the inference involves the conceptualization of a series of events to which the phone ringing has a connection. That is, the perceived situation is construed as the outgrowth of others which are unperceived. Any one of those unperceived circumstances may be selected for overt designation as the inference such as, *That must be Melanie calling, Melanie must be through shopping,* etc.

In actuality, the same perceived circumstances or "evidence" (in this case, the ringing phone) may also arise from a variety of other possible alternate event histories I may not have entertained. It may indeed be Melanie on the phone, but she may have run out of gas and will not be home for some time yet. Or it could even be the police informing me

-chr(a): Inference and Attenuation

that she has been detained for bludgeoning the obnoxious checker at the grocery store with a salami.

In fact any piece of evidence (E) may serve as the entry point for the conceptualizer's reconstruction of any number of possible unknown histories or event chains (EC_a, EC_b, EC_c...). as illustrated in figure (132). Any portion of such a history may then be selected and designated as an inference (I_a, I_b, I_c...).

(132) Alternative histories

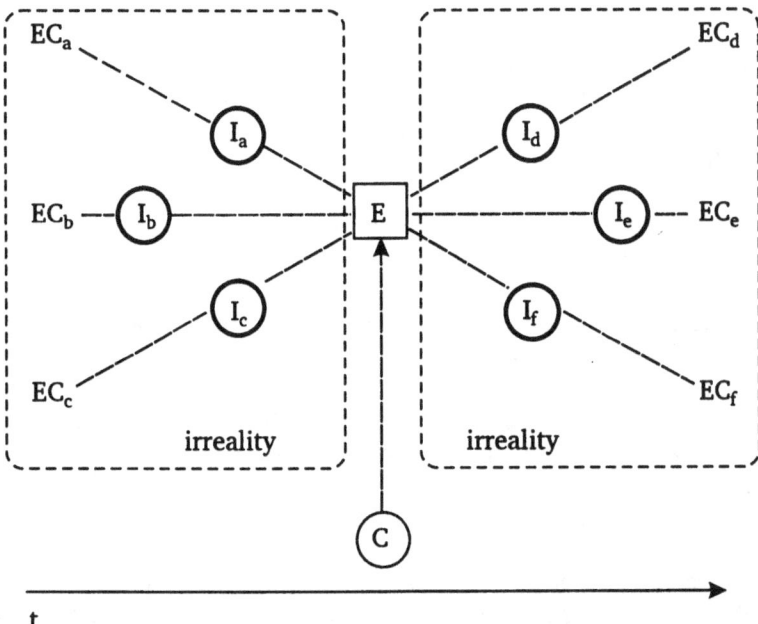

There are two things I wish to emphasize here. First, it is the hypothesized situation, and not the perceived situation, that is marked morphologically as the inference in languages with conjecture evidentials. And secondly, note that the event selected as the inference designates an uncorroborated conceptualization. Even if the extrapolation eventually proves to be factual, from the perspective of the conceptualizer at the moment when the hypothesis is advanced, it is a speculation of an inherently irrealis quality and, therefore, does not comprise part of the speaker's conceptualization of reality at that time.

5.5 Inference versus speculation

Just as there are various kinds of direct experience, it seems reasonable to differentiate between inferences and speculations or guesses, which are conjecture-like in nature but are of a somewhat distinct character. Although Wanka does not morphologically distinguish inferences from speculations, some languages apparently do, e.g., Kashaya and Patwin (cf. Oswalt 1986 and Whistler 1986).

What exactly is the difference between an inference and a speculation? Certainly inferences and speculations are similar in that they are both hypotheses which are advanced about some unexperienced or uncorroborated state of affairs. And in both cases they are associated with the speaker's noncommitment to the truth of the designated proposition. The main difference between them can be appreciated by considering the following:

(133) a. Guess who called today.
　　　b. *Infer who called today.

Guessing or speculating is done against a background of conceptual structure which, when compared to that of an inference, is much more vague and undefined, to the point of making it difficult for one to reasonably extrapolate in any more than haphazzard fashion. Example (133a) assumes the addressee has little or no basis to correctly deduce the target information. One guess is as good as another, and consequently a "correct" guess in this case is viewed as remarkable. Speculating, therefore, fits in expectationally unconstrained circumstances. On the other hand, the context of an inference is much more robust in terms of its conceptual specifications and assumptions, and this has a constraining effect on the content of the inference itself. The context predisposes the conceptualizer to hypothesize along much more narrowly defined lines. In the case mentioned earlier, the ringing phone, the prior arrangement, the time on the clock, etc., all conspire to provide justification for advancing a particular hypothesis about the identity of the caller. However, if I am not expecting a call and the phone rings, a hypothesis about the caller's identity can hardly be more than gratuitous guessing.

So, with an inference some experienced situation interacts with peripheral or background situations to launch a train of thought in a direction that is particularly constrained. Because of this, even though it remains essentially an irrealis concept, an inference is likely to be construed as more probable than a guess would be and, therefore, could have a higher commitment value associated with it than what would be associated with mere speculation.

There is some cross-linguistic support for the special status of inference above other kinds of conjecturing. Kashaya's evidential system, for example, includes a suffix, which "marks an inference based on circumstances or evidence found apart, in space or time, from the actual event or state" (Oswalt 1986:38). The interesting thing is how the evidentials rank with respect to other conjecture-like modals:

> ...all propositions with Kashaya evidentials are presented by the speaker as certain and true. However the evidentials themselves are at the top of a continuing hierarchy of modals expressing increasing uncertainty on the part of the speaker. These include a Suppositional suffix ('I suppose that...'), a Speculative ('I wonder if...'), and Optative ('I hope or wish that...'), and others. (Oswalt 1986:43)

In other words, inference in Kashaya is considered to be more "evidential-like" than other conjectural phenomena and, according to Oswalt, is associated with a greater degree of speaker commitment.

It is not clear how this argues for the prototypicality of either inference or speculation, if indeed there is any need to do so.

5.6 Likelihood

We now consider the association of conjecture with likelihood. In chapter 2, I characterized commitment as the degree to which a conceptualization is incorporated into the speaker's view of reality. Strong commitment equates with full incorporation whereas noncommitment can be understood as nonincorporation. But even if a conceptualization is construed as unreal, it may nevertheless be judged in terms of its *potential* reality. A likelihood assessment does precisely this; it addresses the potential an irrealis conceptualization has for being incorporated into the speaker's view of reality. This is largely determined by the degree to which the two share conceptual structure. In fact, the degree of conformity with respect to a set of constrained expectations provides the third principled basis encompassed by the Wanka evidential system on which a speaker may justify his validational commitment with respect to a proposition. (The other two bases—direct experience and conceptualized control over an event—have been discussed at length in chapter 4.)

Three scenarios were outlined above that equally instantiate possible events leading to the ringing of a telephone. But the closer the inferred event appears to conform to the speaker's view of reality, the more prone he will be to judge it as potentially real. In the case above, Melanie's presence at home conforms more closely to the expectations held by the speaker than either the running-out-of-gas or salami-as-a-weapon scenarios do. Indeed, given the stated set of assumptions, it would be highly unusual to conclude from a phone ringing that Melanie had been arrested, even though it is a conceivable possibility.

An irrealis event may be judged as possible, probable, or necessary depending on its degree of perceived conformity to the expectations resulting from factors previously mentioned such as evolutionary momentum, structure of the world, etc. (Note that I am using necessary in its epistemic, not deontic, sense.) POSSIBILITY is the likelihood value assigned to an inferred scenario that is sanctioned only weakly by the structure of the world, event flow, etc. An event bearing only minimal conformity to these factors prompts the conceptualizer to consider its incorporation into his view of reality as tenuous. PROBABILITY indicates that the designated circumstance conforms more tightly to the structure of the world as the speaker conceptualizes it, and that, in addition, the world is actually more favorably predisposed towards the potential manifestation of *this* situation than it may be to others. Consequently, the speaker is more inclined to consider the circumstance as potentially falling among his inventory of real events and situations. Finally, the assessment of an event as being epistemically NECESSARY involves the available evidence conspiring to point strongly towards a particular conclusion. In other words, the evolution of reality is conceptualized such that it obliges the emergence of the designated circumstance to an even greater extent than is present with either possibility or probability. It is here we find the highest degree of commitment the speaker can have regarding a circumstance that remains construed as inherently irrealis. Beyond possibility would be impossibility: the judgment assigned to a scenario that is completely at odds with speaker's view of reality. Impossibility would be associated with maximum noncommitment. Although scenarios judged as possible, probable, and necessary involve increasing degrees of conformity to the speaker's view of reality, in all cases their full acceptance as realis is held at bay because of some lack of direct corroborative experience or conceptualized control over the event.

In Wanka the conjecture marker may indicate any value along this scale of likelihood. In the majority of cases, *-chr(a)* designates the middle value of probability.

-chr(a): Inference and Attenuation

(134) kuti-mu-n'a-qa-**chr**   ni-ya-a-mi
      return-AFAR-3FUT-now-CONJ say-IMPV-1-DIR
      I think they will probably come back.

(135) aa tardi-man chraa-mu-n tardi-laa-**chra**
      yes late-GOAL arrive-AFAR-3 late-yet-CONJ
      Yes, he'll probably arrive later.

The presence of certain markers elsewhere in the sentence may bias the particular reading in one direction or another. For example, certain loans such as *siguurusi* and *siguuraminti* (both from Spanish *seguro* 'sure') tend to suggest greater certainty on the part of the speaker:

(136) siguuru-si kanan-'a chraa-lu-pti-nchik
      sure-INDEF today-TOP arrive-ASP-DS-12P

   lika-paa-ka-yaa-maa-shrun suma sumaa-**chra**
   see-BEN-REF-IMPV-1OBJ-12FUT very very-CONJ
   Today when we arrive they will surely/probably be looking at [staring at] us.

(137) waala-a   li-sha   siguuru-**chra**
      morning-TOP go-1FUT sure-CONJ
      I'll surely/very likely go tomorrow.

On the other hand, the Wanka word *ichá* 'maybe, or' or the suffix *-pis* 'indefinite' biases the meaning along the more noncommittal possibility lines.

(138) mana-pis-**chra** alli-n-chu ka-nki
      not-INDEF-CONJ good-3-NEG be-2
      You might not be okay.

But *-chr(a)* may have possibility or necessity senses without the presence of these markers:

(139) am kiki-ki-**chr** yachra-ku-nki
      you self-2P-CONJ know-REF-2
      You, yourself, must know [if you are lying].

(140) daañu pawa-shra-si   ka-ya-n-**chra**-ri
      field finish-PART-EVEN be-IMPV-3-CONJ-EMPH
      The field might be finished off [i.e., eaten by animals].

5.7 Discussion of examples

With the preceding discussion as background, then, let us consider some specific examples in more detail with respect to both the inferencing process and concomitant validational values. The context surrounding (141) involves an accusation of theft. A woman (R) has been told that her neighbor (M) was seen working near her house earlier that day. When she discovers that she has been robbed, she accuses M of being the thief. M denies it all, but in addition he replies:

(141) chay lika-a-nii   juk-ta-**chra**-a   lika-la
      that see-NOM-1P other-ACC-CONJ-TOP see-PST
      The witness (lit. 'my seer') must have seen someone else.

M could reconstruct any number of possible histories that might result in his being accused of thievery. Consider two: (1) witnesses actually saw M entering R's house, and (2) witnesses saw someone entering R's house that they mistakenly thought was M. One will mesh with M's view of reality more closely than the other and determines his choice between them. The element of mistaken identity in the second scenario accommodates earlier statements by M that he was nowhere near the house. Because the second history bears more similarity to M's reality, it is chosen and marked as the inference: if the witnesses saw someone and it wasn't M, the only possible conclusion to be drawn is that the witnesses saw someone else. Consequently, M is as convinced as he could possibly be that the witnesses are mistaken given the fact that he was not present among them and does not know who they actually *did* see.

Elsewhere we have seen cases in which the speaker deliberately imposes a certainty construal on a circumstance that is technically irrealis, e.g., the marking of a future event with -m(i). The construal under discussion at present, however, retains the essentially irrealis nature of the conceptualization as part of its semantic base, and this is important in the context of this particular interchange. If M were to give priority to his level of commitment and mark his statement with the direct instead of the conjecture evidential, then it might appear to R that M actually knew who it was that the witnesses saw.

Consider (142) which concerns a woman's suspicions about her husband's infidelity:

(142) walmi   ima-wan-si   puli-n-**chra** ni-k-mi ya'a
woman what^with-INDEF walk-3-CONJ say-1>2 I
I think you are/might be running around with some other woman. (Lit.: [With some woman he's probably walking] I tell you.)

The wider context suggests that the wife's suspicions are based on her husband's recent unexplained prolonged absence and her own observation of a novel change in his general attitudes. Add to this the fact that the husband interjects infidelity into the conversation by first accusing her of flirting with another man the day before. To the wife, this could be construed as a diversionary tactic to draw attention away from his own guilt (the guilty scream the loudest). The presence of another woman in the picture is the factor that in her estimation would make a number of things fit together into a coherent whole. Her inference may or may not accurately reflect the reality leading up to her husband's actions; its corroboration lies outside her experiential knowledge at present. But it points to a circumstance that would explain his odd behavior and would still be consistent with her own experience.

The degree of noncommitment is somewhat indeterminate in this example. Any of the likelihood values would reasonably fit the context, but the fact that so many things are explained by another woman argues strongly for a value away from the relatively noncommital possibility end of the scale. (I add that her suspicions will receive even more support later when he expresses his disenchantment with the way she carries out her household responsibilities and actually threatens to go find another wife.)

One final example is (143) from a text referred to previously in chapter 4, where F's daughter has gone off to another town with her husband. At one point in the conversation F's interlocutor L states:

(143) kay-lla-piita kuti-i-mu-n'a-**chra**-a
here-LIM-ABL return-ASP-AFAR-3FUT-CONJ-TOP
They will come back from this place.

The experiential/perceptual basis for L's conjecture is suggested earlier in the conversation when he points out that many people are going from all over the area to as far away as the United States where they stay two or three years and then return. These "observations" are not themselves immediately perceptible in the sense of unfolding before his very eyes, but exist in L's mind as knowledge of previous events. This is the "perceived" element in the scenario that provides the springboard for the inference.

This then interacts with some underlying set of assumptions, for example, the notion that similar entities will behave in similar ways. There is an obvious parallel between the general situation of local residents leaving for places unknown, and the specific case of F's daughter doing the same. This sanctions a justifiable hypothesis that there should be no difference here-since those in the first group return from so far away it is reasonable to conclude that the daughter will also.

As far as personal commitment is concerned, L is simply stating what he thinks will probably happen. His statement does not project the same degree of certainty that the equivalent sentence marked with -*m(i)* would. This is not to conclude that he is expressing any doubt about the future return of F's daughter; he may actually believe that she and her husband will come back. He simply does not put himself on the line to the same degree he would if he were to mark the utterance with -*m(i)*. He has no reason to. If pressed on the matter the speaker could only state that he does not really know the outcome for sure, so his utterance does not imply any sense of "prediction."

Thus far I have analyzed -*chr(a)* as typically marking an unexperienced situation derived on the basis of some kind of perception-assumption interaction. I have characterized the inferencing process as an attempt by the speaker to fill in some kind of conceptual gap in an event schema. Inferences are distinguished from speculations in terms of how precisely they could conform to such a schema. Validationally, the designated situation is associated with a particular degree of likelihood. But since the coded situation is itself unexperienced, the speaker is precluded from being able to state unequivocally that he knows what the situation was, is, or will be.

5.8 Nonprototypical uses

5.8.1 Mild exhortation.
I have shown how the schematic value of -*chr(a)* is manifested in the domain of commitment. Attenuated commitment equates with nonincorporation into reality, a scalar notion, and is encoded in terms of likelihood values. In the following sections I concern myself with attenuation in other domains. I turn first to directives.

Recall from chapter 4 that a second person future event (2FUT) marked with the direct evidential is usually interpreted as a directive of some sort. A 2FUT event with the conjecture evidential may also be interpreted somewhat along the same lines, but its directive force is markedly diminished in comparison and is consequently the weakest of the directive-type forms, conveying only a sense of mild exhortation or encouragement to perform some action.

I think that the difference in illocutionary strength between 2FUT events with the direct evidential and those with *-chr(a)* involves a couple of factors. I pointed out in chapter 4 that 2FUT events marked with the direct evidential are viewed as being imminent to the speech event, and that this, together with the speaker's conceptualized control over the circumstances, almost invariably results in their interpretation as directives. For a 2FUT event marked with *-chr(a)*, however, I submit that the speaker does not conceptualize the addressee's actions either as falling within his sphere of control or as being temporally imminent. Noncontrol and nonimminence of the speaker's construal of the event lead the addressee to conclude that his own personal response is likewise neither required nor imminent.

As an illustration, consider example (144). The general context involves a husband and wife discussing what the reactions of their family and friends will be in the near future when they return to the village after a prolonged absence. The husband's statement in (144a) concerns how he will stretch the truth when his friends ask him what he did. His wife's response in (144b) essentially echoes the husband's thoughts.

(144) a. M: *pay-kuna-kta-a chay intiiru wanuku-kuna-chru*
him-PL-ACC-TOP that entire Huanuco-PL-LOC

puli-mu-la-a ni-shaa-chra
walk-AFAR-PST-1 tell-1FUT-CONJ
I'll tell them, "I travelled/walked over the whole department of Huanuco."

b. P: *mas kalu-kuna-kta li-la-a ni-nki-chra-ri*
more far-PL-ACC go-PST-1 say-2-CONJ-EMPH
Yeah, tell them, "I've gone farther."[33]

I draw particular attention to the wife's response in (144b). The context does not suggest that her statement is the clear-cut result of the inferencing process, i.e., it does not appear to be a conclusion that she has drawn on the basis of any observation or perception from the

---

[33]Like a number of previous examples, (144a) and (144b) involve embedded speech, the difference here being that there is no evidential grounding for the embedded quotations. This, however, has no bearing on the present discussion, since it is the marking that appears on the quotative verb which concerns us here.

immediate context or otherwise. Its substance is rather the reaffirming and encouraging of the husband's thoughts.

The situation in (144b) is not construed as either temporally or physically imminent; it is merely a possibility envisioned as occurring at some unspecified point in the future, perhaps days or weeks from the time of the speech event, and at a location quite removed from where this conversation actually takes place. In other words, there is a substantial degree of temporal (as well as physical) distance between the speech event and the possible actualization of the event designated by the conjecture-marked utterance.

This separation serves to diminish the speaker's control over the addressee and his actions. Since they are not in a situation where the husband could actually do what the wife is telling him to, she ultimately exerts very little control over what her husband can or will do. Consequently, (144b) is not understood as "requiring" the immediate response of the addressee; he is under little or no obligation to actualize the event. The effect of (144b) may be to encourage the addressee's actions along a particular line, but, according to native speakers, it certainly does not have the strength or impact that the same utterance with the direct evidential would.

Similarly, in the context prior to (145) the wife has expressed doubt about something in her husband's account of a recent trip to a museum. In (145) the husband tells her to ask the friend who was with him at the time so she can verify it for herself.

(145) raasun-chun chay-nu ka-ña ni-nki-**chr**-ari
real-YN? that-SIM be-NPST say-2-CONJ-EMPH
Then ask him if it was really that way. (Lit. Then say to him [was it really that way?])

Since the friend is not present during this conversation, the fulfillment of this directive cannot take place, at least not immediately. So it makes sense to understand (145) as the husband simply encouraging his wife to investigate the issue at some unspecified point in the future. As in the previous example, the speaker does not view himself as exerting any particularly strong degree of control over the addressee's actions, and so her response is ultimately of little consequence to him. It would only concern him if he expected the addressee to do as he suggests. But I do not think that such an expectation is part of the picture.

5.8.2 Acquiescence. In certain contexts -*chr(a)* conveys a sense of acquiescence. Here it points to the speaker's assessment of an event's

-chr(a): Inference and Attenuation

inevitability, and therefore bears links to the necessity end of the likelihood scale. In addition, the likelihood assessment is overlaid with some kind of resistance, disinclination, or diminished enthusiasm on the part of the speaker and can be viewed as the "flip side" of intentionality.

Examples (146) and (147) display the acquiescence use of *-chr(a)*. Both examples occur in a discussion where a woman (L) is demanding compensation from a neighbor (M) whose pigs have just destroyed one of her potato fields. At first, M denies that it could have been his pigs. But when he finally realizes he may be responsible, he states (146) and then later (147).

(146) *paaga-llaa-shrayki-chra-a*
pay-POL-1 > 2FUT-CONJ-EMPH
I suppose I'll pay you, then.

(147) *tapa-chi-mu-llaa-shra   kiki-n   daañiru-ku-u-kaa-ta-chr*
SOW-CAUS-AFAR-POL-1FUT itself-3 damage-REF-NOM-DEF-ACC-CONJ
I guess I'll sow seed right where the damage was.

Recall from chapter 4 that first future events marked with the direct evidential often conveyed a sense of intentionality. In marked contrast, the sense that is conveyed by the conjecture evidential here is one of resignation with respect to the designated event.

Another illustration comes from the domestic argument mentioned above where the man has left his wife for several days. Tired of hearing her complaints about his activities the man mutters (148a) with the direct evidential *-m(i)*. The contrast between this and (148b) with *-chr(a)* is instructive:

(148) a. *kanan li-ku-shraa-ña-m   may-ta-si   uy*
now   go-REF-1FUT-NOW-DIR where-ACC-INDEF oh
Now I'm taking off for anywhere (groan).

b. *kanan li-ku-shraa-ña-chr   may-ta-si   uy*
now   go-REF-1FUT-NOW-CONJ where-ACC-INDEF oh
Now I'm taking off for anywhere (groan).

According to my language help, the difference between (148a) and (148b) with *-chr(a)* is that (b) would suggest the speaker's recognition of "some sort of wrongdoing" or remorse over something that he has done, and is therefore leaving. It would be tantamount to an admission of guilt, which could be reasonably approximated by "Hmmm, I guess I'll leave then." The speaker accepts a forthcoming event as inevitable but does so only reluctantly.

Unlike the intentionality sense of *-m(i)*, acquiescence is not restricted to first person subjects. Mild exhortations discussed earlier may have this sense as well. In the text previously referred to in which the father is trying to convince his daughter to go school, he finally says:

(149) kiida-alu-nki-ña-**chra**-a
       stay-ASP-2-now-CONJ-EMPH
       I guess you'll stay then.

His daughter's refusal to attend classes overcomes his own desires to the contrary.

Notions of force dynamics (Talmy 1985) are directly relevant to the explication of acquiescence. Acquiescence provides a nice contrast to intentionality discussed in chapter 4. As stated there, intentionality does not necessitate the conceptualization of an obstacle in the path of achieving a goal. But if one is encountered, the conceptualizer will expend effort expecting to overcome it, since he envisons his imminently future actions and circumstances as residing within his sphere of influence and hence largely subject to his own control and manipulation. This is shown in (150) with the conceptualizer C as the agonist (indicated by the +), exerting force to overcome a potential obstacle (antagonist) that may stand in the way of some envisioned result.

(150) Intentionality-conceptualizer as agonist

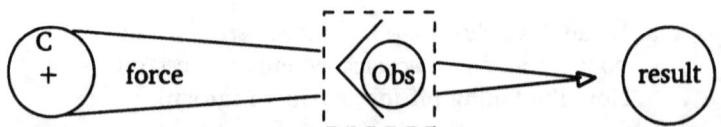

With acquiescence, however, the conceptualizer is what opposes the natural bias of the event flow. Figure (151) shows the force of the event flow as the agonist overcoming the 'antagonist' conceptualizer.

(151) Acquiescence-conceptualizer as antagonist

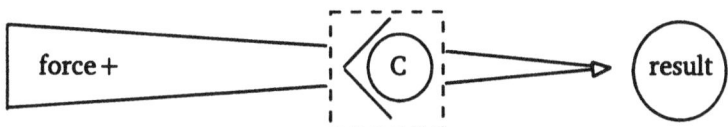

With both intentionality and acquiescence, the obstacle to the flow of events is viewed as yielding. With intentionality the opposing force yields to the conceptualizer; with acquiescence it is the conceptualizer who yields.

5.8.3 Interrogative -chr(a). The conjecture evidential appears in content questions as illustrated by examples (152) through (154)

(152) *pero ima-nuy-pa-chr   walmi-i   daañu-kaa-chi-la*
but   what-SIM-GEN-CONJ WOMAN-1P damage-PSV-CAUS-PST
But I wonder how my wife let them damage [the field]. (Or How did my wife let them damage [the field]?)

(153) *ima-lla-kta-chr   u-yku-shrun   llapa ayllu-kuna-kta-si*
what-LIM-ACC-CONJ give-ASP-12FUT all   family-PL-ACC-EVEN

  chra-alu-l
  arrive-ASP-SS
I wonder what we will give our families when we arrive.

(154) *ima-kta   pinsa-l-chra   chay-nuu-ta suyñu-ku-u-la-nki*
what-ACC think-SS-CONJ that-SIM-ACC dream-REF-ASP-PST-2
What do you suppose you were thinking about to dream that?

In chapter 4 I discussed some of what is entailed in a general analysis of interrogative constructions. In particular, I stated that the construal relationship that holds between a speaker and a proposition in an assertion (figure (155)) is "inverted" and construed to hold between the addressee and a proposition (figure (156)). Specifically, in a question with -m(i) the speaker construes the addressee as being in a direct relationship to the designated proposition and is thus in the position to be able to provide the solicited answer. -m(i)-marked questions thus expect answers.

(155) Assertion schema

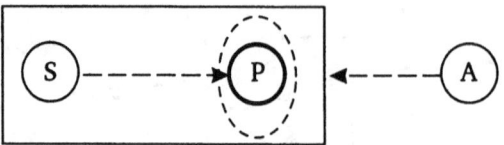

(156) Question schema

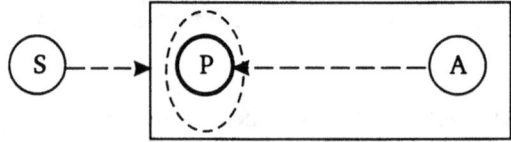

A parallel analysis for a -*chr(a)*-marked question may be argued for. The validational commitment typically associated with conjecture—concommitment—is the operative factor that obtains here. Specifically, the speaker is uncertain or uncommitted about the relationship that exists between the addressee and the proposition. While in reality, the addressee may be in any construal relationship to the designated proposition, i.e., direct, conjecture, or reportative, the speaker simply does not purport to know.

The schematic attenuating effect of -*chr(a)* is precisely what we might expect; unlike questions marked with the direct evidential that require a response, -*chr(a)*-marked questions do not. The difference between questions marked with the direct evidential and those marked with the conjecture marker thus appears to reflect what Lyons describes as the distinction between

> ...asking a question of someone and simply *posing* the question (without necessarily addressing it to anyone). When we pose a question, we merely give expression to, or externalize our doubt; and we can pose questions which we do not merely expect to remain unansered, but which we know, or believe, to be unanswerable. To ask a question of someone is both to pose the question and, in doing so, to give some indication that one's addressee is expected to respond by answering the question that is posed. (1977:755)

In other words, -*chr(a)* sets the stage for a conjecture, but does not actually make one.

-chr(a): Inference and Attenuation

The response predicted for -chr(a)-marked questions is borne out in the following excerpt from a conversation where a father (M) and mother (L) are discussing their son who has borrowed money from a neighbor under false pretexts.

(157) a. M: *may-chruu-chra gasta-y-pa   paawa-alu-n*
where-LOC-CONJ spend-NOM-GEN finish-ASP-3
M: I wonder where he spent it all.

b. *mayan-pa tienda-n-man-chru li-l   ima-k-si*
who-GEN store-3P-GOAL-LOC go-ss what-ACC-EVEN

lanti-mu-la-si
buy-AFAR-PST-EVEN
In whose store would he have gone and bought something?

c. L: *kanan ima-nuy-chra ka-shrun*
today what-SIM-CONJ be-12FUT
L: Now what will we do? (Lit.: Today how will we be?)

The interchange does not point to (157a) as a typical information-seeking question. The speaker of (157a) does not construe the addressee as being in a particularly privileged position to be able to answer his query. Note that he does not wait for a response from L, but instead follows it with another question. M's construal of L's relationship to the proposition, i.e., uncertainty, appears to be justified since her response in (157c) is likewise another -chr(a) question.

A similar situation holds in the following where two individuals are discussing the problems caused by a neighbor who is perpetually drunk. At one point one of the speakers says:

(158) a. *imana-alu-chwan-chra*
what^do-ASP-12POT-CONJ
What can we do?

b. *am-chra lima-pa-nki-man*
you-CONJ talk-BEN-2-POT
You might be able to talk to him.

c. *ya'a mana-m lima-pa-y-ta   yachra-a-chu*
I   no-DIR talk-BEN-INF-ACC know-1-NEG
I don't know how to talk (advise).

Here again, the speaker poses the *-chr(a)* question in (158a) but the fact that she responds to her own question suggests that she does not expect a response from the addressee.

To summarize this section, interrogative *-chr(a)* "poses" rather than "asks" a question. It follows the pattern observed in questions with the direct evidential where some aspect of the prototypical construal is subjectified intra-ground and redirected towards the addressee. For *-chr(a)* questions, since the speaker is uncertain about the relationship the addressee bears to the designated proposition, no response is really expected.

5.8.4 Irony. Sperber and Wilson identify the classical characterization of irony as "saying one thing and meaning, or implicating, the opposite" (1986:240). They point out, however, that a definition such as this is inadequate to characterize the general nature of irony; it does not explain the difference between what we recognize as cases of genuine irony and what would otherwise amount to a "bizarre practice" of irrationally making patently false statements to convey the truth. Instead, they suggest that genuine irony is "echoic," that is, "it is an interpretation of a thought of someone other than the speaker" (1986:241). Haiman expresses a view similar to that of Sperber and Wilson regarding sarcasm (a particularly caustic form of irony)[34] when he says, "Sarcasm is possible-and indeed, almost expected-in only those cases where there is some recognition of two different frameworks: that of the speaker, and of the person quoting the speaker" (Haiman 1989:149).

In irony, then, the speaker echoes the thought or opinion of some individual (or type of individual). But the echoing of an opinion in and of itself does not constitute irony. Sperber and Wilson note that echoic utterances may be found covering the entire range of speaker attitudes "from outright acceptance and approval to outright rejection and disapproval" (1986:240). Irony specifically involves what Haiman (1989) refers to as "alienation," i.e., some kind of emotional or psychological distance between the speaker and the designated situation. Similarly, for Sperber and Wilson, irony is primarily designed to ridicule the echoed

---

[34]Sperber and Wilson (1986) do not discuss any distinctions between irony and sarcasm, presumably because it is not relevant for their purposes. I will adopt the same view here. Haiman (1990:187f.), however, points out a number of differences between them which are worth mentioning. Irony may be innocent; "a speaker need not be aware that his words are 'false'." But in order to be sarcastic, the speaker must know that what he is saying is at variance with the truth. In addition, irony is much milder in its effect, whereas sarcasm is particularly aggressive and caustic. In fact, its etymology (Greek *sarkasmos* related to *sarkazein*, 'to rip flesh') reflects its primary intent to wound, ridicule, or subject another to contempt.

opinion, "The attitude expressed by an ironical utterance is invariably of the rejecting or disapproving kind... The speaker dissociates herself from the opinion echoed and indicates that she does not hold it herself" (Sperber and Wilson 1986:239).

In light of these observations, consider the role of -*chr(a)* in the following line from a text where a father tries to reason with his daughter who is stubbornly refusing to go to school. When she continues to resist the father remarks,

(159) *chay-nuu-pa-chr yachra-nki*
that-SIM-GEN-CONJ know-2
(I suppose) That's how you learn [i.e., that is the way in which you will learn].

There are two possible interpretations of this utterance:

(160) a. As a genuine inference, i.e., perhaps one can indeed learn by refusing to go to school.
b. As irony, i.e., that's an absurd idea.

The first alternative would suggest that, based on some piece of evidence, the father has come to the conclusion that going to school is perhaps a possible way to learn, that there may indeed be others, and that although this conclusion does not reflect his own personal experience, it lies within the realm of possiblity. But the problem with this is that elsewhere he is adamant about the necessity of her attending school. The prototype interpretation thus contradicts the context. This might leave the daughter confused if it were not for the fact that, assuming the principle of relevance (cf. Sperber and Wilson 1986), addressees invariably attempt to relate seemingly disparate propositions into some coherent theme. So although the father himself does not engage in an inferencing process, this is precisely what the daughter must do in order for his statement to make any sense.

I suggest that (159) is best understood as an ironical utterance. In this view, it would be echoic-the father is attributing to the daughter the belief that one can learn by refusing to go to school. In (159) the father echoes that opinion, but clearly does not own it. If (159) is put forth primarily to show just how preposterous the daughter's view is, then its rhetorical punch crucially depends on the intra-ground subjectification of the inferencing process, i.e., on the addressee's ability to infer the speaker's intended metamessage on the basis of the -*chr(a)*-marked statement.

Consider the conversational turn in (161a and b) which follows on the heels of a wife's complaint that her husband has gone off on a drinking binge for several days leaving her to do all the work. Note in particular the wife's response in (161b):

(161) a. M: *pero chay-paa-**chr**-ari walmi-i ka-nki nila*
but that-PURP-CONJ-EMPH woman-1P be-1 so^then

ima-paa-taa karaju aa
what-PURP-SCORN dammit huh
M: But (I suppose) that's what you are my wife for. [If not for that] then what, dammit?

b. P: *nila umri am-si chay-paa-**chra**-ri ka-nki ni-i*
so^then man you-also that-PURP-CONJ-EMPH be-2 say-1

puli-ka-mu-na-yki-pa upya-ka-mu-na-yki-paa-chun[35]
walk-REF-AFAR-NOM-2-PURP
drink-REF-AFAR-NOM-2-PURP-YN?
P: So then I think [I suppose you're a man just for that], to run around and drink?

Example (161a) can be understood as a prototypical inference. If (161b) were similarly understood, it would suggest that the wife had arrived at the conclusion that, although she was not absolutely certain about this, her husband's role in life might actually be to run around and get drunk, and that it deserved at least some consideration as a possible role.

But the context clearly shows that (161b) should be understood as ironic. Although the wife's statement is marked with -chr(a), she does not truly entertain the possibility that her husband's sole purpose in life is to drink it away. Also, it is echoic-when the husband equates the wife's role with her recent hardships, she responds with an analogous association of his role with his recent revelry. The suggestion is that by holding a certain view of her role, he must hold a comparable one about his role as well. Like the previous example, the speaker echoes not the addressee's opinion per se, but an attributed one.

Consider one final example involving a dispute between a man and his wife. Initially, he has complained that she never does any work.

---

[35]In contrast to other cases of embedded speech discussed earlier, this example shows evidential marking only on the embedded quote/thought and not on the matrix verb.

-chr(a): Inference and Attenuation

When she counters with the assertion that she works as hard as any man, the following interchange takes place:

(162) a. M: *i   chay-pi ya'a-ña-tak-**chra** walmi-ki   ka-shra*
            M: and that-ABL I-NOW-FURTH-CONJ woman-2P be-1FUT
            M: And so then (I suppose) I'm your wife.

   b. P: *aa   walmi-i-ña-ri   ka-y*
         P: okay woman-1P-NOW-EMPH be-IMP
         P: All right then, be my wife.

   c. M: *chay-piita am   ima-k   lula-nki-nila*
         M: that-ABL you what-ACC do-2-THEN
         M: So then what will you do?

   d. P: *puñu-shraa-**chra***
         P: sleep-1FUT-CONJ
         P: I'll sleep.

For the husband's comment in (162a) to be understood as a prototypical inference, his thinking would have to go something like this: "Well, if you work hard like a man, and if there is only one man per married couple, and if that's you, then I must be the wife." But obviously, this is not the case; men are not, and cannot be wives. The result of this line of reasoning leads to an absurd conclusion, which is completely in line with Sperber and Wilson's observation that "momentary processing difficulties" such as this one are typical of the best examples of irony (1986:242). But by viewing (162a) as irony, we see its echoic nature in the husband attributing to his wife-albeit tongue in cheek-the view that he should be the wife. He can then freely brand this idea as ludicrous rather than actually considering its possible merits.

By way of summary, then, in an ironic utterance the speaker echoes the opinion of another, but dissociates himself from it in some way. In actuality, the echoed opinion may be one that the speaker only attributes to someone, rather than being one that the other individual truly holds. In Wanka, irony is marked by -*chr(a)*. The examples discussed here do not occur in contexts which support a prototypical inference analysis. Instead the -*chr(a)*-marked utterance invites an inference on the part of the addressee to derive an intended metamessage behind it.

Two final points need to be made before leaving this section. First, I think it is important to note that if considered apart from larger discourse and contextual considerations, the ironic use of -*chr(a)* would remain unaccounted for. I think it is safe to say as a gross generalization that a sentence in isolation marked with -*chr(a)* initially invokes an interpretation along the lines of a prototypical inference. But, as we have observed, if the context shows that the speaker dissociates himself from the content of the inference, then the same marker indicates something quite distinct from the interpretation that would probably be suggested by the identical utterance in isolation.

The second point concerns why the inference evidential should take on the function of irony. Assuming Sperber and Wilson's perspective, there is an obvious connection between *reportative* phenomena and irony, since echoing an opinion could be considered as a special case of hearsay. And indeed there seems to be a certain amount of cross-linguistic confirmation for this. Ballard (1974) notes that it is the hearsay particle which is used to convey irony and sarcasm in a number of Philippine languages, and a similar situation is noted by Blass (1990) for Sissala. The hearsay/inferential particles in Turkish (cf. Slobin and Aksu 1982) and Albanian (called "admirative" by Friedman 1986:180) also may be used to convey irony. Haiman (1990, 1992) has pointed out that even English uses a "spoken rendition of the orthographic quote sign" as a kind of reportative evidential which has an ironic sense, as in (163):

(163)   Your quote (unquote) principles are nothing but snobism.

On the other hand, irony is not merely echoic, but echoic-ness coupled with the speaker's alienation or dissociation from the echoed opinion. The association of irony with the conjecture marker may be equally motivated if we consider the dissociation of the speaker with the content of his utterance as simply one particular manifestation of the schematic conceptual distance that pervades the semantics of the suffix in general (cf. chapter 7). At this point, however, I have no data apart from Quechua to show how common the association of irony and conjecture marking may be cross-linguistically.

5.8.5 First person inferences. In the preceding section we saw that an ironical utterance involved the intra-ground subjectification of the inferencing process and relies upon the *addressee* to "read between the lines" to infer a particular metamessage. This is also what we usually find when -*chr(a)* marks first-person events in either the present or past tense. What initially appears to be the speaker conjecturing about his own present or past experience is in fact something quite distinct. The effect of these "first person inferences" (FPIs) is almost inevitably something along the lines of a rhetorical question (I will return to rhetorical questions below) even though the construction itself is not interrogative.

Formally an FPI involves -chr(a) marking on a first-person subject realis event, as exemplified by (164).

(164) ya'a trabaju-u-ta-**chra**-a upya-ka-mu-u
     I work-1P-ACC-CONJ-TOP drink-REF-AFAR-1
     Lit.: (I suppose) I drink my work (i.e., what I earn).

The context of (164) was introduced in (160) and (161). It is the husband's response to his wife's criticism of his going out on a drinking binge for several days. It seems reasonable to assume that, by itself, the presence of -chr(a) on a first-person subject realis tense verb might initially point to the speaker's hypothesizing about his own past or present actions. A context where (164) could be interpreted as a prototypical inference might involve the speaker realizing that a quantity of money he thought he had is missing; (164) could then be viewed as the speaker's speculations about his own actions in order to account for the disappearance of the money. In this view, *I drink what I earn-chr(a)* is a hypothesis designating an event that lies outside of the speaker's direct experience.

But (164) in fact, occurs in a context in which there is no question in the mind of the speaker about what he has done with his money. Rather, -chr(a) marks a scenario the speaker does know and has experienced, i.e., the obvious fact that he has indeed spent his money on booze. Since the speaker is fully cognizant of his actions he does not need to speculate about his activities in any way. Thus, -chr(a) in conjunction with a first-person present or past tense verb is somewhat anomalous as it creates processing difficulties like those incurred in ironic utterances.

Rather than marking a conceptualization the speaker arrives at via the inferencing process, the actual effect is to force the addressee to speculate and draw conclusions about the relevance of the utterance to the interchange so as to "complete" the picture with the appropriate "missing piece." The net effect of (164) is something along the lines of, *I drink, and what's it to ya?* Or, *So what if I drink what I earn?* The thrust of this verbal joust is the metamessage, i.e., *It's none of your business what I do with my money,* but which is left for the addressee to infer.

We see then that FPIs exemplify the same intra-ground subjectfication evident in the ironical use of -chr(a). Like ironical utterances, the inferencing process is shifted from being speaker-centric to being addressee-centric. Rather than communicating "the speculation is mine,"

-*chr(a)* in this context conveys the idea "the speculation is yours." The difference between FPIs and irony is that with irony, -*chr(a)* marks a scenario that the speaker knows to be patently false, while with FPIs -*chr(a)* marks a scenario that is true in the sense of comprising part of the speaker's experienced reality.

Another example appears in a text referred to previously involving an accusation of theft. At one point the woman claims the man cannot think of doing anything but stealing, to which he replies:

(165) nila talpu-ku-na-a-paa-**chra**   chakma-ka-yaa-mu-u
   so   plant-REF-NOM-1-PURP-CONJ break^ground-REF-IMPV-AFAR-1
   [Lit.] So then (I suppose) I break up the ground (i.e.,"hoe") in order to plant.

As a prototypical inference, this response would require a context in which the speaker was speculating about why one breaks up the ground. In such a context it could be glossed, *So then I suppose that I hoe in order to plant*. But not only does the context not support such a reading, it is ludicrous to suppose that any Quechua would speculate about something so basic to agrarian life.

Assuming, then, that the speaker is perfectly aware of why he hoes, the presence of -*chr(a)* prompts the addressee to find a different interpretation. The effect in this context is more like, *[If I can't think of anything but stealing] then why do I break up the ground to plant?* or *So why do YOU suppose I hoe then?*

That this is indeed the intended sense is borne out by the immediately following utterance in which the accused man specifically recasts (165) as a question.

(166) nila ima-paa-**taa**   chakma-yaa-mu-u   intunsis
   so   what-PURP-SCORN break^ground-IMPV-AFAR-1 then
   So then why DO I break up the ground then?

It is important to note that, just as (165) is not a typical inference, neither is (166) a typical information-seeking question; that much is evident from the scorn marker -*taa* on the interrogative pronoun. A true information-seeking question would be marked with the direct evidential as discussed in chapter 4. The inference to be drawn by the addressee in this case is that the accusation of theft is ridiculous since it is obvious he works and has no need to steal.

-chr(a): Inference and Attenuation 121

Before leaving this chapter, a word is in order about the similarity between FPIs and rhetorical questions. Rhetorical questions (RQs) have been commonly characterized as questions that do not expect a response, in particular those to which the speaker already knows the answer,[36] and are common in discourses that seek to motivate compliance with a particular view, e.g., political talks, advertisements, etc. In fact, Frank (1990:737) suggests (contra Brown and Levinson (1978)), that rhetorical questions do not serve to "normalize social relationships by balancing speaker and hearer 'face' needs...RQ's...were most frequently found in those conversations where conflict was predominant." They appear to be a major device utilized by a speaker to persuade his interlocutor or win the argument. As we have seen above this is certainly the case for FPIs. (See also Haviland (1987) on the connection between evidentials and arguments in Tzotzil and Warlpiri.)

In addition, glosses for FPIs provided by language helpers often have the grammatical form of rhetorical questions. As we have seen, examples (164) and (166) may be glossed as, *So what if I drink what I earn?* Or, *So then why DO I break up the ground then?* Finally, an important similarity between real questions and prototypical inferences parallels the similarity between RQs and FPIs. Both true, information-seeking questions and prototypical inferences point to gaps in the speaker's knowledge, which are filled in distinct ways discussed in various places elsewhere in this study. But RQs (on one definition) and FPIs-both formally identical to their aforementioned counterparts—involve no gap in the speaker's knowledge at all, but are used instead to make some kind of argumentative point. As with irony, the effectiveness of these two constructions depends on the addressee drawing the proper inference, and thus, intra-ground subjectification of some facet of the prototype plays a role here as well.

---

[36]Frank (1990) points out numerous problems in even defining the notion of a rhetorical question. While most people can readily provide examples of them, it is also true that many rhetorical questions can just as easily be interpreted simply as requests for information. "The chief difficulty with identifying R[hetorical] Q[uestions...[is] reliance on analysts' ability to discern speakers' intentions accurately and identify the forces carried by utterances in language 'as it is actually used'" (1990:725). Also, there are conflicting views concerning the function of rhetorical questions. Frank points out that rhetorical questions are used effectively to enable the speaker to make stronger statements than those that are possible via simple assertions (Frank 1990:726). Yet this seems to conflict with Brown and Levinson's treatment of rhetorical questions as accomplishing "face-threatening acts" indirectly (cf. Brown and Levinson 1978), thereby attenuating the strength of the statement.

5.9 Summary

This chapter has presented both schematic and prototypical values of the conjecture marker -chr(a) along with various extensions. -chr(a) attenuates commitment values which are manifested in terms of likelihood assessments. As an information source marker, -chr(a) typically indicates an utterance is the product of an inference. Its attenuating effect can be observed in the diminished illocutionary force of second person future events. With acquiescence we see the reluctant acceptance of an inevitable event. Irony and FPIs involve the intra-ground subjectification of the prototypical inferencing process itself.

6
-sh(i): Hearsay and Revelation

6.1 Introduction

In this chapter[37] I discuss four distinct but related uses of the Wanka reportative suffix *-sh(i)*. Unlike the direct and conjecture evidentials, whose schemas concern commitment values, schematically *-sh(i)* presents information as being "revelatory" in some way, and is not primarily validational at all. The prototypical revelation is HEARSAY, in which the speaker serves as a conduit through which information from another source passes.

The uses of *-sh(i)* derive from the basic conceptualization of an information chain which embodies the nature of reported speech. Two related concepts stand out as being particularly crucial and serve as themes throughout the analysis: (1) the way in which a prior informational "origin" is construed, and (2) the nature of revealed knowledge. With respect to the first point, *-sh(i)*'s extensions all involve some alteration of the prototypically construed origin. Concerning the second point, reported information by nature designates some event that purportedly happened totally outside the speaker's awareness, and to which he bears no evidentiary link beyond having been told by another. This has certain potential ramifications, as other domains pertaining to experience and knowledge beyond normal experiential access are encompassed. In its peripheral uses, the reporative may encode a speech

---

[37]Portions of this chapter are reprinted from Casad (1996), with the permission of Mouton de Gruyter.

event participant's subjective reaction to information from such domains.

As with the direct and conjecture evidentials, -sh(i) has a network category structure with diverse uses motivated from a central prototype or one or more of its extensions. Here as well, intra-ground subjectification is relevant to its nonprototypical senses.

I will also touch on the issue of validation that is frequently associated with evidential phenomena. It will be seen that the Wanka reportative is an evidential in the narrow sense of the word, in that validation is highly peripheral to its characterization. The fact that information has been received from another individual does not preclude the speaker from believing it completely. Thus, in its prototypical use the reportative truly does indicate only information source and does not appear to function as a modal indicating the speaker's degree of commitment to a proposition. In addition, I suggest that, whereas validation may be applicable at some level with respect to the prototype, the concept itself becomes less relevant to its nonprototypical uses, particularly riddles and challenges.

6.2 Reportatives in the literature

The reportative throughout the Quechua language family appears in either of two forms: -shi or -si depending on the dialect. In some dialects the final vowel is deleted following an open syllable (-sh, -s).

In general, evidentials are viewed by Palmer (1986:51) as devices by means of which a speaker signals the degree to which he is committed to a proposition. This tends to be the characterization adopted by Jake and Chuquín (1979), Cole (1985) and Hurley (1991) for the reportative in Imbabura (Ecuadorian) Quichua. Here -sh(i) is characterized as expressing the speaker's uncertainty over the information in the utterance.

Other descriptions of Quechua reportatives usually tend to focus on its prototypical hearsay function. For example, Quesada (1976:157) writes, "Este enclítico indica que lo que afirma el hablante no ha sido conocido directamente por él, sino que lo ha oido o ha tenido noticias. Es decir, afirma algo por información a través de terceros."

Cusihuamán elaborates on the nature of the information source, indicating that it is not restricted to an individual, personal source: "...el hablante está informado...sólo mediante otra persona o a través de otras fuentes de información tales como los libros, periódicos, cartas, radio, televisión, cuentos, historias, conversaciones, etc." (1976:241). He further specifies that the content of the event can be an "interpretation" of what the information source has said or written. In other words, -sh(i) may be used to indirectly quote or paraphrase another information source.

Only Weber (1989), writing on the Huallaga dialect, provides evidence for a situation that is more complicated than that suggested by other authors. He includes examples of riddles, which are marked by -*sh(i)*, under a general discussion of "formulaic expressions" (1989:447f.), as well as an example of an "embedded question complement with -*shi*" (p. 437)-what I have called a challenge. It is worth noting that the formulaic expression beginning a Huallaga riddle—*imataq-shi kaykaa*—is glossed without reference to a second-hand information source as 'What am I?' rather than 'What do they say I am?'. Similarly, no reference to a second-hand information source is suggested by the gloss of the question complement. But unfortunately, in neither case does he explain the motivation for encoding these phenomena with the reportative.

Several somewhat more extensive treatments of reportatives in other languages are found in Slobin and Aksu (1982), Aksu-Koc and Slobin (1986), Blass (1990), and Casad (1992). These studies not only identify a number of seemingly disparate uses, but also attempt to unify them in some coherent way.

Blass (1990) argues cogently against Palmer's (1986) view of the reportative as an evidential with a modal function. The reportative *ré* in Sissala (a Niger-Congo language) has numerous functions; it introduces direct and indirect speech (clearly hearsay-type functions) as well as various propositional attitudes such as *think, believe,* and *want*. In addition it appears in questions. This latter use is completely unexpected in Palmer's account since, as Blass comments, "In asking a question, the speaker does not commit himself to the truth of the proposition expressed, so how could the addition of *ré* weaken the speaker's commitment?" (1990:100). Her solution is to reinterpret the Sissala reportative as an indicator of "interpretive (as opposed to 'descriptive') use" (cf. Sperber and Wilson 1986).

Slobin and Aksu (1982) and Aksu-Koc and Slobin (1986) note that one of the two past tense markers in Turkish, -*mIs*, has senses which include inference, hearsay, and irony, as well as the seemingly disparate notions of scorn and compliments. In their view, what ties all these uses together is that the event is presented as a situation which the speaker was not fully prepared to experience or mentally assimilate at the moment, i.e., "situations on the fringe of consciousness" (1986:163).

Casad identifies six uses of Cora's reportative *yee*, and notes that the conceptual scenes related to each use "are all built on the recapitulation of a verbal, mental or speech event" (1992:176). What results is a network category with members whose senses "differ mainly in that a speaker is free to select for highlighting one set of features or another from a basic conceptual conversational schema" (1992:176). As we have seen elsewhere, multiple senses are included in a single category without requiring the same semantic elements to be present in each sense.

6.3 Uses of -sh(i)

The semantic network for the reportative suffix is given in (167). Schematically, -sh(i) marks information as being revelatory in some way. Revealed information is conceptually different from information one "arrives at" through some experiential or logical process. There is an element of "unveiling" which entails the potential for surprise. These notions will be developed in the course of the discussion.

(167) Semantic network of -sh(i)

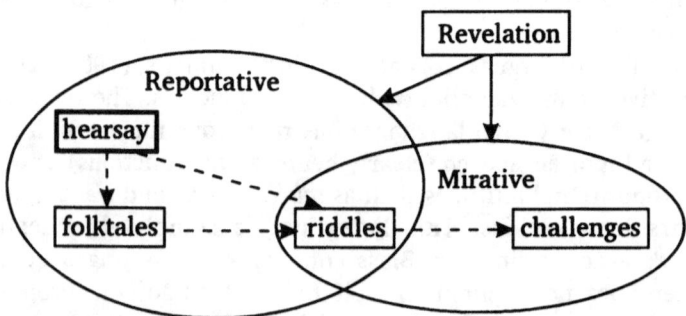

The suffix has four distinct but interrelated uses. It may indicate that an utterance is based on hearsay, it serves as a marker of folktales, it appears on riddles, and is used in what I refer to as a "challenge" question. While there are substantial differences between the hearsay, folktale, and riddle uses, they do share a common "reportative" sense in that at some level they mark information which is second-hand in nature. I consider hearsay to be the category prototype for reasons which I will elaborate next. The folktale and riddle uses can be viewed as obvious extensions of the hearsay prototype. The use of -sh(i) in challenges is not reportative in character at all, but can be understood as an extension motivated from less central characteristics of the other uses, particularly riddles. Both riddles and challenges also involve "mirativity" (cf. DeLancey 1997); they evoke circumstances of "impending revelation"

-sh(i): Hearsay and Revelation   127

and the potential for the subjective reaction of surprise on the part of the speech act participants.

6.3.1 Hearsay. The examples in (168) are typical showing that *-sh(i)* refers to information that has come to the hearer from some second-hand information source.

(168)   a. *shanti-**sh**   prista-ka-mu-la*
        Shanti-REP borrow-REF-AFAR-PST
        (I was told) Shanti borrowed it.

   b. *mana-laa-si   jesucristo   naasi-mu-pti-n-**shi**   chay-kuna*
      not-yet-EVEN Jesus^Christ   born-AFAR-DS-3-REP   that-PL

      lula-shra ka-la
      make-PRT be-PST
      They were made before Christ was born (it is said).

   c. *imay-**shi** yayku-n ya'a-pa umri-i*
      when-REP enter-3 I-GEN   man-1P
      When did (they say) my husband entered [the house]?

The hearsay use serves as prototype for the entire *-sh(i)* category. I maintain this view for a number of reasons. Following Levinson (1983:284) I regard conversation as prototypical of language use in general. Although frequency does not automatically indicate that a certain use is to be identified with the prototype (cf. Shirai 1990 for a counterexample), we find that in Wanka conversation hearsay is the most common meaning for *-sh(i)*, whereas the other uses are much more formulaic and restricted in terms of their usage. In addition, we will see that hearsay forms the basis for extension to the other meanings, a characteristic that has been cited for prototypes (cf. Lakoff 1987). The prototypicality of the hearsay use is particularly supported by the fact that Wanka speakers will themselves recognize the hearsay use as somehow "more basic" than the others. When queried as to what *-sh(i)* means apart from any context, explanations will inevitably point in the direction of hearsay.[38] As Geeraerts states, it is "the prototypical kinds of usage...that reach the introspective consciousness of the language user" (1988a:218). In other words, in the mind of the speaker, the hearsay use

---

[38]The first meaning that is acquired by children also serves to indicate prototypicality. Although I am aware of no studies on this particular issue, I do suspect that the hearsay use is the one which will be acquired first.

is the most prominent and easily identifable. Metonymically, it represents the entire category even though there are other uses that differ from it substantially.

It should seem intuitively obvious what is meant by "hearsay." But careful consideration is not unwarranted, since a simple characterization such as "information which has come to the speaker from some other source" actually involves relations and interactions between various individuals and information content that are quite complex.

Figure (169) shows that hearsay involves a "recapitulated speech event" (cf. Casad 1992) within the current speech event, along with a kind of "role shifting" that takes place as information is transferred between participants in the speech events. In one scenario, a prior speaker serving as information source (which I will refer to as the Origin (OR) is at the deictic center of a speech event in which he communicates some proposition P to an addressee A_1. Hearsay specifically takes place when A_1 becomes the current speaker S communicating (roughly) the same propositional content P' to a distinct addressee A_2. (As elsewhere, correspondences between scenarios are indicated by dotted lines and the designated proposition by the boldface circle.) In other words, a prior communication event forms the conceptual base for the current speech event. Hearsay thus invokes a chainlike configuration in which two participants are made aware of the same piece of information at distinct times.

(169) Hearsay

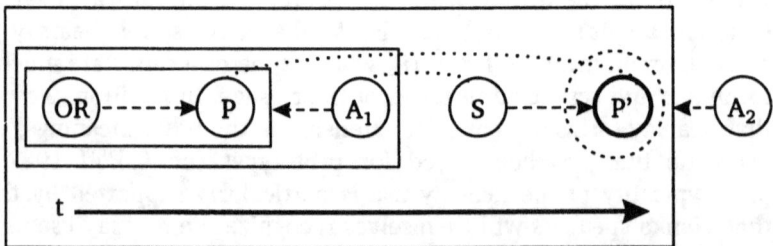

In this characterization, both a speaker's repetition of his own words, and information which has come from the addressee are precluded from being considered as hearsay. In other words, -*sh(i)* marks information exclusively from a noncurrent-speech event participant. This restriction is different from what is allowed in Cora, for example, where a speaker may use the reportative to quote the addressee or even himself (cf. Casad 1992).

Another issue relevant to the general characterization of hearsay concerns the difference between information "revealed" versus information "arrived at." As discussed in preceding chapters, -m(i) and -chr(a) designate knowledge arrived at via some kind of evidence, with which the conceptualizer *personally* interacts either directly or indirectly. In a reportative situation the only link S has to the conceptualization he is passing along is through another conceptualizer, i.e., OR; in other words, hearsay designates a conceptualization for which S has no personal evidentiary access.

From this I conclude that -sh(i) construes a proposition as knowledge revealed, not knowledge "arrived at." Such knowledge is construed as initially confidential, private, or hidden in some way. As information to which the speaker does not ordinarily have access, hearsay provides the potential link to other domains encompassing events or knowledge that are similarly beyond the normal experience of the conceptualizer. This becomes a relevant theme in our understanding of folktales and is particularly important in the analysis of the mirative senses.

One final aspect of construal is noteworthy. We have seen evidence in previous chapters that evidential marking is only partially determined by the actual facts surrounding the nature of an information source. Therefore, nothing precludes S from interacting with the propositional content he has been delivered and imposing his own construal on it in terms of either commitment or noncommitment. But by use of -sh(i) the speaker avoids either alternative and construes himself merely as a conduit through which information passes. He does not assess the propositional content in terms of his own validational perspective; he simply passes it on to the next addressee with the effect that his own validational commitment is largely irrelevant.

Before proceeding further we might consider the relationship between direct quotation and reportatives as a kind of indirect quotation. While a detailed analysis is beyond the scope of the present work, I outline here what I think are the relevant concerns. We may think of direct quotation and a reportative as different perspectives on the same conceptual base of a recapitulated speech event in which the speaker selects particular portions for emphasis. In a direct quote, the OR is overtly designated and is therefore "on-stage." A direct quote is an echoic utterance par excellance (cf. Sperber and Wilson 1986), since the current speaker puts OR's words into his own mouth, so to speak, thereby recreating OR's original construal. As discussed previously in chapter 4, direct quotation involves the current speaker switching his perspective between two distinct mental spaces. This accounts for the fact that, in addition to the expected disparities of temporal and pronominal reference, in a language like Wanka, multiple evidential marking may also occur in the same sentence, which is completely ungrammatical otherwise. Thus, a sentence like *He said, "I will go to Huancayo tomorrow"* appears in Wanka with both the conjecture marker *-chr(a)* and the direct evidential *-m(i)*.

(170) waala-man-**chra**   wankayuu-ta   li-sha   ni-l-**mi**   ni-la[39]
       tomorrow-GOAL-CONJ Huancayo-ACC   go-1FUT   say-SS-DIR   say-PST
       He said, "I will go to Huancayo tomorrow."

The conjecture marker grounds the *going* to the mental space (reality) of the original speaker, whereas the direct evidential grounds the entire prior speech event with respect to the current speaker's reality.

In a reportative situation the perspective shifts from that of the "sender" to that of the receiver. The *OR* is de-emphasized in favor of a focus on the current speaker as the recipient of the information. Because of this, the wording of the original report becomes less important, being distilled into some kind of propositional essence. As a grounding predication, a reportative evidential subsumes the *OR*, the original report, and the current speaker as a recipient as parts of an unprofiled, and subjectively-construed conceptual base. What is profiled is only some distillation of the originally-designated proposition. All other elements are left completely implicit. Thus, in contrast to direct quotation, only one evidential marker is allowed.

(171) waala-man-**shi**   wankayuu-ta   li-n'a
       tomorrow-GOAL-REP   Huancayo-ACC   go-3FUT
       He will go to Huancayo tomorrow (I hear).

I concern myself here only with grammaticalized reportative marking.

I maintain that for the hearsay prototype the speaker construes the *OR* or original information source as a *cognitively-salient,* specifically-identifiable individual. Consider the following excerpt from a conversation where M is telling P about the age of the pottery he saw during a trip to a museum just hours earlier.

(172) a. M: *chay   chay   ka-la   unay   picha   pachrak   walanga*
              that   that   be-PST   long^ago   five   hundred   thousand

---

[39]Direct quotations are also used for thought attribution. This example could also be understood to mean *He thought he would go to Huancayo tomorrow.* (Cf. Larson 1978; for an in depth discussion of the uses of direct quotation in Aguaruna (Shuar).)

    wata-kuna-**sh** pasa-alu-n
    year-PL-REP pass-ASP-3
    M: It was a long, long time ago, 1,500 years-*shi* ago.

  b. mana-laa-si   jesucristo   naasi-mu-pti-n-**shi** chay-kuna
    not-yet-even Jesus^Christ born-AFAR-DS-3-REP that-PL

    lula-shra   ka-la
    make-PART be-PST
    They were made before Christ was born-*shi*.

  c. P: kay peru-kaa-chru ichaa
        this Peru-DEF-LOC or
    P: Here in Peru, or...

  d. M: aa kay peru-kaa-chru kay lima janay chankay
        yes this Peru-DEF-LOC this Lima above Chankay

    ni-sha-n-kuna-chru
    say-NOM-3P-PL-LOC
    M: Yeah, here in Peru, north of Lima in a place called Chankay.

  e. chay-chruu-**shi** mas-ta   lula-paaku-la chay-kuna-kta
    that-LOC-REP   more-ACC make-PL-PST that-PL-ACC
    They made them mostly there-*shi*.

The information that the pots were several centuries old and that many of them were made in what was then known as the Chankay region is based on second-hand knowledge as indicated by the presence of -*sh(i)*.

But to whom does the -*sh(i)* refer? At the beginning of the conversation M specifically identifies a woman that met the tour group at the entrance of the building, who, by implication, is understood to be the tour guide. Although the woman is not overtly mentioned again after her initial introduction into the conversation, the -*sh(i)* that appears throughout the conversation is clearly understood as an oblique reference to her; and since M is passing this information along to P within a relatively short time after he heard it, we can be certain that the woman still figures prominently in his mind as the information source.

We see similarities in the following interchange excerpted from a conversation which again is typical of the hearsay use. The text, already introduced in previous chapters, involves an exchange between a father and his daughter who refuses to go to school because she claims her teachers beat her. The father responds,

(173)   *kanan prufisura-yki-ta ni-mu-shra   ancha-p-shi*
        today teacher-2P-ACC say-AFAR-1FUT too^much-GEN-REP

> *wa'a-chi-nki wamla-a-ta ni-mu-shra*
> cry-CAUS-2   girl-1P-ACC say-AFAR-1FUT
> Today I'll tell your teacher...I'll say "(I hear) you make my daughter cry too much."

Two distinct time frames are referred to in this sentence which must be kept clear. The statement marked with the reportative is what the father intends to tell the teacher later that day. But this statement is based on the present conversation in which the daughter is informing him of the treatment she receives in school. In other words, the father is prefiguring the future recapitulation of the current speech event.

The point I wish to emphasize, however, is that when the present report is recapitulated in the teacher's presence, even though the information source is not overtly identified, we know from the present context it is the daughter, and can therefore be certain that she figures prominently in the speaker's mind as he anticipates the confrontation.

Finally, consider (174), from a previous text involving an accusation of theft, which also illustrates how *-sh(i)* prototypically presumes a specifically-identifiable information source.

(174)   a. R: *wasi-i-ta   am-shi yayku-llaa-la-nki*
            R: house-1-ACC you-REP enter-LIM-PST-2
            R: (They say) you entered my house.

       b. M: *mayan-taa ni-n*
           M: who-SCORN say-3
           M: WHO says that?!

      c. R: *nuna   lika-a-niki ka-ña achka-m*
           R: person see-AG-2P be-NPST much-DIR
           R: There are lots of people who saw you.

There are two indications that *-sh(i)* is evoking a cognitively salient individual as the information source. The first is that this is what M seems to understand as the implication of (174a): in his response in

-sh(i): Hearsay and Revelation   133

(174b) he demands to know the identity of the specific person or persons at the source of these accusations. In addition, note the presence of the direct evidential in R's reply in (174c). Although the identity of the original information source is never mentioned anywhere in the context, my language consultant informs me that the direct evidential clearly implies that the speaker has had personal contact with them and knows who they are.

So then, in its first reportative use, *-sh(i)* recapitulates a prior speech event in which, for the speaker, the information source is a cognitively salient, specifically-identifiable individual.

6.3.2 Folktales, myths, and legends. In its second reportative use *-sh(i)* marks folktales and legends. Example (175), an excerpt from "The Fox and the Rabbit," is typical of this genre. (In the interest of space I will not include morpheme-by-morpheme glosses.)

(175)   ªUnay-***shi*** pulila juk atu llaki llaki mikanaashra mikuyta ashishtin. ᵇChay pulishanchruu-***shi*** tinkuulun kuniijuwan....ᶜChaychruu-***shi*** kuniiju nin, "Uy kunpaari, kay wankaapa luliininmanmi jiyakuykun jatu jatun llutu. ᵈChalashra niyaa mikunaykipaami. ᵉ¡Yanapaamay!" ᶠNiptin-***shi*** atuuka: "¿Rasunpa?" ᵍ"Rasunpam. ʰMaapis kayta chalaykuy." ⁱNilkul-***shi*** kuniiju tan'alaachin alli allikta wichayman. ʲ"Uy, yaañatakmi yaykushra chay llutu chalamu." ᵏNiptin-***shi*** atuuka chalalayan chay wankaata...

   ªA long time ago-***shi*** a starving fox was going around looking for food. ᵇAlong the way-shi he met a rabbit....ᶜThen-***shi*** the rabbit says, "Hey, brother, a really big quail just went under this boulder. ᵈI was thinking about catching him for you to eat. ᵉHelp me." ᶠ"Really?," the fox says-***shi***. ᵍ"Really! ʰHere, hold this." ⁱSaying this-***shi***, the rabbit has him there pushing it [the boulder] way up. ʲ"Now I'm going in to get that quail." ᵏAnd so-***shi*** the fox is there holding up that boulder....

The folktale use bears one main similarity to the prototypical hearsay use. Legends and folktales are of course typically passed by word of mouth from generation to generation and are therefore second-hand information. In fact, according to Utley (1965:13) the defining characteristic of folk literature is its oral transmission.

But I do not hold the view that folktales are instances of hearsay, since such an analysis overlooks certain relevant differences. A cursory comparison of the "Museum" and "Fox" texts, for example, reveals that

"Museum" is formally characterized by successive turn-taking typical of most conversations, whereas "Fox" is monologic, even though it was produced in the context of a conversation. (Perhaps "Fox" could be thought of as an extended turn.) On the formal side, then, the quantity of information passed along in any one turn varies, from isolated single bits to much larger spans. Another formal difference concerns the frequency of the evidential marking itself, a point to which I will return.

The nature of the subject matter is also very different between the two texts. "Museum" is much like narrative accounts of any mundane, quotidian experience grounded in reality—what one did, what was seen, who was there, what they said, etc. However, the events in folktales usually have some particular uniqueness about them that distinguishes them from ordinary mundane narratives. For example, Bascom notes,

> ...characters in folktales and myths may do things which are regarded as shocking in daily life. To cite only one example, Old Man Coyote has intercourse with his mother-in-law, whereas in ordinary life the American Indian who finds amusement in these tales must observe a strict mother-in-law avoidance. (1965:33)

Likewise, in the Wanka text ("Fox") there is a significant deviation from experienced reality; animals are not observed to carry on conversations with each other.

The connection between reportative marking and this quality of "alien-ness" in a folktale has been observed in Turkish:

> There are some kinds of events for which one is always unprepared events which partake of a quality of unreality or other-worldliness. Thus the -mIs form [of the past tense/reportative morpheme] is always used in such narratives as myths, folktales, and fairy tales, and this is the form used for recounting those parts of dreams which are most alien to everyday experience. (Slobin and Aksu 1982:198).

Note that I am not equating alien-ness with nonbelievability since many Quechuas believe that at one time animals did talk even though they do not now.[40] The great temporal separation between the present and the time when animals did talk precludes personal verification of the recounted events; but this has not necessarily resulted in making the account unbelievable for the speakers themselves.

---

[40]Eugene Casad (p.c.) informs me that this is a wide-spread belief in Amerindian cultures.

The frequency of the evidential marking itself is another formal differentiator between hearsay and folktales. Coombs, Coombs, and Weber (1976:149f.) note the variation in the frequency of the use of direct and reportative evidentials among speakers of San Martin Quechua (presumably with respect to conversation although it is not entirely clear). They explain the variation partially as a function of redundancy reduction, "Por cierto, sería redundante indicar en cada oración la modalidad de un texto entero. Una vez que se establezca la modalidad de una unidad del habla no será poco común que el hablante cese de usar los enclíticos -mi y -shi."

The elimination of unnecessary redundancy may play a part in the sporadic evidential marking evident in Wanka, at least with respect to the conversational genre. For example, in the entire "Museum" text, which is comprised of some 245 sentences, -sh(i) actually appears only 16 times (6%), in spite of the fact that almost all of what M relates to P is second-hand information. Another text (not included in this study) concerns the actual retelling of an overheard conversation of medium length. This would be a prime candidate for -sh(i) marking. Yet, it is significant that in the entire text only one example of the reportative occurs.

The principle of fixing the evidential orientation of a text also seems to be operable with respect to folktales in some languages. Schlichter observes that the reportative in Wintu "is not suffixed to every single verb of a story known through hearsay, but rather only to the verb in the first sentence...establishing a frame for the whole story" (1986:49). Similar observations have been made for Pomo folktales (cf. McLendon 1982).

In contrast, the marking in Wanka folktales is almost completely regular. An examination of "Fox" shows the following: of the 86 sentences in the text, 43 are direct quotations and would not be marked with -sh(i) anyway. Ninety percent of the remaining nondirect quotations (i.e., 39 out of 43) are marked with -sh(i). (Zero marking will not be dealt with here.) Folktales obtained from a variety of different speakers show comparable tendencies.

If the early establishment of the evidential orientation of a text obviates the need for continuous marking as Coombs, Coombs, and Weber (1976) suggest, what do we make of the Wanka data? Why should virtually each sentence in a folktale be marked as hearsay? I would like to suggest that what we have here is a sort of discourse level grammaticalization. Reportative marking here is principally a characteristic feature of the genre, not an indicator of hearsay. Strong evidence for this view comes from the observation during writer training workshops where language consultants made up original stories but nevertheless marked them as reportative.

This is not to deny the very obvious connection between hearsay and folktales. By virtue of sharing the oral transmission feature of hearsay, folktales are naturally and logically associated with reportative marking. Willett's (1988) distinction between second- and third-hand information is relevant in this regard. Second-hand information is that which has been obtained from a direct witness, whereas third-hand information comes from an indirect witness. Folktales would seem to come quite naturally under this latter category.

This similarity to hearsay notwithstanding, what I want to emphasize is that the cognitive salience of the information source in the hearsay use has been bleached out of the folktale use. To speak of a uniquely identifiable information source in a folktale is missing something of the very character of the genre. Myths and folktales are corporate enterprises that evolve over long periods of time as they are told and retold by multiple speakers, each one making slight modifications and embellishments in the process, the product of "anonymous creativity" (Bascom 1965). With each successive recounting of the story, its originator becomes increasingly more removed both physically and temporally. In a real sense, then, the original information source is lost (Sparing 1984:5) and is thus beyond anyone's mental recoverability.

It is in this specific sense that the meaning of -*sh(i)* in a folktale is different. I do not think that with each and every use of -*sh(i)* the speaker is harking back to a particularly identifiable information source any more than the individual listening to the story would be prompted to be continually asking the question, "WHO said this?" expecting that an answer would ever be given.

It seems, then, that a major difference between the conceptualization of the information source in hearsay and that in a folktale is that the OR in hearsay is a specific, cognitively salient individual, whereas in a folktale the OR is diffused among a multiplicity of individuals.

Finally, consider the relationship between speaker and addressee. With prototypical hearsay the speaker and addressee are in a very asymmetrical relationship. The speaker holds the status of a prior initiate in the information chain, as exclusive possessor of "new" knowledge which "informs" the addressee, and in that respect he can be considered as having some sort of "privileged" status over the addressee. However, as part of the oral literature of a culture, a folktale is not necessarily privileged information. It is much more likely to be known by more than just one or two individuals in a communication chain. Folktales are knowingly told to people who already know them. Witness children's unceasing

-sh(i): Hearsay and Revelation

requests for the same bedtime stories. Prior to a specific event of the telling of a folktale, then, the possibility exists that even the hearer is likely to have already heard it, thus putting him more on a "knowlege-par" or equal footing with the speaker.

A schematic characterization of the folktale use is given in (176). OR, S, and A are in verbally mediated relationships, as they are with hearsay, but OR is a diffuse and nonunique entity rather than a specific one. We might view OR as a conglomerate of multiple prior instances of the hearsay use. Furthermore, OR's relationship is not uniquely with S, but potentially with both S and A since the addressee may already know the folktale. Note also that the overall configuration does not form a chain as much as it does a network of simultaneously existing relationships.

(176) Folktales

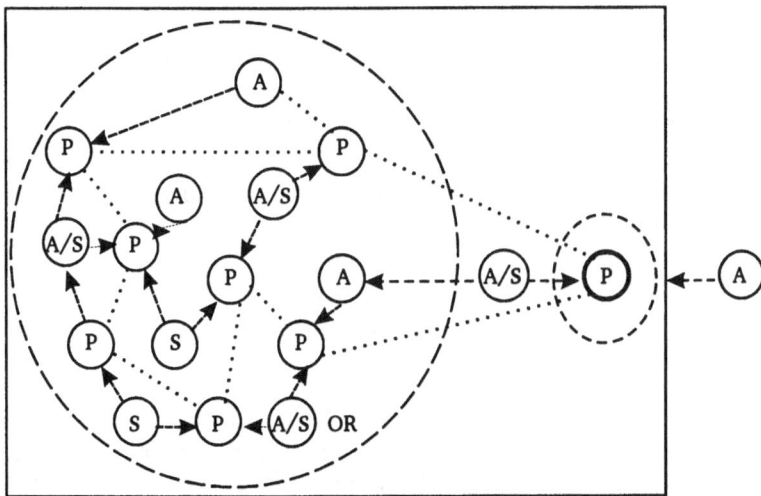

So then, hearsay and folktales are distinguished with respect to the following parameters: quantity of turn, regularity of evidential marking, the degree to which subject matter deviates from observed reality, the degree to which the prior information source is cognitively salient to the speaker, and whether or not the speaker has a privileged status over the hearer. However, I would not want to imply that the division between an instance of hearsay and a folktale is clear cut. These parameters interact to different degrees to form intermediate cases.

Consider example (177), for example, which is from the beginning of a text where a woman relates why her father has a deformed foot:

(177) ªUnay-*shi* papaaniipa maman ishyaylla ishyala. ᵇChay-*shi* jampikuuwan jampichipaakula. ᶜChay-*shi* jampikuuka "jintilkaami daañashra; ᵈchaypa tullunta apamay" nila. ᵉNiptin-*shi* jintilkaapa chay machrayninkunaman luli Irba Bwina laadukunakta lipaakula. ᶠChaychruu-*shi* tullunta takwaypa ashipaamushranchru uchuk wakuychallakta talipaamula. ᵍChiwakuy chayta-*sh* apamula. ʰChay uywapaakula chay wakuychaata....ⁱJinaptin-*shi* mana-*sh* maman saanalachu. ʲChaypiimi papaaniisi chraki paltan nanayta allaykuykula. ᵏNanala nanala chay alalaychru nila-*sh*. ˡPay chay unuk uu nawan watala imaymanawan watapaakula...

ªA long time ago-*shi*, my grandmother was really sick. ᵇSo-*shi* they took her to a healer to cure her. ᶜThen-*shi* the healer said she had been hurt by the "ancient ones" and to ᵈbring him one of their bones. ᵉSo-*shi* they went to the cave of the "ancient ones" down by Hierba Buena. ᶠThere-*shi* as they were digging through the bones they found a small pot. ᵍThe Chiwakuy [a kind of bird] had brought it-*shi*. ʰSo they took that pot.... ⁱAfter that-*shi* she still didn't get well. ʲThat's when the bottom of my father's foot began to hurt. ᵏIt would hurt and hurt like when it got cold-*shi*. ˡHe would wrap it up with anything that was warm...

When we compare this example to the previous ones a number of similarities and differences emerge. This text is a specific turn in a conversation, but is an extended, more monologic turn, and, like the "Fox" text, exhibits the regular marking of a folktale. With respect to the cognitive salience of OR in "Foot," there is no information source specifically mentioned, either in the question which prompted the story or in the story itself. Yet, pragmatically-speaking it is not unreasonable to assume that it is most likely either her own father who recounted this story himself, or that she was told by an immediate family member who was well acquainted with the facts. If so, then we can assume that for the speaker the OR is a relatively salient, potentially identifiable individual. Regarding the nature of the subject matter, the "Museum" text as a whole is essentially an account of a mundane personal experience. The content of "Foot" is likewise mundane (even though the events are not the speaker's personal experiences)-diseases, cures, and deformities are commonplace. Furthermore, certain facts can be corroborated by members of the community at large: that the father went on a trip, that indeed he now has a deformed foot, that he complains about it hurting in cold weather, etc. This type of corroboration is not characteristic or

-sh(i): Hearsay and Revelation

even required of folktales. So there is an sense of "ordinary reality" that attaches to those aspects of the narrative. Nevertheless, there are other elements which are more "other-worldly" or in some sense peripheral vis-à-vis common experience, e.g., the "magic" associated with the bones of the gentiles and the role played by the *Chiwakuy*.

We see then that there are certain similarities between "Foot" and the hearsay prototype in terms of the cognitive salience of the information source. On the other hand, its structural characteristics appear more folktale-like, and its subject matter occupies some intermediate ground.

Consider next an excerpt from a text about a *kundinaadu*, a zombie-like being, typically a person who in life committed certain kinds of immoral acts, particularly incest, and as punishment is forever condemned to walk the earth after death.

(178) ªTiyuu willamaala kaynuuta. ᵇUnay-**shi** wik ... Andahuaylaslaajuchru trabajala. ᶜTrabajaalul-**shi** chaychru lipaakun byajikta kun achka muulawan.... ᵈIntonsi tutay muyun liyalkan kargawan.... ᵉJukllay muulalla-**sh** punta puntakta lin. ᶠIpanta-**sh** lipaakun parti. ᵍChay punta liikaalla-**sh** ima kaptin suspichakun. ʰChay-**shi** tutapaalun liyalkaptin. ⁱIntonsi kumu dyes unsi de la nuuchiñatak punta muula liikaa puntaman lin ipaman kutikuyan, puntaman lin ipaman kutikuyan. ʲChay-**shi** "¿Imatan?" nin. ᵏChay-**shi** duyñu, muulakunap duyñunñatak nin tiyuuta: "Kundinaadu siguuru shrayaamun. ˡManam lin'achu masta," nin.... ᵐLlapan llapan puntaka shraykuuluptin llapan muulaka shraykuulun. ⁿChay-**shi**... "Wik punta punta muulap linlintam likanki. ᵒNinam waalaalun'a asul asulta kundinaadu kaptin'a" nin. ᵖChaypii-**shi** mana pay kriyinchu....

ªMy uncle told me this. ᵇA long time ago-***shi*** he worked in Andahuaylas. ᶜAs part of their work-***shi*** they went on trips with lots of mules. ᵈThey went all day and all night with their loads. ᵉOnly one mule-***shi*** was in front. ᶠThe rest followed behind-***shi***. ᵍThe one out in front-***shi*** suspects if there is anything wrong. ʰThen-***shi*** as they were going it got dark. ⁱAbout 10, 11 o'clock at night the first mule shot out in front and then came back, went forward and came back. ʲThen-***shi*** "What's that?" he [the uncle] said. ᵏThen-***shi*** the owner of the mules told my uncle, "A kundinaadu is probably coming. ˡThe mule won't go any farther." ᵐWhen the first mule stopped, all the others stopped. ⁿThen-***shi*** "Look at that first mule's ears. ᵒThey'll glow blue like fire if there's a kundinaadu." ᴾSo-*shi* he [my uncle] didn't believe him....

Like both the "Fox" and "Foot" texts, "*Kundinaadu*" is a monologue, exhibiting the same formal regularity of evidential marking: *-sh(i)* appears on almost every sentence that is not a direct quote. The speaker's information source is clearly cognitively salient since he identifies his uncle as the one who told him the story; and, like "Foot," the text concerns the personal experiences of a member of his immediate family. Furthermore, the events of the story are novel for the hearer, so the speaker has a privileged status, more like typical hearsay. The nature of the subject matter, however, is more like "Fox" than "Foot." *Kundinaadus* have more of an alien, "other-worldly" quality about them than does the protagonist suffering from physical ailments of the type in "Foot." Here again, I underscore that its "alien" quality does not equate with being fictitious. Quechuas believe in *kundinaadus;* they constitute part of their world view, and many, like the speaker's uncle, claim to have had personal encounters with them. However, such encounters appear to be the exception; most people have not had experiences of the kind related here, and thus the phenomenon lies beyond personal verification for the majority.

The texts we have considered could be "categorized" as indicated in figure (179).

(179) Categorization of texts

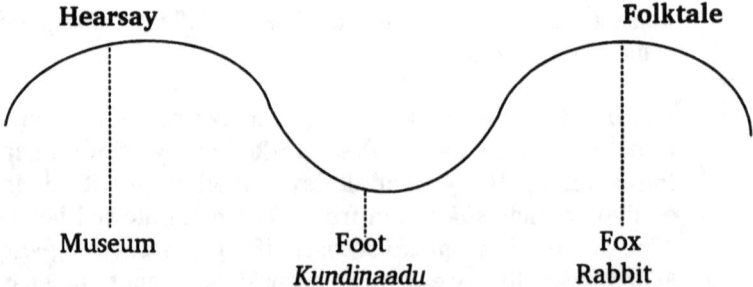

The figure represents HEARSAY and FOLKTALE as genres with prototypical, identifiable "peaks" (determined on the basis of specific structural and semantic characteristics). We see that "Museum" and "Fox" are representative of their respective hearsay and folktale "categories," while "Foot" and *"Kundinaadu"* have some intermediate status since they show similarities to both uses but in different ways.

-sh(i): Hearsay and Revelation   141

To summarize thus far, I have considered examples of text material in terms of several parameters: quantity of turn, regularity of evidential marking, the degree to which the content diverges from observed reality, the cognitive salience of the information source as a specific individual, and the degree to which the speaker's information is privileged.

The hearsay prototype is characterized by short turns and irregular evidential marking and the subject matter is mundane. The prior information source is a specific, cognitively-salient nonspeech-event participant, and the speaker is the possessor of privileged information. On the other hand, a folktale is characterized as an extended monologic turn with very regular evidential marking with content that is typically alien to normal everyday experience. The information source is diffuse and distributed across a multitude of anonymous individuals over time. And the speaker may not necessarily hold a privileged position as possessor of new information. But category membership is ultimately a matter of more-or-less and not either-or, since the parameters may interact to varying degrees to produce intermediate cases.

The hearsay and folktale uses share a reportative sense by virtue of presupposing actual communication by a specific individual or, in an extended sense, by presupposing prior communication by an anonymous collectivity of individuals.

6.3.3 Riddles. The third reportative use is found in riddles. A typical riddle in Wanka is comprised of a conventional formulaic interrogative expression marked with *-sh(i)* followed by a description of some object. Examples include the following (from Flores Canchanya 1983):

(180) *ima-lla-sh   ayka-lla-sh*
       what-LIM-REP   how^much-LIM-REP

      chrunka pun-nin-chru suuta killa-n-chru
      ten   day-3P-LOC   six   month-3P-LOC

      wata-n-chru wa'a-ku-n wa'a-ku-n
      year-3P-LOC cry-REF-3 cry-REF-3

What is it? How much? It cries on its tenth day, its sixth month, and its first year? [ans: a bell]

(181) *ima-lla-sh   ayka-lla-sh*
what-LIM-REP how^much-LIM-REP

> *wishya-n mana shimi-yu*
> whistle-3 not mouth-having
>
> *alli-kta li-n mana chraki-yu*
> fast-ACC go-3 not feet-having
>
> *ma'a-shrunki kaara-yki-chru*
> hit-32   face-2P-LOC
>
> *mana-tak ima-kta-si   lika-nki-chu*
> not-FURTH what-ACC-INDEF see-2-NEG

What is it? How much? It whistles without a mouth. It goes fast without feet. It hits you in your face, but you don't see anything. [ans: the wind]

(182) *ima-lla-sh   ayka-lla-sh*
what-LIM-REP how^much-LIM-REP

> *juk machray-chru puñu-ya-n puka waaka*
> one cave-LOC   sleep-IMPF-3 red cow

What is it? How much? A red cow is sleeping in a cave. [ans: a tongue]

References to the use of *-sh(i)* in riddles are scant in the Quechua literature been available to me.[41] Although Weber (1989:448) mentions them in connection with other formulaic expressions for the Huallaga dialect, he does not elaborate on the function of the evidential marking nor on their glossing, which, as I mentioned previously, makes no reference to a second-hand information source.

Riddles bear numerous semantic similarities to hearsay and folktales, perhaps the most obvious one being the fact that they are included among the genres that are typically passed from person to person by word of mouth (Dundes 1965:3). A riddle is similar to the hearsay prototype in terms of the asymmetrical relationship that the speaker has with the addressee. Recall that in hearsay the speaker is a communication link between a prior information source and the addressee, and thus, from the addressee's perspective, he has a privileged position of knowledge. The same is true for a riddle; the speaker holds a privileged position as

---

[41] Beuchat (1965) has described in detail the nature and structure of Bantu riddles, but I have found no comparable study on riddles from a language with a grammaticalized evidential system.

"knower" of some information, i.e., the answer that is imminently forthcoming.

In addition to the similarities between riddles and folktales, already mentioned, both use -*sh(i)* as a grammaticalized marker of the genre. This is supported in two ways: like a folktale, the evidential in a riddle has been bleached of a cognitively salient prior information source; I do not believe that the teller of a riddle is mentally calling to mind a specific individual who previously told it to him, since riddles more typically stem from an amorphous, anonymous, public domain-type source. In addition, the answers to the riddles do not directly respond to the second portion of the introductory expression, *How much?* This suggests that at least that much of the formulaic expression has become conventionalized without strict regard for word-for-word meaning. But perhaps more significantly, riddles made up on the spot will have the same form as those that a speaker may have heard elsewhere. In other words -*sh(i)* in a riddle does not strictly evoke the conceptualization of an information chain; identification of a prior information source is essentially irrelevant.

Another similarity is that riddles like folktales involve the presence of elements or events that contravene normal expectations. It is this characteristic, with its potentially concomitant MIRATIVE reaction, that introduces the next major area of semantic space in which we find uses for -*sh(i)*.

6.3.4 Mirativity. Mirative utterances (also called "admirative" or "surprisal") involve the potential conflict between an expectation and an actual outcome. For example, Slobin and Aksu (1982) describe the surprisal use of the Turkish evidential/perfect as marking an event or situation which the speaker was not mentally prepared to receive. And although DeLancey (1986) explains the Tibetan evidential system partially in terms of "new information," the insight is essentially the same. Mirativity is frequently, but not exclusively associated with reportative marking. In Jaqi the same remote past tense marker used for myths, legends, and tales of spirit encounters is also used to express surprise (Hardman 1986). Situations about which the speaker has become belatedly aware are indicated by forms of the inferential in Makah and Kashaya (see Jacobsen 1986 and Oswalt 1986). (Cf. DeLancey 1997 for further discussion.) We may consider mirativity, then, as referring to the subjective counterpart to the speaker's objective assessment of elements as "other-worldly" or mismatched in its context.[42] It is easy to see, then, how folktales, myths, and legends often provide the elements that are

---

[42] I am endebted to Ron Langacker for this insight.

objectively assessed as "other-worldly" to which the speaker subjectively reacts with surprise. I argue that in addition to these, other genre riddles involve mirativity as well.

6.3.4.1 Riddles revisited. An appreciation for the mirativity of a riddle can be gained by considering the following example from Flores Canchanya (1983):

(183)   a. *ima-lla-sh*   *ayka-lla-sh*
          what-LIM-REP how^much-LIM-REP

    b. *chraki-n chay-chru ñawi-yu*
       foot-3P   there-LOC eye-having

      ishkay tupshu-yu   uma-n-chru
      two   beak-having head-3P-LOC
      What could it be, what could it be? Its feet have eyes. Its head has two beaks.

The formulaic expression in (183a) evokes the riddle genre and sets up the expectation that the description that follows-which taken by itself could be that of some monstrous creature in a child's nightmare-cannot be taken at face value. The solution to the riddle involves making the proper metaphorical connections from specific elements in the riddle to features of some object that could, if viewed from the proper perspective, constitute a likely candidate for an answer. In example (183), the item being described has features to which the speaker attributes the qualities of "foot-ness," "eye-ness," "head-ness," and "beak-ness." When either the addressee makes the appropriate metaphorical connections between the actual words of the riddle and perceived similarities to their intended referents, or the answer is subsequently revealed to him by the riddler, it has the potential for being a surprise.

In the case of (183), the answer is "scissors." Figure (184) shows the associations that can be motivated between the riddle and its intended referent. The "feet with eyes" are the handles with finger holes, and the "two beaks" are the blades-associations which are based on perceived similarities of shape. The "head" is identified principally by virtue of being the opposing pole in a canonical foot-head configuration, and not because of any overt similarities to the appearance of a typical head.

(184) Scissors

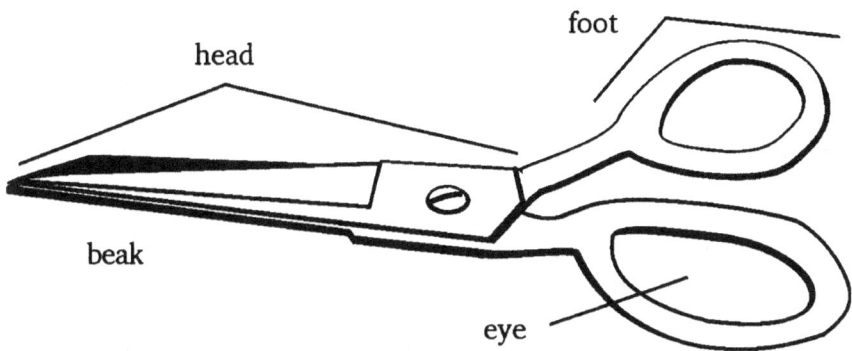

A clever riddle will be one where connections like these are sufficiently obscure so as to make its solution difficult, but not so obscure that it totally inhibits any plausible associations. Ultimately, it is the unexpected result achieved by bridging the gap between description and referent that makes the riddle what it is.

Riddles are thus similar to (some) folktales in that both typically involve a significant deviation from the path of normal expectation. For folktales the deviation concerns the domain of routine experience. In the course of one's daily life one does not ordinarily expect to have encounters with a para-human being like a *kundinaadu*. For riddles the deviation is restricted to the linguistic domain of word referents. Outside the context of a riddle, for most speakers the term *ñawi* 'eye' will normally evoke the conception of the organ of sight, not a hole in a piece of metal.

6.3.4.2 Riddles and questions: the intra-ground subjectification of mirativity.
Intra-ground subjectification has played a large role in our analysis of questions. We, therefore, need to consider it in the present case since by their very nature riddles are interrogative.

As discussed previously, in questions the speaker construes the addressee as lying in a relationship to a designated proposition that parallels what he-the speaker-normally bears to a proposition in an assertion. With prototypical information-seeking questions the addressee is presumed to be in a direct experience relationship to the designated proposition, and with *-chr(a)*-marked questions, the speaker is uncertain about the addressee's relation to the proposition. We expect, therefore, the prototypical hearsay relation of a *-sh(i)*-marked assertion to be reflected in *-sh(i)*-marked interrogative forms. This is indeed what we find. Consider (185).

(185) imay-***shi*** yayku-n ya'a-pa umri-i
when-REP enter-3 I-GEN man-1P
At what time did they say my husband entered [the house]?

Typical -*sh(i)*-marked questions follow the same pattern and subjectify the prototypical assertion construal: the speaker construes the addressee as being in a hearsay-type relationship to the designated proposition.

Now if mirativity, and not necessarily hearsay, were to comprise an aspect of construal associated with -*sh(i)* in some class of assertions, then based on what we have seen elsewhere with questions, we might expect addressee-based mirativity to be involved in some interrogative -*sh(i)* forms as well. At this writing I have no clearcut cases of a -*sh(i)*-marked assertion with mirativity as a prominent aspect of its construal. However, there is evidence that the reportative may code an unexpected situation in some Quechua dialects. Christa Toedter (p.c.) notes that in Pastaza Quechua -*sh(i)* may occur in statements like, "May the mountains fall on us if we do not do such and such." She describes it as marking "circumstances involving the impossibility of fulfillment or unattainable desire." Also, I recall one instance that arose during the translation of the Wanka Gospel of Mark where -*sh(i)* marked the disciples' reaction to Jesus walking on the water.

Addressee-based mirativity appears to be precisely what is involved in riddles, with one slight adjustment. Note that mirativity as already discussed usually refers to an after-the-fact phenomenon, i.e., the speaker indicates his surprise at what he has already observed or has just realized. But the situation with a riddle is much different; the speaker tells a riddle already knowing the answer, assuming, furthermore that the addressee does not know. Granted, it could be argued that the evidential marking on a riddle reflects, not only its hearsay-type origin, but also the speaker's mirative reaction. While this is certainly plausible, it must be remembered that riddles made up on the spot will also have the same marking, which militates against both strict hearsay and speaker-based mirativity views.

To summarize this section, I have argued for the motivation of reportative marking in riddles on several grounds. Like hearsay and folktales, riddles are information that is typically transmitted orally. Riddles bear another similarity to folktales in that the information source has been bleached of any identification as a specifiable person. In addition, I have shown that riddles, hearsay, and folktales involve revealed knowledge that has the potential for a subjective mirative reaction on the part of the speaker. The reportative marking on a riddle is consistent with the analysis of questions and facets of the prototype in that it anticipates the

-sh(i): Hearsay and Revelation   147

addressee's reaction of surprise when the semantic conflicts presented in the riddle are resolved. Thus, the same process of intra-ground subjectification that has been observed in the extended senses of the direct and conjecture evidentials is operative here as well.

Throughout the discussion I have shown how the notion of information source changes from being a personal, identifiable prior speaker in hearsay to a depersonalized, anonymous public domain-type entity in folktales and riddles. In the next section I turn to a use of *-sh(i)* in which the information source undergoes complete dehumanization, being construed simply as an abstract region wherein a revelation resides. Furthermore, its primary link to the category is through the mirativity of riddles, since it is not reportative in either the hearsay or folktale/riddle sense.

6.3.4.3 The challenge construction. The mirative sense that is characteristic of a riddle is also seen in what I will refer to as the challenge construction.

Before proceeding I should clarify what I mean by a challenge. The word commonly evokes a conceptualization involving opposition and animosity between two individuals and some impending mutually hostile activity, as in *I challenge you to a duel.* Although some cases do involve opposition, a challenge as I am using it is not restricted to such. Rather, I intend a challenge to be understood in more general hortatory terms, as giving encouragement to the addressee to join in with the speaker in some corporate endeavor.

The challenge construction is a formulaic expression involving the particle maa followed by *-sh(i)* attached to an interrogative pronoun:

(186)   maa INTERROGATIVE-*sh(i)* VERB

Although *maa* is consistently translated in Spanish as *a ver* 'let's see', it should be noted that it is an interjective particle and not a verbal form. It could equally be translated in some contexts as "hmmm."

The challenge construction is not mentioned by Parker (1976), but it reportedly exists in the Callejon de Huaylas dialect.[43] Willem Adelaar's observation (p.c.) that in Tarma Quechua *-sh(i)* may signal the anticipatory outcome of an experiment suggests something along similar lines is found there as well. Weber (1989:437) specifically mentions the challenge construction (as a particular kind of embedded question) in the Huallaga dialect, but does not discuss the motivation for its evidential

---

[43] I thank Mike Miller for this observation.

marking. I maintain that even though the challenge construction has no reportative sense whatsoever, its inclusion in the -*sh(i)* category is sanctioned on the basis of the potential for mirativity it shares with riddles and is consonant with the general notion of "revealed information."

Although somewhat rare in the conversational data base, an example of the challenge use of -*sh(i)* appears in a folktale, the context for which is introduced in (187). A fox meets a condor who tells him he is going to the mountain across the valley to look for a sheep to eat.

(187) ªA*tuu-shi* puliña unay. ᵇ*Chay pulishanchruu-shi* tinkuulun juk kundurwan. ᶜ*Chaychruu-shi* nin: ᵈ-Uy, kumpaari kundur, maytata liyanki? ᵉKundur nin: ᶠ-Ya'a liyaa wik chimpakta-*m*, uwish ashii-*mi*, ᵍmikunaapaa-*mi*...

> ªOnce a fox-*shi* was going along. ᵇAs he was going along-*shi* he met a condor. ᶜThen-*shi* he said: ᵈ"Hey, brother condor, where are you going?" ᵉThe condor says: ᶠ"I'm going across-*mi* over there ᵍto look-*mi* for a sheep, so I can eat-*mi*..."

The fox accompanies the condor and together they catch a sheep. In an effort to trick the fox into relinquishing his share of the sheep, the condor challenges him to an all night vigil on a mountain top. Whoever withstands the cold and is alive in the morning gets to eat the entire sheep. The condor delivers the challenge as follows:

(188) maa mayan-ninchik-*shi* waala-shrun
PART which-12P-REP dawn-12FUT
Let's see which of us-*shi* lasts till morning.

It should be noted that the -*sh(i)* of the challenge is distinct from either the -*sh(i)* that marks the narrative as a folktale or the -*sh(i)* of hearsay. Observe that in (187) the folktale -*sh(i)* occurs on the narrated events and serves to ground the telling of the story to the real-time narrator in a real-time setting. The challenge -*sh(i)*, on the other hand, appears in the dialogue within the "mental space" of the two protagonists (cf. Fauconnier 1985). The shifting of mental spaces is evident, not only from the explicit quotative verb *nin*, but also by the fact that, except for the challenge, the dialogue is marked by the direct evidential -*m(i)*. In other words, the evidential marking on the dialogue refers intrinsically to the world of the protagonists of the story, not to that of the narrator of the folktale. Our understanding of *-sh(i)* in example (188), then, must be within the confines of the protagonists' mental space.

Neither can the *-sh(i)* of (188) be understood as indicating hearsay. For (188) to be an instance of hearsay, we would have to assume that the issue of the condor and fox engaged in an all night vigil had already been discussed in some previous context by someone besides the speech event participants and that this had already been communicated to the speaker of (188), the condor. In such a case the *-sh(i)* could refer back to that discussion. But the linguistic context provides no hint of any kind of an interchange which the condor might be assuming by his use of *-sh(i)*. Conversation has only taken place between the condor and the fox; this is the very first mention of any vigil.

Furthermore, if this were a typical hearsay use a gloss something like "Hmm, which of us *do they say* will last till morning?" would be appropriate. Yet speakers do not gloss the challenge construction with any reference to a second-hand information source as they regularly do when dealing with instances of hearsay. Indeed such a gloss is explicitly rejected when suggested. The translations of Weber's examples of challenges and riddles (Weber 1989:437, 448) are relevant here since they also indicate no reference to a second-hand information source.

Mithun (1986:110) attributes the consistent lack of translation of evidential particles in Northern Iroquoian to their low cognitive salience, as does Casad (1992:167) for Cora. The translation issue is important in that in this case it provides evidence for nonprototypicality (cf. Geeraerts 1988a). Thus, there is no report or second-hand information source which appears to figure prominently in the mind of the speaker for this construction.

Consider another example (189) where the more general, nonconfrontational sense of challenge obtains. In this text two parents are discussing an incident where their son has lied to a neighbor claiming that they have sent him to borrow money. The neighbor foolishly gives it to the boy and has now asked the parents to pay it back. The parents decide to try to recover the money, which by now has been spent and so the father says to the mother:

(189) *maa mayan-man-shi chay illay-kuna-a-ta u-ña*
PART who-GOAL-REP that money-PL-DEF-ACC give-NPST
Let's find out who he gave the money to. (or Hmm, to whom did he give the money?)

In this challenge the speaker is not pitting himself against the addressee. Instead the the father enjoins the mother to aid him in an investigation. It invokes a situation where both speaker and addressee are pitted together against some unknown.

Note this does not mean, "Let's see, *who did he say* he gave the money to?" as though some instance of hearsay were involved. Since the child has not even told his parents about what he has done, there can be no conversation between him and his parents which is being referred to by *-sh(i)*. Nor does the *-sh(i)* refer to the report from the victimized neighbor who originally told them about this, since he does not know what the boy has done with the money either.

Both (188) and (189) constitute challenges in the sense of being injunctions to the addressee to enter into a joint venture together with the speaker for some specified purpose. In each case the *-sh(i)* evokes the concept of a circumstance which involves some sort of impending revelation—in one case, it is the outcome of an all night vigil, in another, the result of an investigation. In neither does *-sh(i)* refer to a prior communication event.

The motivation for the inclusion of challenges in the *-sh(i)* category comes primarily from their similarity to riddles principally with respect to their mirative character. Both riddles and challenges share the anticipation of a result, of some forthcoming resolution to a conflict. We can view the ultimate outcome of the challenge as the conceptual equivalent of the answer to the riddle, and for challenges, as with riddles, the potential for surprise exists to the extent that there may be a mismatch between the preconceived outcome and the actual result.

According to Slobin and Aksu (1982) a surprise interpretation is potentially applicable in Turkish for any sentence marked with the reportative that is extracted from its context. Surprise thus seems to have a very salient role to play in the category for Turkish. But given the contexts in which this use of *-sh(i)* occurs in Wanka, however, it seems more accurate to say that *-sh(i)* does not encode surprise per se, but rather the potential for surprise. Surprise implies a de facto result; for riddles and challenges the result is still forthcoming.

However, the origin of the resolution, i.e., the domain in which the resolution resides, is different for a challenge than for a riddle. In a riddle the answer lies with the speaker; one does not normally tell riddles to which he does not know the answer. But with a challenge, the resolution is completely unembodied and lies solely in the domain of the abstract, unknown future. This carries with it the consequence that the revelation in a challenge will not be verbal, but rather "event"-ful as circumstances unfold.

-sh(i): Hearsay and Revelation

Since the resolution impinges upon the awareness of *both* speech act participants, not just the addressee, the speaker does not hold a privileged position of knowledge as he does with a riddle. In other words, neither participant knows what the resolution will be. Knowing that foxes do not live at high altitudes, the condor may be fairly confident that he will come out victorious, but he does not know the outcome of the challenge as an accomplished fact.

Note that both the formulaic expression introducing riddles and the form of the challenge construction are syntactically interrogative. That this sense of an impending revelation occurs only with interrogative forms should not be surprising since riddles, challenges, and questions are anticipatory in nature. With an interrogative form a speaker prototypically solicits information unknown to him and awaits a forthcoming response from his interlocutor. In riddles and challenges the speech event participants are awaiting an "answer" of sorts in the form of the resolution of either some linguistic conflict or the results of the challenge.

Finally, one could also build a case that *-sh(i)* is a grammaticalized marker of the challenge construction as a whole. First it is associated with a specific formulaic expression, just as it is with riddles and, at a somewhat more abstract level, with folktales (if we can consider virtually absolute regularity as formulaic). Furthermore, there is no sense in which a challenge question merits the name of a specific individual as an appropriate response.

The diagram in (190) illustrates the essential elements involved in a challenge.

(190) Challenge

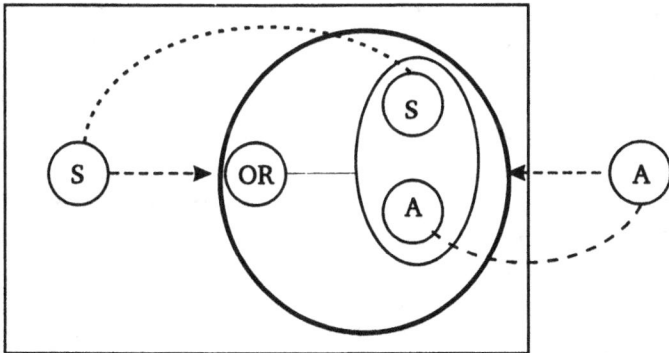

The *OR* is neither a specific individual nor a multiplicity of individuals. OR simply exists as a region of undefined nature. It is thus even more diffuse in its character than the *OR* in the folktale or riddle uses. It nevertheless has the potential for containing information or elements that will come into the awareness of the speech act participants. Also note that *both* speech-act participants are subject to surprise, not just the addressee. This is indicated by the *OR* impinging on their common domain of awareness. Since *OR* is not specified as human, the relationship between *OR* and *S* is necessarily nonverbal, and hence not "reportative." It is "event"-ful. Finally, since *OR* "resides in the future" in some sense, it intrudes into the speech-act participants' domain of awareness from the other end of the time spectrum. The cumulative effect of the various extensions is a configuration quite different from that of the hearsay prototype, but which nevertheless shows numerous family resemblances to other members of the reportative category.

6.4 The relevance of validation

In previous chapters I have argued for the schematic characterization of the direct and conjecture evidentials in validational terms. The direct evidential *-m(i)* is strongly associated with certainty, and the conjecture marker *-chr(a)* is generally associated with noncommitment-assessments of likelihood which range from possibility to necessity. In his review of Palmer (1986) Salkie states, "If a language has a grammatical system (a set of auxiliaries...or particle) which for the most part have modal uses, this is at least *prima facie* grounds for supposing that the other members of the system have some kind of link with modality in a wide sense" (1988:241). Based on this, we therefore have reasonable justification for assuming that *-sh(i)* might have some validational notion associated with it as well. There appears to be some supporting evidence for this view. Weber states, for example, that although in Huallaga Quechua *-sh(i)* primarily indicates information source, it can be interpreted validationally as meaning "unconvinced" (1986:142). In addition, commenting on Pastaza Quechua, Zahn (n.d.) notes that Quechua translators of Biblical narratives occasionally show reluctance to use it to mark long streams of text which the speaker believes.[44] These data seem to set *-sh(i)* up in opposition to *-m(i)* on a validation scale.

However, there are a couple of issues militating against this view. First, the entire range of commitment is already covered by *-m(i)* and

---

[44]My own experience corroborates this. Eugene Casad likewise informs me that the same has been noted among Bible translators in Mexican languages.

-*chr(a)*. If -*sh(i)* may mean 'unconvinced' as Weber (1986) suggests, then what would be the difference between the 'unconvinced' of -*sh(i)* and the 'noncommitment' value of the conjecture marker?

Evidence supporting this position comes indirectly from an investigation originally undertaken to address an entirely different (structural) issue. I was concerned with the constraints on the positioning of the evidentials in a sentence. In order to investigate this I constructed a "cloze" test: I removed all the evidentials from a number of conversational texts and gave the transcriptions to a language consultant to see if he would supply the original evidential in its original position.

Instead of revealing anything particularly novel about positional constraints (cf. chapter 2), something else emerged which was somewhat unexpected. I had always assumed that the direct and conjecture evidentials encompassed very different regions of semantic space. I was, therefore, surprised by the apparent fluctuation in some cases between these two. Often in place of the direct evidential of the original text, the "reconstituted" version showed the conjecture evidential. In other cases an original conjecture evidential was replaced in the reconstituted text by the direct evidential. As I will discuss more fully in chapter 7, the fluctuation between -*m(i)* and -*chr(a)* stems from their schematic characterization as validation markers. There is some portion of validational space to which both of these evidentials have potential access.

The present concern, however, is with the validational status of the reportative. The interesting thing is that in the reconstituted texts, there was no fluctuation between -*chr(a)* and -*sh(i)*. If a validational meaning of "unconvinced" were central to the characterization of the reportative, it seems like some substitution between these two would have occurred.[45]

Secondly, reportative markers in some languages apparently convey no sense of lack of speaker commitment at all. This seems to be the case in Guaraní (Maura Velázquez, p.c.), Kashaya (Oswalt 1986), and Tuyuca (Barnes 1984 and p.c.). There is, therefore, no a priori reason to assume that the Wanka reportative must necessarily have a validational sense. And finally, the facts concerning how -*sh(i)* is actually used lead to the conclusion that it has no particular degree of speaker commitment inherently associated with it.

---

[45]The results of this particular aspect of the investigation are inconclusive. The concept of cloze testing itself is relatively abstract even when supplying lexical items, and much more so when supplying suffixes. An endeavor such as this is a totally foreign concept to Wanka speakers who do not play these kinds of games with their language. In addition, because the fluctuation phenomenon occurred late during my last stay in Peru, I simply did not have time to train a sufficient number of speakers in the concept in order to draw any substantial conclusions. Nevertheless, the initially provocative results suggest lines for future investigation.

Let us consider a few examples from the perspective of validation. In the "Museum" or "Foot" texts discussed previously there is no indication that -*sh(i)* is automatically or necessarily associated with a speaker's lack of commitment. For example, in "Foot" there is no suggestion that the woman telling the story doubts the veracity of what she has been told, even though all the events are tagged with -*sh(i)*. When asked if it seems that the woman believes the events she has related, my language help responded affirmatively. This may be due to the fact that this individual knows both the teller of the story as well as its protagonist, and may himself believe it to be true. However, the important thing to note is that the presence of the reportative marking does not inherently create a conflict between personal commitment and the second-hand nature of the story.

Recall as well the text involving the borrowed money. When the man is first informing his wife that their son has gone to the neighbor asking for a loan, he says,

(191) kay walashr-ninchik-*shi* juk bisiinu-nchik eugenio-pi
this boy-12P-son-REP one neighbor-12P Eugenio-ABL

prista-ka-mu-ña illay-ta
borrow-REF-AFAR-NPST money-ACC

(It is said) this boy of ours borrowed money from our neighbor Eugenio.

The -*sh(i)* does not seem to suggest any particularly strong lack of commitment to the proposition whatsoever on the part of the father. In fact, the rest of the conversation shows that the parents do indeed believe the report since they take appropriate actions as a result of hearing it.

Finally, consider a case where a man has confronted a neighbor with the accusation that her husband has broken into his house and has stolen a number of things.

(192) a. wayapa-yki-*shi* wasi-i-ta yayku-ulu-l
man-2P-REP house-1P-ACC enter-ASP-SS

llapa nuna-kuna-m lika-a-nin ka-ña
all person-PL-DIR see-AG-3P be-NPST
(They say) when your husband entered my house...everybody was a witness.

b. *bwinu ya'a-kta-si nuna   lika-a-kuna-m ni-ma-n*
   well I-ACC-EVEN person see-AG-PL-DIR say-1OBJ-3
   Well, the witnesses even told me.

c. *falta-n radyu-u llapa-n maakina-a*
   lack-3 radio-1P all-3P machine-1P
   I'm missing my radio, all my tools.

d. *llapa moodana-a-ta apa-ka-mu-ña*
   all   clothes-1P-ACC take-REF-AFAR-NPST
   He took all my clothes.

e. *chay-shi lika-la*
   that-REP see-PST
   That's what they saw (they say).

f. *llapa nuna-kuna lika-ña pay-ta*
   all person-PL see-NPST he-ACC
   Everyone saw him.

This example shows that there is no inherent conflict between *-m(i)* and *-sh(i)* with respect to validation. The accusation based on hearsay (a and e), together with his own interaction with the witnesses as specified in (b), move the speaker to action. The reported speech is actually used to muster evidence on his behalf, rather than indicate his lack of commitment to any propositional content.

So then, the fact that a statement *is* based on reported information does not mean that the proposition is necessarily either believed or disbelieved. This being the case, I can only conclude that validation is simply the wrong lens through which to view what *-sh(i)* is essentially about. However validation relates to the characterization of the reportative, it is certainly not central.

In previous chapters I have tried to emphasize the idea that validation is essentially a conceptualizer-centric notion that is largely related to and supported by the degree to which the conceptualizer/speaker personally interacts with evidence to arrive at a conclusion. I think this is why commitment notions attach so obviously and strongly to the direct and conjecture evidentials; the prototypes for *-m(i)* and *-chr(a)* rely on the presence of some kind of evidence which either directly or indirectly forms the basis for a statement. The prototype for *-sh(i)*, on the other hand, depends exclusively on a prepackaged, preprocessed report inherited from a prior conceptualizer-a report which, incidentally, could have any evidentiary basis, i.e., direct experience, inference, or still another previous report. There is no actual evidence for the current conceptualizer/speaker to interact with. The speaker simply passes information on to another addressee, and serves as a *conduit* for a report, not as the processor of evidence.

I view validation as an orthogonal issue for the reportative, the sense of noncommitment possibly stemming from a couple of sources. Slobin and Aksu (1982) suggest that the validational sense of the Turkish reportative may be attributed to the pragmatic knowledge that second-hand information simply may not be reliable to begin with. In addition, I suggest that any commitment value could be a by-product of how the speaker construes the origin and its relationship to the proposition(s). That is, it is an implicature deriving from the speaker's construal of the origin's relationship to the designated conceptualization. If the speaker thinks that the origin believes the account is trustworthy, then the speaker will also be predisposed to believe the account himself.

This might explain the fact that different degrees of speaker commitment are associated with the "Foot" text and the folktale of "The Fox and the Rabbit." In the former, since the story concerns a personal event in the life of the speaker's father, the speaker is more likely to judge the relationship between her information source (presumably her father) and the events in the story to be direct. In "The Fox and Rabbit," however, the origin is diffuse with no one individual bearing a direct eyewitness relationship to the events of the folktale, hence no real responsibility for their veracity. Therefore, the speaker is not as likely to commit himself either. This implies that the content of a folktale would more likely be doubted than an instance of hearsay. (But, once again, unbelief is not necessitated; as we have seen, even aspects of folktales may be believed.)

Competing construals of the origin may account, at least in part, for native translators' hesitancy to mark as reportative certain kinds of passages. The translator must seek to capture not only the original author's actual evidential relationship to the designated events, but also his validational construal. Since biblical Hebrew and Koiné Greek had no evidential marking the biblical manuscripts provide no help in solving this thorny coding issue.

Consider, for instance, the problems encountered in rendering the genealogy at the beginning of the Gospel of Matthew:

(193) Abraham was the father of Isaac, Isaac the father of Jacob, Jacob the father of Judah and his brothers...

Which evidential should be used? Questions to Quechua co-translators framed in terms of prototypes like, "Was the author present? or Did he hear this from someone else?" virtually pre-determine the limits within which any answer will be given. Obviously, unless the author was 2,000 years old at the time this was written and actually had opportunity to base the passage on direct experience, he must have been told by someone else. So, according to the "rules" (which have some basis as far as the prototype is concerned), second-hand information *should* be encoded with -*sh(i)*, producing something along the lines of:

(194) "...Abraham was the father of Isaac-*shi,* Isaac the father of Jacob-*shi,* Jacob the father of Judah-*shi* and his brothers..."

Upon reflection, however, the Quechua speaker may decide that the resulting product, because of such regular evidential marking, sounds just like a folktale, whose origin is diffuse and impersonal, and which by its very nature is more removed from everyday experience and hence is not necessarily believed. At this point, his knowledge that the original author was convinced of the truth of the passage may reassert itself, prompting him to change the marking to -*m(i)*.[46]

In this respect, I mention Rosch (1978:36) who states that either/or categorical questions such as these are the cause of much confusion over the notion of prototype. The notion has tended to become reified as though it meant a specific category member of mental structure. Questions are then asked in an either/or fashion about whether something is or is not the prototype or part of the prototype in exactly the same way in which the question would previously have been asked about the category boundary. Such thinking precisely violates the Wittgensteinian insight that we can judge how clear a case something is and deal with categories on the basis of clear cases in the total absence of information about boundaries.

An alternative view of -*sh(i)*'s relationship to the validational domain might be to consider the reportative as indicating some "intermediate" level between full-commitment (as codified by -*m(i)*) and noncommitment (-*chr(a)*). This has some measure of intuitive appeal. It is certainly reasonable to assume that if, say, the prior information source was a direct witness of the encoded event, then there are indeed grounds for the speaker to accept the proposition as true, but that his own lack of direct experience

---

[46]It goes without saying that the very act of focussing on a grounding element in this way violates something of its inherently subjective nature. A consideration of a similar approach toward verb tense in English may helpful. If we interrogate naive English speakers about the "correctness" of a sentence like, "He comes tomorrow," it just might occur to them that since comes is present and tomorrow is future the sentence must be bad.

in the matter prevents him from committing himself to the same degree as he would otherwise.

My problem with this view for *-sh(i)* is not that it is not a plausible perspective, nor even that this might not be the analysis for the reportative in some other language, but rather that it attributes to *-sh(i)* an *inherent* validational function rather than considering any validational value as an indirect incidental result of other factors, as I prefer. I base my view primarily on the fact that with the other evidentials, validation emerged even in extended senses, supporting this parameter as a prominent aspect of their schematic characterizations. In contrast, I have no examples in my data base where *-sh(i)* is used strictly to indicate validation; any validational sense emerges only as a side effect. Mirativity, on the other hand, is what DOES pervade the extensions of the reportative, arguing in favor of this as its schematic characterization.

Mirativity is like validation in that it involves a codified subjective reaction to a proposition and—thus it bears a relationship to modality at large—but it is not a reaction of the speaker's willingness to commit himself to a proposition. It bears greater similarity to other more "broadly modal" notions often associated with evidential marking that, like mirativity, also appear to be subjective reactions to information "breaking into" or "invading" the speaker's reality from the "outside," e.g., in Menomini, disappointment (Hockett 1958:237-8), in Apalai, pity and irritation (Koehn and Koehn 1986), *inter alia*. The schematic value for the reportative—"revelation"—thus pertains to a domain that may intersect validation at some point, but is not coextensive with it.

The point I wish to emphasize, however, is simply the marginal status that validation has with respect to the overall characterization of the reportative. In some sense this is at variance with the view in which evidentials are viewed primarily as devices for commenting on the degree of commitment a speaker has with respect to a proposition (cf. Palmer 1986); in this view, the reportative (along with the conjecture marker) would serve to relinquish personal responsibility for the contents of an utterance. My view is not that reportatives are deliberately and actively used to relinquish the speaker's responsibility, but rather, responsibility may appear to be relinquished as the result of passing along information.

6.5 Summary

In this chapter I began with the examination of the Wanka reportative suffix as an indicator of hearsay, which I concluded was the prototype

-sh(i): Hearsay and Revelation 159

for the category. Extensions included *-sh(i)* as a marker of folktales and its uses in riddles and the challenge construction. These uses fall into reportative and mirative (surprisal) categories.

At the heart of an instance of hearsay is a prior communicative act between the speaker and a specific individual that reveals information to the speaker. A major theme that derives from this prototype is woven throughout *-sh(i)*'s semantic network, i.e., how the informational origin is construed. We observe a progressive "dehumanization" of the origin from use to use. In hearsay the origin is conceptualized as a specifically identifiable individual, whereas in folktales and riddles the origin has been bleached of its individuality, becoming more of an amorphous nonindividuated public domain-type entity. This dehumanization finds its fullest expression in the challenge construction where the the "origin" is a completely dehumanized, unembodied, and abstract region.

The other principal theme that emerges concerns the nature of revealed knowledge (as opposed to knowledge arrived at). I claimed that revealed knowledge is construed as being the kind to which the conceptualizer does not normally have experiential and evidential access. This provides a potential link to domains involving events or knowledge beyond the bounds of normal experience that potentially admit the presence of elements that contravene normal expectation. Mirativity is the subjective reaction to this aspect of the prototypical construal. I concluded the chapter providing evidence for the marginal status of validation to the characterization of the reportative.

7
On Directness, Proximity, Ground Domains, and Evidentials

7.1 Introduction

This study is motivated in part out of the observation that evidentials in Wanka (as well as in other languages) do not co-occur randomly with person and tense marking. Rather, there are distinct tendencies which must have some coherent explanation. In this chapter I explore a tentative explanation of this phenomenon based on the assumption that conceptualization affects linguistic structure. The central idea is that schematic notions of directness and proximity are related concepts that serve as organizing principles for deictic domains as well as for facets of the Wanka evidential system. Directness and proximity are first examined in terms of their common conceptual basis. I then relate these abstract notions to aspects of deixis that have been relevant throughout the study, namely, the nature of the experiences that evidentials typically encode and our conceptualization of the domains that constitute the fabric of the ground, i.e., the speech event.

Evidentials are often characterized in terms of directness (cf. Willett 1988). I explain this characterization as how directly or immediately the speaker experientially "contacts" the designated scenario. Our conceptualization of ground domains, on the other hand, is generally construed in terms of proximity. I will show that ground domains are not notionally homogeneous, but rather are viewed in terms of subdomains or subregions which reflect some schematic notion of "proximity." Correlations between directness and proximity suggest a motivated alternative characterization of the Wanka evidential system in terms of the latter. I will suggest that such a characterization is valuable in explaining the propensity of evidentials to co-occur with markers for particular ground subdomains. I begin with a discussion of the abstract notions of directness and proximity.

7.2 Directness

Schematically, directness concerns the nature of the path between two entities-in particular, the presence or absence of a mediating element. I take abstract directness as having its conceptual basis in our rudimentary comprehension and experience of spatial expanse. In its most generalized sense, directness involves the assessment of the positions of differentiated entities with respect to each other. Schematically, the relative positions of the two entities are left unspecified. There are, of course, innumerable instantiations of this schematic relation, several of which are indicated in (195)-(199).

I follow Langacker (1985:146) in translating maximal proximity between two entities into coincidence. The limiting case is depicted in figure (195) where there is complete isomorphism between A and B. Figure (196) depicts the partial overlap between A and B, marking a departure from the previous configuration towards individuation and separation of the two entities. Figure (197) illustrates two highly differentiated entities in minimal tangential contact. And figures (198) and (199) depict fully differentiated entities separated by varying distances.

(195) Coincidence of A and B

(196) A overlaps B

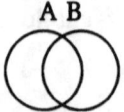

(197) A tangential to B

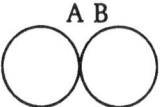

(198) Gap 1

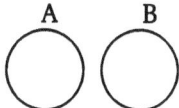

(199) Gap 2

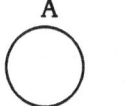 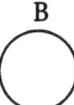

A couple of observations concerning the configurations in (195)–(199) are in order. It seems to me that the greater the degree of coincidence between the two entities, the more likely the overall configuration can be perceived in some unitary fashion as a gestalt. But this becomes more difficult with increased differentiation and distance between the entities, as can be appreciated in (198) and (199) where there is a measure of separation between A and B.

The separation is what ultimately opens the door for the perception of a path between the entities. The loss of the point of contact between A and B is accompanied by increased difficulty in perceiving the entities in a unified fashion. Therefore, if there is a connection between them, it must be supplied by the conceptualizer. In other words, as the relationships among the entities change, there is a sense in which gestalt perception gives way to processual scanning. The notion of an incipient path enters, then, as scanning of the area between the two entities occurs (cf. figure (200)).

(200) Path

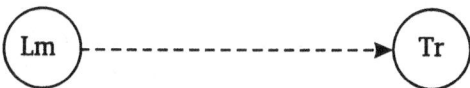

The conceptualizer scans the configuration taking one of the entities as his starting point. This entity serves as a landmark (Lm) in relation to which the other entity, the trajector (Tr), is located.

Given any measure of distance between two entities, a direct path is readily understood as the shortest route (the most "immediate") from one to the other. (Thus, Go directly to jail; do not pass 'GO'; do not collect $200.) But significantly the presence of a gap between two entities admits the intervention of other elements which potentially block direct progression from point A to point B. In this case, scanning from A to B necessarily includes scanning of an intervening entity X (cf. (201)).

(201) Indirect path

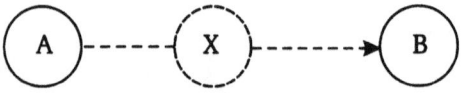

The same spatial imagery may be metaphorically extended into nonspatial domains, e.g., time, as in I'll be there directly (i.e., immediately, without delay). Or in the communication domain, DIRECT ANSWER, for example, equates a spatial path with qualities of truthfulness, frankness, and efficiency; a direct answer, therefore, is one that comes "straight to the point" (more spatial imagery) and is without hemming and hawing. An INDIRECT ANSWER, on the other hand, involves unnecessary complications and additional elements which distract from or hide the central point.

7.3 Proximity

Related to directness, is the notion of proximity. Schematically, it is a relation where one entity is taken as a reference point for the description or location of another in some domain; but the two entities are situated with respect to each other along some parameter which is construed as being scalar and analogous to spatial distance.

Like directness, I take abstract proximity as having its conceptual basis in our experience of the spatial domain. Spatial proximity is readily comprehended as having to do with the relative measurable distance between two objectively-construed entities. The same array of configurational relationships relevant to directness in (195)–(199) is applicable here as well, where individuated entities are located with respect to each other in a variety of ways. Spatial proximity specifically involves the assessment of any such relationship relative to some relevant scope. In the case of an assessment as "proximal/near" (example (202)), the distance between the trajector and the landmark comes nowhere near exhausting the relevant scope, whereas it does in "distal/far" in (203).

(202) Proximal

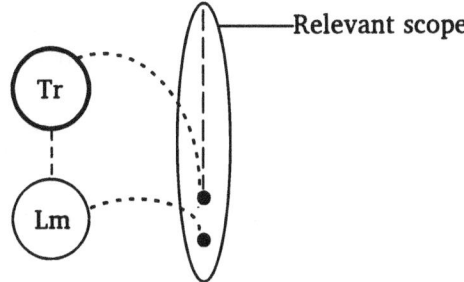

(203) Distal

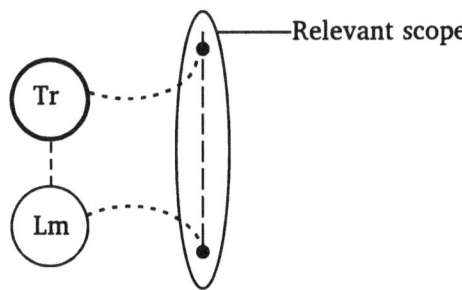

The scale onto which the entities are mapped enabling the proximity assessment is, in principle, measurable. Measurements of physical space, of course, include conventionalized units such as millimeters, miles, and light years. But it is important to note that near and far are not directly equated with any specific difference between points on the scale. In other words, near does not necessarily equal a *distance of two millimeters* any more than far necessarily equates with a *distance of 200 light years*. *Near* and *far* are subjective judgments about the distances between landmark and trajector with respect to *potential* dimensions within the relevant domain. By saying that the Burger King is near the Texaco, I am saying that the distance between Burger King and Texaco is less than some undefined expected norm given the potential distance there might be, say, within the scope of the city as a whole. *Fort Worth is near Dallas* suggests that given the potential for distances within, say, the scope of the state of Texas, the distance between Dallas and Fort Worth is considerably less. The same judgment of near is used in both cases even though the measurable space is remarkably different-100 yards versus 30 miles more or less. If the actual distance between Burger King and Texaco was the same as the distance between Dallas and Fort Worth it is not likely that the relationship between them could be felicitously termed as near.

The metaphorical extension of spatial proximity into the temporal domain is well noted (for example, Fleischman 1989) and is evident in examples such as *He'll be home close to 9,* where spatial distance terminology (analogous to near) is utilized to describe a time span. The temporal duration between the landmark "9:00" and the trajector, i.e., the point at which the subject arrives home, is assessed with respect to an undefined temporal scope, but which presumably is construed as extending some measure beyond the bounds of the duration itself (cf. (204)).

(204)   Close to 9

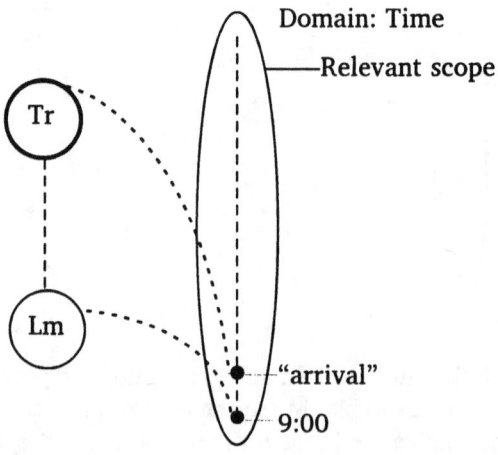

Conversely, in *He'll be home long past 9* a distal temporal counterpart of *far* describes the temporal duration between landmark and trajector.

On Directness, Proximity, Ground Domains, and Evidentials 167

(205) Long past 9

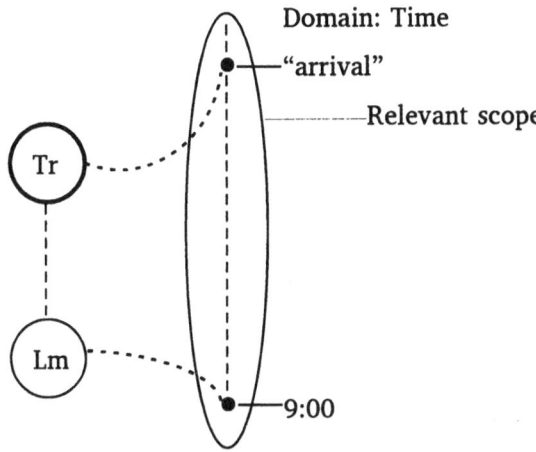

It is likely that physical and temporal proximity coincide to some degree. The assessment of the distance between two points in the spatial domain involves the conceptualizer's mental scanning which may be thought of as subjective motion as he "travels" from one point to the other. But scanning also entails some kind of processing time. Compare the following two diagrams:

(206) Proximity comparisons

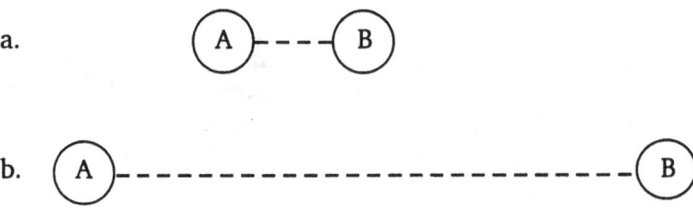

It may be that one of the reasons we judge the distance in (206b) to be greater than that in (206a) is the fact that the path in (206b) takes a greater amount of time to traverse mentally, since it is less easily apprehended as a unit.

Contrasting schematic directness with proximity, the former is conceptually simpler than the latter since it invokes no scale of any type onto which landmark and trajector are mapped. Schematic proximity, on the other hand, not only avails itself of a scale and a mapping procedure, but also assumes some relevant scope within which the scale is applied. Nevertheless, there are certain correlations between the two which are noteworthy and become important to the discussion later on. Direct and proximal relationships correspond in the following way (cf. (207)). The essence of an assessment of a relationship between entities as direct is that, regardless of the actual space between the entities, schematically there is no allowance for intervention by a third. This admits the possibility of actual contact between the entities (perhaps even merger), resulting in a highly proximal relationship. Indirect and distal relationships are likewise similar. For either the relationship of indirect or distal to obtain, the entities must not be in contact; there must be a gap between them.

(207) Directness/Proximity correspondences

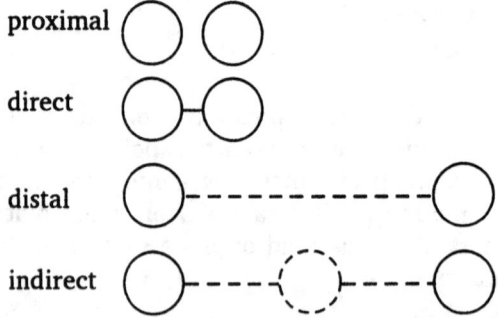

In the next section I consider in some detail the nature of the ground domains, first in general terms, then from the perspective of the schematic notion of proximity just outlined. When a ground element is taken as the landmark, ground domains are conceptualized as being egocentrically organized, with certain regions being more "proximal" to the conceptualizer than others. In section 7.6 the nature of the experiences that evidential markings typically encode are examined from the viewpoint of both schematic directness and proximity.

7.4 Ground domains

As shown throughout this study, evidentials are deictic expressions which make implicit reference to some aspect of the ground. The nature of the ground, however, has been assumed and left largely unexplicated. Following Langacker (1987a:126), I have been using the term "ground" to refer collectively to the speech event in all its facets. In general terms, the characterization of the ground involves reference to domains of reality-irreality, location in time and space, as well as speakers and hearers, their knowledge and objectives in communicating, their interactions, and a potential host of other domains.

Langacker (1991) details some of what enters into the characterization of the ground at a very basic level, focusing specifically on a speech event's location in the domains of reality and time. The two are so inextricably interwoven that it is somewhat difficult to conceive of one without the other, but for purposes of the present discussion I will assume that they may be conceptualized separately.

At this basic level, reality involves the array of situations and circumstances that a conceptualizer accepts as factual, "what a particular person knows (or thinks he knows)" (Langacker 1991:242, footnote 1). It involves multidirectional spatial expanse as the domain in which tangible objects are located and events occur. While we interact with things that do exist, we also imagine things that do not. We recognize that hopes, dreams, and desires, for example, partake of some quality that is markedly different from that of bricks, food, and pain. Therefore, in some primary, elemental sense we make a distinction between reality and irreality. Example (208), based on Langacker (1991:242),[47] shows the division of conceptual space into regions of reality (depicted as a cylinder) and irreality, with the conceptualizer (C) situated within the former.

(208) Basic epistemic model: Reality/irreality

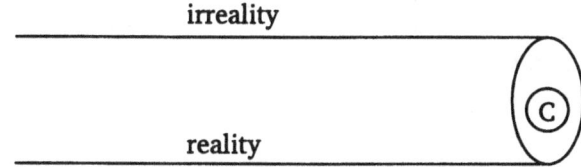

This basic epistemic model is elaborated to incorporate what might be understood in some sense as a kind of "intermediate" domain between reality and irreality. This domain, which Langacker (1991:243) refers to as "unknown reality," reflects the conceptualizer's realization that there

---

[47]I should point out that the model I have suggested here differs from Langacker's in one respect. In Langacker's basic epistemic model reality is represented as a cylinder evolving along some axis, with "immediate reality" described as "reality at the latest stage of its evolution" (Langacker 1991:243). But it seems to me that the idea of evolution already presupposes the imposition of a concept of time which he specifically invokes later on as necessary for a distinct elaboration of this basic model.

are aspects of reality which he may suspect or potentially contemplate but whose reality has not been established, as well as those aspects of reality about which he is completely unaware. Thus, what is referred to as "irreality" in the basic epistemic model is conceptualized here as incorporating some subregion of unknown reality. The elaborated epistemic model in (209) illustrates these different domains.

(209) Elaborated epistemic model

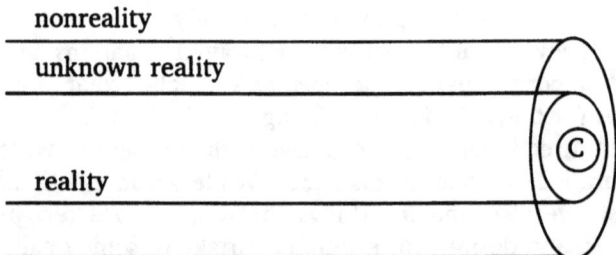

In addition to this basic conceptualization of reality and irreality is the recognition that the world is biased toward the occurrence of certain events and situations as opposed to others (Langacker 1991:276). Certain events arise or are precluded from arising simply because of the way the world is. An event may be conceptualized as being within some domain of potential reality due to certain incidental factors consistent with the structure of the world. On the other hand, another event may be conceptualized as more directly arising out of the structure of the world (together with certain expectations about the normal "flow of events") and is consequently predictable to some degree, placing it within a domain of projected reality (cf. (210)).

(210) Projected and potential reality

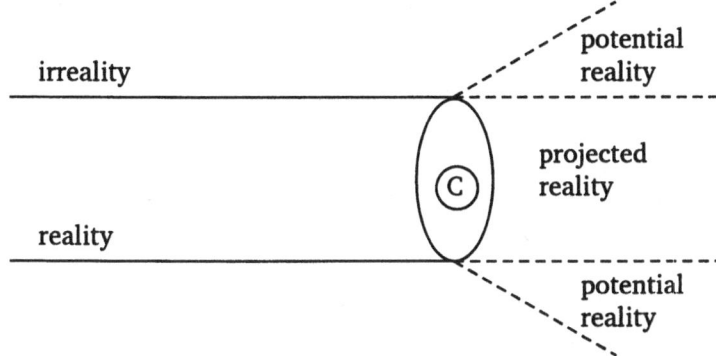

As Langacker points out, reality is not static, but is ever-evolving. Thus, in addition to the fundamental notions of reality and irreality noted above, the basic epistemic model is elaborated by the addition of time, conceptualized as "the axis along which reality evolves" (Langacker 1991:243). Reality at its latest stage of evolution is referred to as "immediate reality."

(211) Reality and time

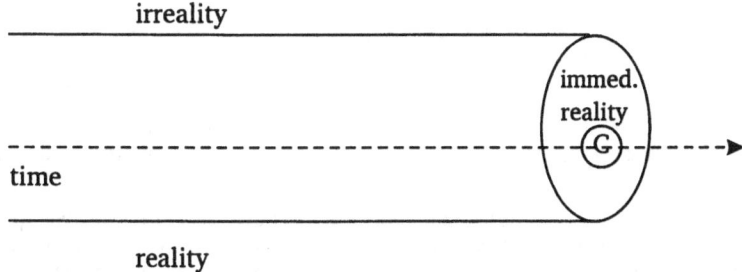

Finally, the very concept of a speech event presupposes a speaker and potential addressees. I take the view that the primary purpose of language is communication. Speakers seek to express ideas, to accomplish tasks, to establish and preserve relationships, etc., But whatever the particular goal, a speaker normally directs his message toward some other entity, typically toward entities like himself which are conceptualized as being capable of comprehending the message. I will say more about this later in relation to the empathy hierarchy. For the present, however, it will suffice simply to state that a speech event inherently involves a domain of potential participants in that event-a speaker and entities who are capable of comprehending the speaker's message.

An adequate characterization of the ground thus incorporates conceptual models from different domains: reality/irreality, space, time, and speech event participants. Reality can be understood as the summation of consecutive immediate realities which the conceptualizer has available to his awareness, lying along the axis of time. The ground is the location of the conceptualizer and other speech event participants within reality at its latest stage of development. It is from the perspective of the ground that a speaker conceptualizes the world and communicates his assessments of it to others in a speech event.[48]

The schematic notion of proximity sketched out in section 7.3 serves as a general organizing principle for these domains. In the following section I show that when a ground element figures as a reference point for the assessment of an entire ground domain, the result is that the domain is viewed as being composed of subregions or subdomains lying in various degrees of "proximity" to the speaker, the most "proximal" of which have particular characteristics.

7.5 Subdomain proximity

It has been noted by many (Lakoff and Johnson 1980, Fleischman 1989 *inter alia*) that language and linguistic structure consistently reflect an egocentric, speaker-based orientation. We live in a world of spatial relationships. Since we are not omnipresent, everything is not equally physically tangible. Neither can we attend psychologically to all entities simultaneously to the same degree. Rather, the physical relationships

---

[48]Since deictic expressions like *tomorrow* or *here* make reference to particular aspects of the ground, and since evidentials are likewise deictic expressions, the question may arise as to whether or not evidentiality is a conceptual ground-defining domain on the same level as (ir)reality, time, and speech event participants. The same question could be raised with regard to the conceptual domains of other deictics such as honorifics and speaker gender. I do not think that evidentials are ground-defining domains for two reasons. While social distance and speaker gender are obviously related to facets of the ground, they are not as conceptually fundamental as the other domains outlined above. I view evidentiality, honorifics, etc., as being conceptually dependent on a more fundamental domain in that they already presuppose a participant.

Furthermore, the difference in status between domains needed to characterize the ground and those like evidentiality, honorifics and speaker gender is observed cross-linguistically. All languages have indications of speaker and addressee, but not every language has morphologically encoded male/female speech distinctions. Furthermore, many languages have grammaticalized tense. I suspect that far fewer languages grammatically encode evidential distinctions, although this awaits more investigation.

between entities affect how we perceive them; at any one moment some may be more salient, tangible, etc., than others simply due to their physical proximity. Subdomain proximity is the reflection of this principle in the conceptual domains that comprise the ground.

Simply put, the reality, space, time, and participant domains are not conceptually "homogeneous masses." Rather, from the perspective of the conceptualizer, each domain has some aspect, facet, or region that emerges as particularly cognitively accessible or proximal in some sense.

7.5.1 Reality/irreality and proximity. It seems intuitively sound to assert that within the conceptual domain of reality/irreality, reality is the region that is the most psychologically proximal to the conceptualizer. At its most basic level, reality is the "stuff" that stimulates our perceptive faculties and includes the world of tangible objects, experienced events, personal knowledge, etc., Immediate reality, i.e., the spatio-temporal location of the speaker within reality, is more cognitively accessible to the conceptualizer than other points within the reality domain because it is the domain from which interaction with tangible objects in the world around occurs and the position from which experiences are typically assessed.

Irreality, then, is more distal. Entities which "are not" cannot be as tangible as those which "are." Things about which the conceptualizer has no awareness must necessarily hold a different cognitive status from those about which he is fully cognizant.

In spite of the intangible nature of irreality, it is not an undifferentiated conceptual mass (Langacker 1991:243ff). In section 7.4, irreality was characterized as a multifaceted domain encompassing real entities of which the conceptualizer was unaware, those that partake of some projected or potential (but as yet unestablished) reality, as well as those which are clearly counterfactual or nonexistent. That different kinds of nonreality can be distinguished formally is evident from the following Wanka Quechua examples.

(212) a. *li-ku-n-chra*
       go-REF-3-CONJ
       He'll probably go. (projected reality)

   b. *li-ku-n-man-chra*
       go-REF-3-POT-CONJ
       He might go. (potential reality)

c. *li-ku-n-man-chra ka-la*
   go-REF-3-POT-CONJ be-PST
   He should have gone. (counterfactuality)

(These examples hint at the correlation between the domain of reality/irreality and that of time, which is considered in section 7.5.3.)[49]

So then, entities which fall into the region of potential reality, for instance, have a distinct cognitive status from those that are nonreal or false. Since the conceptualizer has potential access to knowledge of entities in the domain of potential reality, it seems reasonable to assume that this domain may in some sense be judged as more proximal to the conceptualizer than that of nonreality.

7.5.2 Space and proximity. Encodings for distinct regions of spatial expanse are common in linguistic descriptions and do not require a great deal of elaboration. In (213) I illustrate that the tripartite spatial deictic distinction found in Wanka Quechua conforms to a common pattern of egocentric organization found cross-linguistically.

(213) Wanka spatial deictics

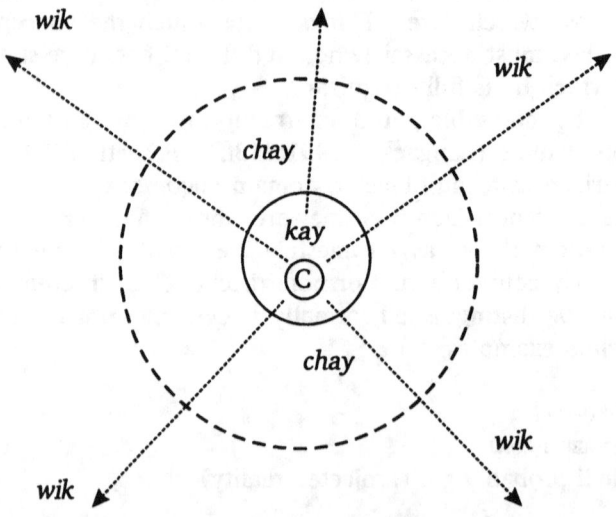

---

[49]It should be also noticed that the conceptual distance from immediate reality and the different "irrealities" are iconically represented in the markings themselves by means of linguistic distance: *-n-chra* 'projected reality'; *-n-man-chra* 'potential reality'; *-n-man-chra kala* 'counterfactuality' (cf. Haiman 1985).

Note that the regions designated by these terms encompass different spatial "quantities." *kay* 'here/this' indicates spatial immediacy and may be thought of as roughly the area spanned by an arm's length in all directions and then some. It is the most proximal and also the most restricted in areal scope. *chay* 'there/that (proximal)' designates a larger and less rigidly-defined area, one that is not necessarily immediately accessible tactilely, but is usually limited at its greatest extent to what actually falls within the speaker's field of vision. So, whereas both vision and physical contact delimit the region designated by *kay*, vision serves as the principal determiner of the region encompassed by *chay*. The greatest areal region is designated by *wik* 'there/that (distal)'. *wik* is not limited to the speaker's field of vision and typically extends beyond it, but may overlap with the area designated by *chay*. Rather than vision being the determining factor, we may think of *wik*'s area as that which is accessible by some mental analog of vision, "conceptualizable" even if not actually seen.

We observe parallels to this pattern in how the temporal domain is conceived.

7.5.3 Time and proximity. Time, like space, is not conceptualized as an undifferentiated mass, but is comprised of regions or subdomains that are viewed as lying in varying degrees of proximity to the conceptualizer. I suggest that for the conceptualizer/speaker the present is the subdomain of which he is most cognizant. From a fundamental intuitive standpoint, it is the only portion of the time domain which he actually "occupies." The present is the point at which the speaker's reactions, assessments, and processing of all that has preceded are actually manifested. It is the point from which the temporal orientation of all other events is typically calculated. It is the moment that, as a speaker, he is engaged in the physical effort of vocalization. And it is the moment that demands the attention of the addressee in terms of interaction, cognitive processing, etc.

The past is less proximal than the present. It has some measure of tangibility since it consists of the collective set of previous consecutive "present," hence real, moments. But as experienced events become memories of past history which are no longer fully experientially tangible, they also become conceptually more remote (cf. Fleischman 1989).

The future concerns actual moments that are expected to unfold. But since moments subsequent to the present have not yet been experienced, the future bears the status of being more inaccessible still, coinciding in large measure with the domain of irreality. In fact, Chung and Timberlake (1985) point out that although it does occur, the encoding of three separate tenses (i.e., past, present, future) in a given language is not particularly common. It is more usual to find tense distinctions aligning or overlapping with the reality-irreality domain in some way, e.g., along lines such as past/nonpast or nonfuture/future, such as is illustrated in (214).

(214) Time and reality correspondence

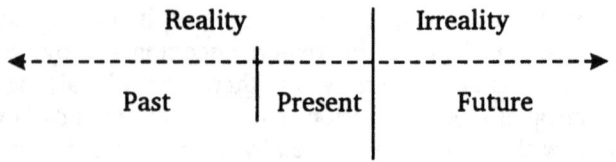

Note that past and future regions encompass vast portions of the total temporal expanse. Both are bounded by the moment of speech (i.e., present) on one end, but are infinitely open ended as one moves away from the moment of speech in either past or future directions. Note that the moment of speech itself is not strictly a punctiliar event, but has temporal duration (cf. Langacker 1991:243). "The present" may actually appear in either category. Presumably, one reason for this has to do with the difference between the perfectivity of an event, which most typically correlates with past, and irreality, a quality which events in the future would clearly have. Events that are currently being experienced (hence in the present tense) are not completed and, therefore, fit less easily into the prototypical "real event" category. On the other hand, there is a sense in which the irreality of an anticipated event is different from that of an event that simply has not been completed.

Since past and future encompass such large temporal expanses it follows that these subdomains in their entirety would not be equally psychologically proximal to the conceptualizer; rather within them, particular subregions could vary in cognitive proximity. For example, some region of "recent past" should be more cognitively accessible than "distant past" simply because of its temporal proximity to the moment of speech; recollection of events in that time period would be clearer than those from earlier periods.

Similar comments apply to the temporal subdomain of future; some region of "imminent future" would have a degree of conceptual accessibility or proximity greater than that of "remote future." A certain degree of predictability of subsequent states or events is sanctioned, even if those states or events are unknown or as yet unexperienced (cf. Langacker 1991:275ff.). The accuracy of a prediction regarding the near future seems more likely assured than that of a prediction targeting some time far in the future, since the greater the temporal expanse between the moment of prediction and the target time, the greater the possibility for more elements to intervene and alter the resulting picture.

Division of the temporal domain in terms of proximal/nonproximal subregions is reflected in the formal tense distinctions found in a number of languages. For example, Wanka Quechua differentiates "recent" from "remote" past tenses. Haya (cf. Comrie 1985:29) makes a three-way past tense distinction: earlier in the day, yesterday and before yesterday. The Wasco-Wishram dialect of Chinook morphologically distinguishes four past tenses: immediate, recent, far, and remote (Silverstein 1974).

Comrie observes that multiple temporal distance distinctions are more common in the past than in the future (Comrie 1985:87), which I interpret as providing evidence for the greater conceptual proximity of past over future temporal subdomains. More rare are languages with parallel distinctions in both past and future, but they can be found. Givn (1972), for example, describes ChiBemba as distinguishing four degrees of remoteness in both past and future subdomains, and also provides some specification of the actual degree of remoteness from the present.

(215) remote past   before yesterday
       removed past   yesterday
       near past   today
       immediate past   e.g., within the last three hours
       immediate future   very soon, within three hours
       near future   later today
       removed future   tomorrow
       remote future   after tomorrow

Figure (216) plots ChiBemba's temporal distinctions along a time line calculated from "0," the moment of speech.

(216) ChiBemba tenses

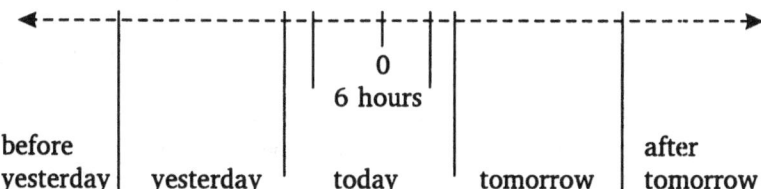

ChiBemba's system parallels the nature of spatial proximity that I argued for in section 7.5.3. Like other languages with multiple remoteness distinctions, ChiBemba divides the entire expanse encompassed by "past" into chunks of varying, not equal, temporal extents. The closer to the present, i.e., the deictic center, the narrower the time frame becomes. Furthermore, the majority of temporal distinctions in the past are made for a period that falls within a very small "time window" with respect to the actual moment of speech. Events occurring a few minutes ago, earlier today, and yesterday will all be encoded differently, whereas events happening the day before yesterday and 200 years ago would be encoded in the same fashion. Similar comments can be made for the encoding of future events as well.

I suggest that the fine-grained differentiations made in the temporal window around the deictic center are parallel to what we find in the spatial domain which, as we saw, are closely related to visual perception. In addition, there may also be some conceptual parallel to the temporal duration of the speech event; the speech event itself has duration, but is much shorter in time span compared to those encompassed by other temporal divisions. Experience informs us of the fact that certain details in any object become increasingly more evident at close visual range. Up to a certain point, the number of discernible details in some object under scrutiny increases as the distance between viewer and object decreases. Consequently, greater differentiation of its parts becomes possible. Clarity increases up to an optimal point, after which details once again become fuzzy. If linguistic structure reflects cognition, we might expect there to be certain kinds of distinctions appearing in the more proximal domains than in those that are less so, since the more proximal domains would be subject to a greater degree of "scrutiny" and dissection than would be possible with the more distal domains.[50]

7.5.4 Participants and proximity. The ground domain of speech event participants also appears to distinguish proximal and distal subdomains. One evidence of egocentricity in this domain found in Quechua and many other languages is the inclusive/exclusive plural distinction, whereby "we" which includes the addressee is differentiated from "we" excluding the addressee. Even though the speaker and addressee both

---

[50]One wonders if, in addition to tense, there might not be some reflection of a similar egocentric conceptual bias vis-à-vis aspectual distinctions. I mention in passing Adelaar's (1988) observation that in Tarma Quechua, perfective and imperfective suffixes cannot occur with a negated (hence, conceptually distal) verb. This would appear to be an example of a conceptual distinction allowable in a more proximate domain of reality that was disallowed in the more distal irrealis domain.

comprise part of the ground, the inclusive/exclusive distinction always takes the speaker as the point of reference, not the addressee.

Another reflection of subdomain proximity in the speech act participant domain concerns what has gone by various names (animacy hierarchy, Silverstein hierarchy), but what will be referred to here as the empathy hierarchy, given in (217)) (cf. Langacker (1991:306). The essential idea behind the hierarchy is a ranking of the various sorts of entities that populate the world in terms of an egocentric assessment of the potential they have to attract our empathy, usually based on matters of likeness and common concerns with respect to ego (Langacker 1991:307). Entities are thus located at varying degrees of "empathetic distance" from the speaker. We may interpret this as a manifestation of conceptual proximity in the empathy domain.

(217) The empathy hierarchy

    speaker > hearer > human > animal > physical object > abstract entity

The hierarchy reflects our prototypical conceptualizations of agents and patients. We recognize ourselves as agentive, volitional, directed beings capable of exerting influence over other entities, etc. The more that an entity exhibits such characteristics the more likely it will be conceptualized as an agent, and consequently, the more likely it will be cross-linguistically encoded as a subject. Conversely, the more an entity appears to be influenced by other forces, the more likely it will be conceptualized as patient-like and encoded grammatically as an object or some other oblique role.

As Langacker points out, if empathy is based on likeness and common concerns, then it follows that the highest degree of empathy (i.e., proximity, in my view) that the speaker can achieve is with himself (1991:307). The difference in empathetic status between humans and those entities farther down on the scale, i.e., animals, physical objects, etc., is clear and its motivation needs no elaboration. Deserving of some consideration, however, is the special status of the addressee.

Assuming that addressees are typically human, the question arises as to why the speaker would have more empathy with the addressee than with other humans.[51] I believe that there are at least two reasons why this is so.

---

[51]Of course, not all addressees are human. Within the context of a speech event, the speaker's intent to communicate imposes a kind of empathy on the addressee. Humans often direct communication to entities much farther down on the empathy hierarchy, e.g., pets or plants. The object of communication is "drawn up," so to speak, into the level of the speaker in some sense. Differences are minimized conceptually as the speaker construes an entity as having communicative abilities, hence empathy, regardless of whether or not they in fact exist.

One is due to simple cognitive limitations. A conceptualizer is incapable of fully attending to an unlimited number of entities simultaneously. When he focuses his attention on one thing, other things are necessarily excluded or ignored. Merely by being the focus of the speaker's attention in a speech event the addressee occupies a more prominent, immediately relevant conceptual status than other nonaddressee humans.

The second reason is related. Face-to-face interaction provides the speaker with a potentially greater amount of knowledge about the addressee. The point has already been made that the speaker knows most about himself. He has inside knowledge of his own subjective thoughts, memories, activities, etc., which may not be apparent to others but are nevertheless very present and very real. Although the speaker does not have direct access to the internal states of either the addressee or a third person, he has sufficient reason to assume a great deal about them from the beginning simply because they also are human. He may assume with a fair degree of certainty that others experience external reality in a fashion that is not wholly unlike himself and that internally they are subject to the same or similar emotions, thoughts, etc., A particular facial expression or gesture, for example, may give a clue as to what the nonspeaker is experiencing internally. By simple analogy, therefore, the speaker can justifiably and reasonably speculate about the significance of some outward sign in light of what he knows about himself. In this respect both addressee and human third persons are alike to the speaker.

But face-to-face communication provides the opportunity for the speaker to obtain verbal and nonverbal input, correction, etc., immediately and directly from the addressee. In other words, the speaker's knowledge of the addressee is somehow more dynamic and capable of being altered, adjusted, and fine-tuned on the spot. This is not the case with a human third person who is typically not present during the speech event. The speaker's knowledge about him is essentially static and less susceptible to immediate adjustment.

So within the domain of potential participants in a speech event, the speaker is most proximal to himself. Out of the mass of distally-construed "others," one (or more) is selected for particular attention and interaction, who thereby achieves the status of addressee and is thus conceptually and empathetically closer to the speaker than others.

By way of summary thus far, the domains that comprise the ground-reality/irreality, space, time, and participants-are composed of subdomains that differ with respect to the conceptualizer in terms of their cognitive accessibility: the subdomain of immediate reality, the location of the conceptualizer, the moment of speaking, and the conceptualizer himself. Other subdomains are more conceptually remote.

On Directness, Proximity, Ground Domains, and Evidentials   181

In the next section I consider the nature of the experiences typified by evidential encodings from the perspective of both schematic directness and proximity. I consider an interpretation of the traditional classification of evidentials along directness lines, but ultimately I will suggest one that takes into account schematic proximity.

7.6 Evidentiality, directness, and proximity

The Wanka evidential system can be understood in terms of both abstract directness and proximity. Directness captures aspects of the system related to information source, while proximity addresses its validational character.

Directness applies in several ways. First the evidential markers can be viewed as desginating a chain of events where a perception event and a speech event are the beginning and endpoints of a path along which some original perception is "processed" or "interacted with" in one of several ways. As its name suggests the direct evidential indicates a process between the perception event and the speech event that is unmediated in character, where the speech event flows directly from the perception event. In addition, there are correlations between principal entities in each event. Note in (218) the conceptualizer C in the perception event and the speaker S are the same individual. In addition, there is a direct correspondence between the object of perception O and the designated proposition P of the speech event.

(218)   Direct experience: -mi

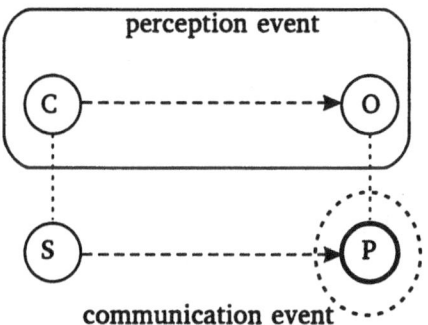

Consider also that in a typical direct perception scenario the speaker is the original perceiver who is "in on" the history of the utterance from beginning to end; he fixes his attention on some event, he processes it, and then comments on it. DeLancey (1986) has talked about the importance of this for the Tibetan evidential system in terms of the distinction between "old and new knowledge." Here the speaker is identified with the location at which the "processing" of a perception begins, a point that will become relevant to the issue of validation.

Compare these observations with indirect evidentials (the term used by Willett 1988 to refer collectively to reported and "inferred" evidence) in which some other type of event intervenes between perception and speech events, and which further involve some kind of a mismatch between elements in these events instead of correspondence.

Consider a typical hearsay situation, for instance in (219). Assuming for the sake of discussion that the scenario designated in a hearsay utterance is based on someone's actual perception, hearsay involves at least one intervening speech event between a perception event and the current speech event.

As far as correspondences among elements across the perception and current speech events are concerned, the original perceiver and the current speaker are not the same individual. The current speaker's relationship to the designated scenario O is therefore only indirect, i.e., it has been mediated through another individual. Alternatively, the current speaker can be viewed as the mediating entity between the designated scenario of the prior speech event and the designated scenario of the current speech event.

(219) Hearsay: -sh(i)

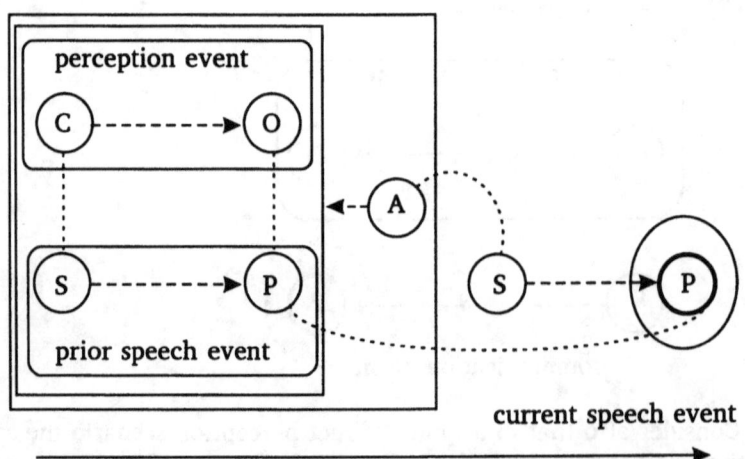

An inference involves a perception event followed by an inferencing event prior to the speech event (cf. (220)). In addition, a different set of indirect relationships between perception, speaker, and designated scenario obtains. Recall from chapter 5 that an inference is an irrealis scenario whose conceptualization is prompted by a perception/experience in conjunction with certain assumptions about the structure of the world. The conceptualizer of the scenario that underlies the inference and the speaker are the same individual. But the perception itself is not actually reflected by the designated proposition, since an inference is a hypothethized scenario. Inferences are thus indirect since an inferencing event intervenes between the perceived scene and the designated scenario of the speech event.[52]

(220) Inference: *-chr(a)*

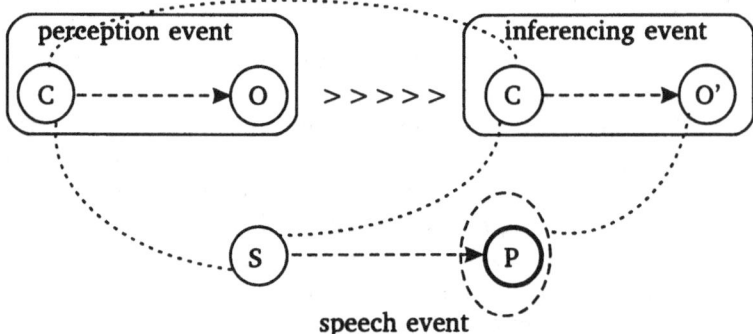

Figure (221) summarizes the correspondences observed for the evidential situation types. For the direct evidential, we observe direct and immediate (nonmediated) correspondences between elements in perception and communication events. There is a direct correlation between the perceiver in the perception event and the speaker in the communication event, as well as between an original perception and the scenario designated in the utterance. Indirect evidentials, on the other hand, involve the presence of mediating entities and noncorrespondences between elements in perception and communication events. For hearsay,

---

[52]A test could be constructed where the directness of the processing path would correlate with response times to particular kinds of questions. For example, the test subject could be shown a picture of a boy wearing a knit cap, gloves, and a sweatshirt. I predict that the question *What do you see?* (soliciting direct evidence) will be answered more quickly than *Is it cold there?* or *How old is the boy?* The answers to these latter questions require that the picture first be scanned for relevant information and then inferences be drawn on that basis. The temperature may be inferred from the fact that the boy is wearing a hat, gloves, and a sweatshirt, and his age from his general physiognomy.

the original conceptualizer does not correspond to the speaker of the current speech event, and for an inference the original perception does not correspond to the designated scenario.

(221) Correspondences between perception events and speech events.

	Conceptualizer/Speaker	Original perception/ designated Proposition
Direct	C = S	O = P
Hearsay	C ≠ S	O = P
Inference	C = S	O ≠ P

Directness, then, is particularly appropriate for explicating the more or less "objective" aspects of the process through which information is prototypically obtained. It captures the fact that for -sh(i) (hearsay) and -chra (inference) some entity interrupts a smooth transition between an original perception and a spoken proposition, whereas no such interruption exists for -mi (direct).

On the other hand, the system can also be looked at in terms of proximity notions presented above in section 7.3. As expected, the direct evidential typically reflects conceptualizer-centric elements on several levels. First, some rudimentary concept of spatial proximity is evoked, since for the conceptualizer to be an eyewitness of the designated event (prototypically-speaking), he must have been relatively near the locus of activity. We may consider the speaker to be in a relationship of maximal proximity to the locus of events when he describes a state or experience internal to himself.

In contrast to the direct evidential, the experiences encoded by indirect evidentials are conceptually distal on a number of levels with respect to the relationship that the speaker has to the designated scenario. For instance, in neither hearsay nor inference circumstances is the conceptualizer actually in the position to be an eyewitness (or direct experiencer) of the designated event. Even though reportative situations may at some level truly involve the direct evidence perspective of some conceptualizer, the one who bears that perspective to the designated scenario is not the speaker of the current speech event. All this to say that the event occurred at a location removed from the speaker's reality.

The same point can be made for an inference. Recall that an inference was characterized in part as the reconstruction of a hypothetical circumstance that could plausibly explain some kind of presently available evidence. While the evidence may be proximal to the speaker in the same way that any other directly observed situation is, the scenario designated by the inference itself is not, since it is purely speculative. It, too, is located outside the speaker's reality.

I mentioned in conjunction with direct evidence that the speaker has the status of the perceiver in the original perception event. And because he has perceptual access to the original scene, particular facets can be highlighted or defocussed at his discretion in order to package the utterance in accordance with his purposes. He is thus in the optimal position to control the construal of the original perception that is ultimately presented to the addressee. Control, as discussed in chapter 4, presumes entities located within a restricted sphere of dominion (hence, spatially or metaphorically proximal) which the conceptualizer has the potential to manipulate. Direct evidence, then, involves a high degree of conceptualizer-centricity, not only situationally, but in terms of other factors of a highly personal nature as well, such as knowledge of utterance history and construal imposition, etc.

I think it can be argued that inferences, like direct evidence situations, concern activity that is largely conceptualizer-centric and conceptualizer-driven, stemming from the fact that the speaker is the perceiver in the original perception scenario. I have argued in chapter 5 that an inference involves the conceptualizer's own perceptions/experiences, and his own extrapolations on the basis of his own assumptions. Like a direct evidence scenario, inferences concern the mental activity of the conceptualizer proper-perception begets processing begets utterance. So, as with direct evidence, the "history" of an inference is accessible to the speaker in a way that is not true of reportatives. Therefore, it seems reasonable to view an inference as a product of the speaker's uniquely personal interaction with a particular set of circumstances.

On the other hand, it does not seem to me that hearsay involves this kind of personal interaction. In a hearsay situation, the scenario designated in the utterance has been bequeathed to the speaker as a pre-packaged image. As a "nonoriginal construer" of sorts, the speaker is limited by the structure of the conceptualization he has inherited, in that he is not able to pick out, emphasize, or deemphasize facets of the original scenario at his own discretion. Ultimately, he holds a qualitatively different status than he would as the designer of an utterance concerning a perception of his own. When he passes on the information to the addressee of the current speech event, he serves principally as a sort of link in an information chain, as an intermediary rather than as an originator. By using *-shi*, the speaker, albeit in an unprofiled way, evokes his prior addressee role, as well as the fact that some other conceptualizer was involved even before he was. He thus construes himself as removed from "original perceiver" status.

The original perceiver, then, is in the optimal position to process and manipulate facets of the original perception in terms of construal imposition. This leads directly to the issue of validation. I have characterized validation as the extent to which a proposition is incorporated into the speaker's reality. It seems to me that the potential for such incorporation is something that cannot be determined extrinsically; it must be assessed by one who has "inside information" and who is, therefore, in the position to be able to judge how closely a particular proposition meshes with his current state of knowledge. This suggests that the more conceptualizer-centric an evidential process is, the more likely such a judgement could be potentially effected.

Because proximity evokes a scale and a relevant scope of some kind, it seems particularly well-suited for addressing the evidential system's schematic validational facets. By taking the speaker as the landmark, and his reality as the relevant scope against which proximity assessments are made, then the full commitment associated with -mi can be straightforwardly understood as locating a proposition within the region indicated in (222). On the other hand, -chra locates the proposition not just outside the speaker's reality, but outside of it to varying degrees (cf. (223)), in terms of necessity, probability, and possibility.

(222) Validation and -m(i)

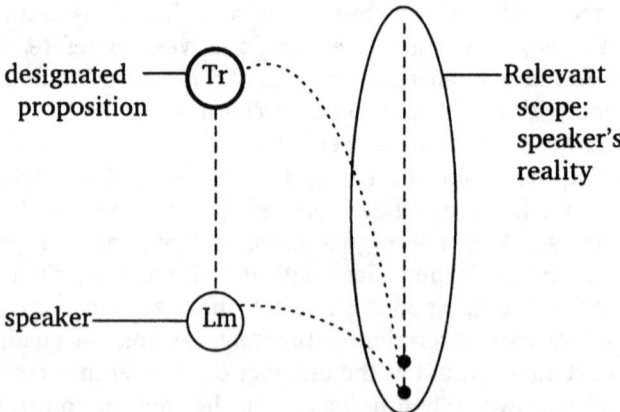

(223) Validation and -chr(a)

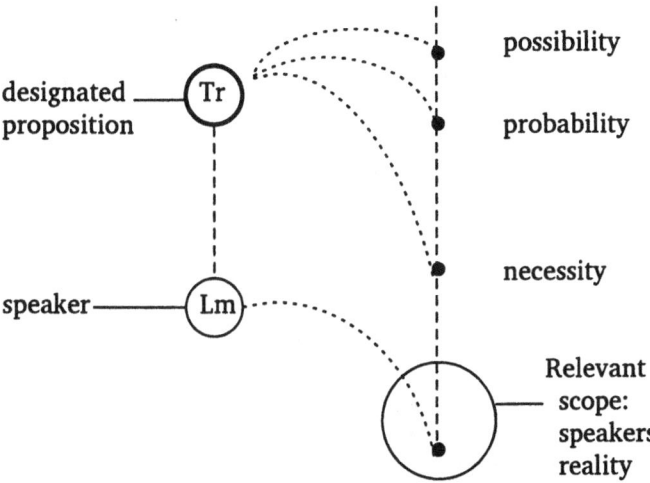

The fact that the entire validational range is encompassed by these two evidentials once again recalls the issue of -sh(i)'s validational status and could be viewed as one more factor arguing in favor of an essentially nonvalidational view of the reportative.

Whereas both -sh(i) and -chr(a) indicate 'distal' values in a gross sense of a proposition's nonincorporation into the speaker's reality, there is a difference. It is a matter of -chr(a) indicating that a proposition is unincoporated to X degree versus what -sh(i) communicates, namely that a proposition is a revelation, and is therefore unincorporated. They share the aspect of unincorporation but along entirely different parameters. For -chr(a), the status of the proposition as lying outside the speaker's view of reality is taken as the principal semantic factor; for -sh(i), 'outness' is a by-product of "revelatoriness," and is thus secondary. This is reflected in the fact that -chr(a) has a range of noncommitment values associated with it, whereas -sh(i) does not. Again, unlike -chr(a), none of the extensions of the reportative are exclusively validational in character.

And finally, the cloze testing mentioned in chapter 6 provides additional support for the characterization of -m(i) and -chr(a) as distinct from -shi along some parameter. I mentioned there that occasional substitutions between -m(i) and -chr(a) were observed, whereas substitutions were not observed between -chr(a) and -sh(i).

In chapter 4 we saw cases, albeit rare, in which an event that is technically irrealis (the typical domain of -chr(a)) has been marked nevertheless with the direct evidential. And although relatively infrequent,

-chr(a)'s values of 'necessity' indicates a region of semantic space that lies just beyond the border of commitment. So while direct evidence and conjecture are quite distinct in many ways, this fluctuation suggests that there is some region of semantic space that both -m(i) and -chr(a) may mutually access. While I have not examined all the factors involved, I do suspect that the explanation of this phenomenon will involve the conceptualizer-(non)centric.

A conceptualizer-centric characterization of validation is supported cross-linguistically. I am aware of no language having a set of grammatical markers precisely parallelling evidentials that encodes the commitment of a nonspeaker. The Nambiquara system may be considered as a move in this direction in that it expresses evidential relationships (in terms of data source) not only for speaker, but also for first person inclusive. The characterization as given by Palmer (1986:77) is unclear as to the extent to which validational associations actually accompany the individual markers. But even if there are such associations, the Nambiquara system is still speaker-centric. It does not, for instance, ground a proposition (in terms of experience and perhaps validation) to a third person to the exclusion of the speaker. This restriction on grounding is completely in line with the characterization of evidentials as grounding predications. Since third persons do not comprise part of the ground, it is not expected that a grounding predication would take a third person as a deictic reference point.

Recapping briefly, thus far I have presented schematic characterizations of directness and proximity, and then applied these concepts to the characterization of ground domains and evidentials. In the final section I will suggest that the co-occurrence tendencies between evidentials and markers for particular ground domains fall out as a natural consequence of the way in which the evidential and ground domains are construed.

7.7 Conceptual proximity and subdomain alignment

Conceptual proximity is characterized by Haiman as follows:
Two ideas are conceptually close to the extent that they
a. share semantic features, properties, or parts;
b. affect each other;
c. are factually inseparable;
d. are perceived as a unit, whether factually inseparable or not.
(1985:106ff.)

The idea that conceptual proximity may be relevant to linguistic structure is not new. Bybee's cross-linguistic examination of verb stems and inflectional categories (Bybee 1985a, b) shows that conceptual closeness has an overt iconic manifestation; the more semantically relevant (i.e., "conceptually close") an inflectional category is to the verb, the more likely it is to occur as verbally-bound morphology. Furthermore, the most relevant categories will occur closest to the stem, and this in turn will be reflected in greater morpho-phonological fusion with the stem. Fleischman (1989) details how markers of temporal distance have been pressed into service to express distance in other conceptual domains, such as modality, assertiveness, social/interpersonal distance such as politeness and evidentiality. Haiman (1989) shows how linguistic manifestations of sarcasm reflect an inherent "detachment, alienation, or emotional distance" between the speaker's words and his actual meaning.

If ground domains are egocentrically-conceptualized in terms of various subregions, then there is an inherent semantic affinity among domains that are construed as proximal, as well as a similar affinity among distal domains. These affinities fit into an idealized cognitive model of conversation where a cross-subdomain confluence such as that given in figure (224) would be evident. According to this model, we would expect that statistical counts done on conversational texts in a given language would show that speakers talk more about what they do or have done than about what someone else will do. As a further consequence, we would expect to find nonrandom co-occurrences between markers for proximal subdomains, as well as for those corresponding to distal subdomains.

(224) Proximal and distal subdomain alignment

PROXIMAL	DISTAL
1st person	3rd person
present	future
realis	irrealis

By construing evidentials in proximal/distal terms, then it seems plausible to expect nonrandom correlations between evidentials and markers for these ground subdomains as well.

I examined a corpus of fifteen conversations for co-occurrences between subject, tense and evidential marking. The corpus contained a total of 1,344 utterances. Of these, I excluded utterances with no evidential marking (414), utterances with incomplete arrays of evidential, person, and tense marking (147), and questions marked with evidentials (262). Examples (225) and (226) are based on the remaining 521 utterances, all of which indicate evidential, person of subject, and tense overtly. Example (226) gives the correlations between evidential and tense marking.

(225) Correlation of evidential and tense marking

	-m(i)		-chr(a)		-sh(i)	
	no.	%	no.	%	no.	%
fut	30	10.56	105	**49.76**	1	3.85
pot	21	7.39	38	**18.01**	0	0.00
prs	135	**47.54**	47	22.27	4	15.38
pst	98	**34.51**	21	9.95	21	**80.77**
total	284		211		26	

Out of the total number of utterances marked with the direct evidential -m(i), the vast majority, approximately 82%, appear with realis tenses (either past or present), whereas only about 18% occur with irrealis tenses (i.e., future and potential). The converse situation holds for the conjecture marker; out of the total number of utterances marked with -chr(a), roughly 68% occur with irrealis tenses, but only 32% with realis. Finally, 96% of the total number of tokens of -sh(i) occur with realis verb forms.

These figures are very much in line with what should be expected given an idealized cognitive model of conversation with subdomain alignment as a prominent feature. Present and past-the most proximal subregions of the time domain from the perspective of the speaker-bear a natural semantic affinity with proximal evidentiary experience. Similarly, future and potential regions are nonproximal with respect to the speaker, which is also a dominant characteristic of the evidentiary experience typically encoded by the conjecture marker. I suspect that the high correlation of -sh(i) with realis tenses (especially past) reflects the prototypical case, namely, that hearsay involves a prior report of a previous actual event.

The correlations between evidential marking and grammatical subject are given in (226).

(226) Correlation of evidential and subject

	-m(i)		-chr(a)		-sh(i)	
	no.	%	no.	%	no.	%
1	152	53.52	70	33.18	0	0.00
2	26	9.15	71	33.65	4	15.38
3	104	36.62	63	29.86	22	84.62
12	2	0.70	7	3.32	0	0.00
total	284		211		26	

Most utterances marked with -m(i) also have first-person subjects (roughly 54%), approximately 37% have third-person subjects, and a mere 9% have second-person subjects. The total number of -chr(a)-marked utterances are relatively evenly divided between first-, second-, and third-person subjects. Of the total number of -sh(i)-marked utterances, the vast majority (85%) occur with third-person subjects. Finally, first inclusive subjects (12) occur only 9 times, most of which occur in utterances marked with -chr(a).

I attribute the strong correlation between the direct evidential and first person marking to the proximal aspect shared by both. The high number of third-person subjects among -sh(i)-marked utterances is, once again, presumably due to the nature of prototypical hearsay which almost always concerns activities of nonspeech event participants. At present it is unclear why the -chr(a)-marked utterances would have a roughly equal distribution of subject markings, although this may be due to the simultaneously proximal/distal character of the conjecture evidential.

I take co-occurrences such as these to be nontrivial manifestations of particular aspects of conceptualization that are brought to bear on these domains. Subdomain alignment comprises part of a more encompassing idealized cognitive model of conversation. It suggests furthermore that the prototypical meanings of evidentials will be found within certain subdomain alignments, e.g., proximal evidential meanings should occur with proximal subdomain alignments. We have found this to have some basis, as indicated by examples presented previously.

(227) a. *pata-yuu-ña-m-ari   ka-ya-a ya'a*
         stomach-HAVE-now-DIR-EMPH be-IMPV-1 I
         I sure AM pregnant.

b. *kuti-mu-n'a-ña-chr*
return-AFAR-3FUT-NOW-CONJ
He will probably come back.

c. *luisa-sh prista-ka-mu-la*
Luisa-REP borrow-REF-AFAR-3PST
(I was told) Luisa borrowed it.

The corollary, namely, that nonprototypical meanings will be found in noncanonical subdomain alignments, also appears to have some validity. Recall from the discussion of the conjecture evidential in chapter 5 that Weber (1989:425ff.) notes a number of cases where the conjecture marker achieves various so-called "rhetorical effects."

(228) a. *chay-ta musya-yka-:-chi*
that-ACC know-IMPV-1-CONJ
I know that. [but with rhetorical force of: So you think I know? I don't know a thing about it!]

b. *noqa aywa-yka-:-chi qam-paq-qa*
I go-IMPV-1-CNJ you-PUR-TOP
'I'm going on your behalf.' [but with rhetorical force of: 'You might have thought I was going there, but I'm not.']

c. *sapu-ta-chi ima-chi haru-riyku-: hahaa hahaha*
frog-ACC-CONJ what-CONJ step-ASP-1 (laughs)
It seems I've stepped on a frog, hahaha.

Two things should be apparent from these examples: (1) they all convey a sense of irony or sarcasm, a meaning that in the present analysis is considered an extension from the prototype of inference, and (2) they all involve first-person subject marking in conjunction with the conjecture evidential, which could be considered as a radically noncanonical subdomain alignment since speakers do not normally hypothesize about their own activities.

While I do not have a great deal of data from outside the Quechua language family to establish firm cross-linguistic patterns, some support for the correlation between noncanonical domain alignment and nonprototypical meanings comes from Kogi (Chibchan, Colombia), where schematic proximity appears to play a prominent role within the evidential system. According to Grace Hensarling (p.c.) two of the evidential particles "are distinguished on a scale of 'closeness'—whether by first-hand knowledge, by physical proximity, by temporal proximity, or by familiarity." Another set of markers expresses various kinds of "lack of knowledge," a kind of nonproximity. Among this group is the question particle -sh(i) (not related to the reportative -sh(i) of Quechuan languages), which may technically occur in conjunction with any person or tense, but is markedly less frequent with first person. This parallels the Wanka tendency to use -chr(a) with first person less frequently than with -m(i). However, Hensarling reports that in one Kogi example where the first person does occur in conjunction with -sh(i), the result is specifically a "sarcastic, rhetorical" sense.

Admittedly, much work remains to be done in this area. But there is at least tentative evidence to suggest that an adequate theory of evidentiality should take into consideration the central issue of this chapter-that schematic directness and proximity are principles organizing the conceptualization and interaction of evidentials and related domains.

7.8 Areas for further study

There are a number of issues that have arisen during the course of this investigation which bear on our overall understanding of evidentiality at large and the Wanka system in particular, but which have fallen outside the limits of the study and, therefore, have not been researched with any degree of depth. Four principal topics come to mind: (1) how the position of an evidential affects the interpretation of the sentence, particularly in the case of multi-clausal sentences; (2) the semantic relationships between the evidential suffixes and nonevidential suffixes that indicate other aspects of epistemic modality, e.g., scorn; (3) zero-evidential marking; and (4) restrictions on the evidential marking of Question-and-Answer pairs. It is hoped that future work, either by myself or by others will contribute to our understanding of these areas.

7.9 Conclusion

This study presents a multifaceted picture of the Wanka evidential categories structured around prototypes, schemas, and well-motivated conceptual links between the various members within each category.

I have showed that evidentiality pertains to the semantic domain of epistemic modality, that each evidential involves some notion of data source at its semantic core, and that the prominence of validation is not the same for each evidential.

Palmer states that it may be difficult or even impossible to identify a prototype modality given its complexity (1986:3). The idea that all of modality is handled under the rubric of "speaker attitude," for example, is perhaps too schematic to be of much relevance or use. I hope to have shown that at least one subdomain of modality can be insightfully described in terms of networks of related senses organized around prototypes, and that, in principle, such an approach is applicable to the field of modality as a whole.

References

Adelaar. Willem. 1977. Tarma grammar: Grammar, texts, dictionary. Lisse: Peter de Ridder.
———. 1988. Marcadores del aspecto en el quechua del centro de Peru. Lingüística de las Américas. 45º Congreso Internacional de Americanistas. Bogotá: Ediciones Uniandes.
Akatsuka, Noriko. 1985. Conditionals and the epistemic scale. Language 61:625–39.
Aksu-Koc, Ayhan and Dan Slobin. 1986. A psychological account of the development and use of evidentials in Turkish. In Wallace Chafe and Johanna Nichols (eds.), 159–67.
Anderson, Lloyd. 1986. Evidentials, paths of change and mental maps: Typologically regular asymmetries. In Wallace Chafe and Johanna Nichols (eds.), 273–312.
Anderson, Stephen and Edward Keenan. 1985. Deixis. In Timothy Shopen (ed.), Language typology and syntactic description, vol. 3: Grammatical categories and the lexicon, 258–308. Cambridge: Cambridge University Press.
Aoki, Haruo. 1986. Evidentials in Japanese. In Wallace Chafe and Johanna Nichols (eds.), 223–38.
Ballard, Lee. 1974. Telling it like it was, part 1:4, The 'hearsay particle' of the Philippine languages. Notes on Translation 51.
Barnes, Janet. 1984. Evidentials in the Tuyuca verb. International Journal of American Linguistics 50:255–71.

Bascom, William R. 1965. Folklore and Anthropology. In Alan Dundes (ed.), 25–33.
Berlin, Brent and Paul Kay. 1969. Basic color terms: Their universality and evolution. Berkeley: University of California Press.
Bertonio, Ludovico. 1603. Arte y grammatica muy copiosa de la lengua aymara. Rome: Luis Zannetti.
Beuchat, P. D. 1965. Riddles in Bantu. The study of folklore. In Alan Dundes (ed.), 182–205.
Blass, Regina. 1990. Relevance relations in discourse. Cambridge: Cambridge University Press.
Boas, Franz, ed. 1911. Handbook of American Indian languages, part 1. Smithsonian Institution, Bureau of American Ethnology, Bulletin 40. Washington, D.C.: Government Printing Office.
———. 1922. Handbook of American Indian languages, part 2. Smithsonian Institution, Bureau of American Ethnology, Bulletin 40. Washington, D.C.: Government Printing Office.
———. 1947. Kwakiutl grammar, with a glossary of the suffixes. Transactions of the American Philosophical Society 37(3):201–377.
Borgman, Donald. 1990. Sanuma. In Desmond Derbyshire and Geoffrey Pullum (eds.), 15–248.
Brown, Gillian and George Yule. 1983. Discourse analysis. Cambridge: Cambridge University Press.
Brown, Penelope and Steven Levinson. 1978. Universals in language usage: Politeness phenomena. In Evelyn Goody (ed.), 56–289.
Brugman, Claudia. 1989. The story of over: Polysemy, semantics and the structure of the lexicon. New York: Garland.
Bybee, Joan. 1985a. Morphology: A study of the relation between meaning and form. Typological Studies in Language, vol. 9. Amsterdam: John Benjamins.
———. 1985b. Diagrammatic iconicity in stem-inflection relations. In John Haiman (ed.), Iconicity in syntax, 11–47. Amsterdam: John Benjamins.
Bybee, Joan and William Pagliuca. 1985. Cross-linguistic comparison and the development of grammatical meaning. In Jacek Fisiak (ed.), Historical semantics, historical word formation, 59–83. Berlin: Mouton.
Carpenter, Lawrence. 1982. Ecuadorian Quichua: Descriptive sketch and variation. Ph.D. dissertation. Gainesville: University of Florida.
Casad, Eugene. 1984. Cora. In Ronald Langacker (ed.), Southern Uto-Aztecan grammatical sketches, 151–459. Dallas: Summer Institute of Linguistics and University of Texas at Arlington.
———. 1992. Cognition, history and Cora yee. Cognitive Linguistics 3:151–86.

———, ed. 1996. The radial structure of the Wanka reportative. Cognitive linguistics in the Redwoods: The expansion of a new paradigm in linguistics. Berlin and New York: Mouton de Gruyter.
Cerrón-Palomino, Rodolfo. 1973. Evolución del fonema */q/ en Ya?a Wanka. Documento de Trabajo No. 15. Lima: CILA, UNMSM.
———. 1975. Hispanismos en el quechua wanka. Documento de Trabajo No. 30. Lima: CILA, UNMSM.
———. 1976a. Gramática quechua Junín-Huanca. Lima: Ministerio de Educación e Instituto de Estudios Peruanos.
———. 1976b. Diccionario quechua Junín-Huanca. Lima: Ministerio de Educación e Instituto de Estudios Peruanos.
———. 1977. Huanca Quechua dialectology. Ph.D. Dissertation. Urbana-Champaign: University of Illinois.
———. 1987. Lingüística quechua. Cuzco: Centro de Estudios Rurales Andinos "Bartolomé de las Casas."
Chafe, Wallace. 1976. Givenness, contrastiveness, definiteness, subjects, topics and point of view. In Charles Li (ed.), Subject and topic, 25–55. New York: Academic Press.
———. 1986. Evidentiality in English conversation and academic writing. In Wallace Chafe and Johanna Nichols (eds.), 261–72.
Chafe, Wallace and Johanna Nichols, eds. 1986. Evidentiality: The linguistic encoding of epistemology. Advances in Discourse Processes, vol. 20. Norwood, N.J.: Ablex.
Chung, Sandra and Alan Timberlake. 1985. Tense, aspect, and mood. In Timothy Shopen (ed.), Language typology and syntactic description, vol. 3: Grammatical categories and the lexicon, 202–57. Cambridge: Cambridge University Press.
Cole, Peter. 1985. Imbabura Quechua. London: Croom Helm.
Comrie, Bernard. 1985. Tense. Cambridge: Cambridge University Press.
Coombs, David, Heidi Coombs, and Robert Weber. 1976. Gramática quechua San Martín. Lima: Ministerio de Educación e Instituto de Estudios Peruanos.
Cowan, Marion. 1969. Tzotzil grammar. Norman, Okla: Summer Institute of Linguistics.
Cusihuamán, Antonio. 1976. Gramática quechua Cuzco-Collao. Lima: Ministerio de Educación e Instituto de Estudios Peruanos.
Dahl, Östen. 1990. Review of Wallace Chafe and Johanna Nichols, eds., Evidentiality: The linguistic encoding of epistemology. Journal of Pragmatics 14:682–86.
Dedenbach-Salazar Sáenz, Sabine. 1991. El punto de vista y la evidencialidad en los textos de Huarochirí (Per·, Siglo 17). Paper presented at the International Symposium: Textuality of Amerindian

Cultures: Production, Reception, Strategies. Institute of Latin American Culture Studies, King's College, London, May 1991.
DeLancey, Scott. 1986. Evidentiality and volitionality in Tibetan. In Wallace Chafe and Johanna Nichols (eds.), 203–13.
———. 1990. Ergativity and the cognitive model of event structure in Lhasa Tibetan. Cognitive Linguistics 1:289–321.
———. 1997. Mirativity. Linguistic Typology 1:33–52.
Derbyshire, Desmond. 1979. Hixkaryana. Lingua Descriptive Series 1. Amsterdam: North Holland.
———. 1986. Comparative survey of morphology and syntax in Brazilian Arawakan. In Desmond Derbyshire and Geoffrey Pullum (eds.), 469–566.
Derbyshire, Desmond and Geoffrey Pullum, eds. 1986. Handbook of Amazonian languages, vol. 1. Berlin: Mouton de Gruyter.
——— and ———. 1990. Handbook of Amazonian languages, vol. 2. Berlin: Mouton de Gruyter.
Dinsmore, John. 1979. Pragmatics, formal theory, and the analysis of presupposition. Ph.D. dissertation. San Diego: University of California.
Dundes, Alan, ed. 1965. The study of folklore. Englewood Cliff, N.J.: Prentice-Hall.
Everett, Daniel. 1986. Pirahã. In Desmond Derbyshire and Geoffrey Pullum (eds.), 200–325.
Fauconnier, Gilles. 1985. Mental spaces. Cambridge, Mass: MIT Press.
Firbas, Jan. 1971. On the concept of communicative dynamism in the theory of functional sentence perspective. Studia minora facultatis philosophicae universitatis brunensis. u.p.
Fleischman, Suzanne. 1989. Temporal distance: A basic linguistic metaphor. Studies in Language 13:1–50.
Flores Canchanya, Roberta. 1983. ¿Imallash aykallash? Seminario de Autores Quechua Hablantes., Chupaca, Perú. Huancayo, Perú: Dirección Departamental de Educación, Huancayo e Instituto Lingüístico de Verano.
Floyd, Rick. 1985. -tan and the grammatical encoding of contextual dependency for question interpretation in Wanka. Paper presented at the 45th International Congress of Americanists, Andean Linguistics Symposium. Bogotá, Colombia, July 1985.
———. 1989. A cognitive analysis of evidentiality in Wanka. Fourth Meeting of the Pacific Linguistics Conference, 134–53. Eugene: University of Oregon.
———. 1993. The structure of Quechua evidential categoreis. Ph.D. dissertation. San Diego: University of California.

Frank, Jane. 1990. You call that a rhetorical question? Forms and functions of rhetorical questions in conversation. Journal of Pragmatics 14:723–38.
Friedman, Victor. 1986. Evidentiality in the Balkans: Bulgarian, Macedonian, and Albanian. In Wallace Chafe and Johanna Nichols (eds.), 168–87.
Geeraerts, Dirk. 1988a. Where does prototypicality come from? In Brygida Rudzka-Ostyn (ed.), 207–29.
———. 1988b. Cognitive grammar and the history of lexical semantics. In Brygida Rudzka-Ostyn (ed.), 647–77.
Givón, Talmy. 1972. Studies in ChiBemba and Bantu grammar. Studies in African Linguistics, supplement 3:1–247.
———. 1982. Evidentiality and epistemic space. Studies in Language 6:23-49.
———. 1984. Syntax: A functional-typological introduction, vol. 1. Amsterdam: John Benjamins.
———. 1990. Syntax: A functional-typological introduction, vol. 2. Amsterdam: John Benjamins.
Goody, Evelyn, ed. 1978. Questions and politeness: Strategies in social interaction. Cambridge: Cambridge University Press.
Goddard, Pliny Earle. 1911. Athapascan (Hupa). In Franz Boas (ed.), 85–158.
Gordon, Lynn. 1986. The development of evidentials in Maricopa. In Wallace Chafe and Johanna Nichols (eds.), 75–88.
Greenberg, Joseph. 1966. Some universals of grammar with particular reference to the order of meaningful elements. In Joseph Greenberg (ed.), Universals of Language, 73–113. Cambridge: MIT Press.
Gregores, Emma and Jorge A. Suárez. 1967. A description of colloquial Guaraní. The Hague: Mouton.
Grice, H. Paul. 1975. Logic and conversation. In Peter Cole and J. Morgan (eds.), Syntax and semantics 3: Speech acts, 41–58. New York: Academic Press.
Haas, Mary. 1941. Tunica. Handbook of American Indian languages, vol. 4, 1–143. New York: J. J. Augustin.
———. 1976. Boas, Sapir and Bloomfield. In Wallace Chafe (ed.), American Indian languages and American linguistics, 59–69. Lisse: Peter de Ridder.
Haiman, John. 1980. Dictionaries and encyclopedias. Lingua 50:329–57.
———. 1985. Natural syntax. Cambridge: Cambridge University Press.
———. 1989. Alienation in grammar. Studies in Language 13:129–70.
———. 1990. Sarcasm as theater. Cognitive Linguistics 1:181–205.

———. 1992. Moods and metamessages: Alienation as a mood. Paper presented at the Symposium on Mood and Modality, Albuquerque, N.Mex., May 1992.

Hardman, Martha. 1986. Data-source marking in the Jaqi languages. In Wallace Chafe and Johanna Nichols (eds.), 113–36.

Hargreaves, David. 1991a. The concept of intentional action in Kathmandu Newari. Ph.D. dissertation. Eugene: University of Oregon.

———. 1991b. The conceptual structure of intentional action: Data from Kathmandu Newari. Berkeley Linguistics Society 17:379–89.

Haviland, John. 1987. Fighting words: evidential particles, affect and argument. Berkeley Linguistics Society 13:343–54.

Hensarling, Grace. 1982. The Kogi verb phrase. Ms.

Hess, H. Harwood. 1968. The syntactic structure of Mezquital Otomí. The Hague: Mouton.

Hockett, Charles. 1958. A course in modern linguistics. New York: Macmillan.

Holland, Dorothy and Naomi Quinn, eds. 1987. Cultural models in language and thought. Cambridge: Cambridge University Press.

Hopper, Paul. 1991. On some principles of grammaticalization. In Elizabeth Traugott and Bernd Heine (eds.), Approaches to grammaticalization, vol. 1, 17–35. Amsterdam: John Benjamins.

Hopper Paul and Sandra Thompson. 1984. The discourse basis for lexical categories in universal grammar. Language 60:703–52.

Hurley, Joni Kay. 1991. Expressing certainty and doubt in Quichua: The use of validators. Paper presented at the International Conference on Language, Language Policy and Education in the Andes, Oct. 28–30. University of Delaware, Newark.

Hutchins, Edwin. 1980. Culture and inference: A Trobriand case study. Cambridge: Harvard University Press.

Hymes, Dell. 1981. In vain I tried to tell you. Philadelphia: University of Pennsylvania Press.

Inoue, Kyoko. 1978. Speaker's perspectives and temporal expressions—A case study from Japanese and English. University of Michigan Papers in Linguistics, 105–15.

Jacobsen, William. 1986. The heterogeneity of evidentials in Makah. In Wallace Chafe and Johanna Nichols (eds.), 3–28.

Jake, Janice and Carmen Chuquín. 1979. Validation suffixes in Imbabura Quechua. Chicago Linguistic Society 15:172–84.

Jakobson, Roman. 1971 [1957]. Shifters, verbal categories, and the Russian verb. Selected writings, vol. 2, 130–47. The Hague: Mouton.

Kakumasu, James. 1986. Urubu-Kaapor. In Desmond Derbyshire and Geoffrey Pullum (eds.), 326–403.
Kay, Paul. 1987. Linguistic competence and folk theories of language: Two English hedges. In Dorothy Holland and Naomi Quinn (eds.), 67–77.
Koehn, Edward and Sally Koehn. 1986. Apalai. In Desmond Derbyshire and Geoffrey Pullum (eds.), 33–127.
Kuroda, S. Y. 1973. When epistemology, style and grammar meet—A case study from Japanese. In Paul Kiparksy and Steven R. Anderson (eds.), A Festschrift for Morris Halle, 377–91. New York: Holt, Reinhardt, and Winston.
Kwong, Luke Kang. 1989. The Cantonese utterance particle LA and the accomplishment of common understanding in conversation. IPrA Papers in Pragmatics 3:39–87.
Labov, William and David Fanshel. 1977. Therapeutic discourse: Psychotherapy as conversation. New York: Academic Press.
Lakoff, George. 1987. Women, fire and dangerous things: What categories reveal about the mind. Chicago: University of Chicago Press.
Lakoff, George and Mark Johnson. 1980. Metaphors we live by. Chicago: University of Chicago Press.
Landerman, Peter. 1979. 16th-Century sibilants in Spanish, Quechua and Aymara: A three-sided puzzle. Paper presented at the Workshop in Andean Linguistics, Congress of Americanists, Vancouver, BC.
——. 1991. Quechua dialects and their classification. Ph.D. dissertation. Los Angeles: University of California.
Langacker, Ronald. 1978. The form and meaning of the English auxiliary. Language 54: 853–82.
—— 1985. Observations and speculations on subjectivity. In John Haiman (ed.), Iconicity in Syntax (Typological studies in language, vol. 6.), 109–50. Amsterdam: John Benjamins.
——. 1987a. Foundations of cognitive grammar, vol. 1: Theoretical prerequisites. Stanford: Stanford University Press.
——. 1987b. Grammatical ramifications of the setting/participant distinction. Berkeley Linguistic Society 13:383–94.
——. 1988a. A Usage-based model. In Brygida Rudzka-Ostyn (ed.), 127–61.
——. 1988b. A view of linguistic semantics. In Brygida Rudzka-Ostyn (ed.), 49-90.
——. 1990. Subjectification. Cognitive Linguistics 1(1):5–38.
——. 1991. Foundations of cognitive grammar, vol. 2: Descriptive application. Stanford: Stanford University Press.

Larson, Mildred. 1978. The functions of reported speech in discourse. Dallas: University of Texas, Arlington and The Summer Institute of Linguistics.

Laughren, Mary. 1981. A preliminary description of propositional particles in Walpiri. In Steven Swartz (ed.), Papers in Walpiri grammar, In memory of Lothar Jagst, 129–63. Darwin: The Summer Institute of Linguistics-Australia.

Lee, Hyo Sang. 1985. Consciously known but unassimilated information: A pragmatic analysis of the epistemic modal suffix -*kun* in Korean. Pacific Linguistics Conference 1. Eugene, Oreg.: University of Oregon.

Lehmann, Christian. 1985. Grammaticalization: Synchronic variation and diachronic change. Lingua e Stile 20(3):303–18.

Levinsohn, Steven. 1975. Functional perspective in Inga. Journal of Linguistics 11:1–37.

———. 1979. Pragmatics and social deixis: Reclaiming the notion of conventional implicature. Berkeley Linguistics Society 5:206–23.

———. 1983. Pragmatics. Cambridge: Cambridge University Press.

Lindner, Susan. 1981. A lexico-semantic analysis of verb-particle constructions with up and out. Ph. D. dissertation. San Diego: University of California.

Longacre, Robert. 1976. An anatomy of speech notions. Lisse: Peter de Ridder.

Lowe, Ivan. 1972. On the relation of the formal and sememic matrices with illustrations from Nambiquara. Foundations of Language 8:360–90.

Lyons, John. 1977. Semantics, vols. 1 and 2. Cambridge: Cambridge University Press.

Maldonado, Ricardo. 1992. Middle voice: The case of Spanish *se*. Ph.D. dissertation. San Diego: University of California.

Matteson, Esther. 1965. The Piro (Arawakan) language. Berkeley: University of California Press.

McLendon, Sally. 1982. Meaning, rhetorical structure, and discourse organization in myth. In Deborah Tannen (ed.), 284–305.

Miller, Cheryl. n.d. Some aspects of negation in Callejon de Huayllas Quechua. Ms.

Mithun, Marianne. 1986. Evidential diachrony in northern Iroquoian. In Wallace Chafe and Johanna Nichols (eds.), 89–112.

Nichols, Johanna. 1986. The bottom line: Chinese Pidgin Russian. In Wallace Chafe and Johanna Nichols (eds.), 239–57.

Ochs, Elinor. 1979. Planned and unplanned discourse. In Talmy Givón (ed.), Syntax and semantics, vol. 12: Discourse and syntax, 51–80. New York: Academic Press.

Orr, Carolyn and Robert Longacre. 1968. Proto-quechumaran. Language 44:528–55.
Oswalt, Robert. 1986. The evidential system of Kashaya. In Wallace Chafe and Johanna Nichols (eds.), 29–45.
Palmer, Frank R. 1986. Mood and modality. Cambridge: Cambridge University Press.
Parker, Gary. 1963. La clasificación genética de los dialectos quechuas. Revista del Museo Nacional (Peru) 32:241–52.
———. 1976. Gramática quechua Ancash-Huailas. Lima: Ministerio de Educación e Instituto de Estudios Peruanos.
Payne, Doris L. and Thomas E. Payne. 1990. Yagua. In Desmond Derbyshire and Geoffrey Pullum (eds.), 249–474.
Quesada, Felix. 1976. Gramática quechua Cajamarca-Cañaris. Lima: Ministerio de Educación e Instituto de Estudios Peruanos.
Ráez, José Francisco María. 1917. Gramáticas en el Quichua-Huanca y en el de Ayacucho. Lima: Sanmarti y Ca.
Rosch, Eleanor. 1978. Principles of categorization. In Eleanor Rosch and Barbara B. Lloyd (eds.), Cognition and categorization, 27–48. Hillsdale, N.J.: Lawrence Erlbaum Associates.
Rudzka-Ostyn, Brygida, ed. 1988. Topics in cognitive linguistics. Current Issues in Linguistic Theory 50. Amsterdam: John Benjamins.
———. 1989. Prototypes, schemas, and cross-category correspondences: The case of ask. Linguistics 27:613–61.
Sacks, Harvey and Emanuel Schegloff. 1979. Two preferences in the organization of reference to persons in conversation and their interaction. In George Psathas (ed.), Everyday language: Studies in ethnomethodology, 15-21. New York: Irvington.
Sacks, Harvey, Emanuel Schegloff, and Gail Jefferson. 1978. A simplest systematics for the organization of turn-taking in conversation. In Jim Scheinkein (ed.), Studies in the organization of conversational interaction. Language, thought, and culture. New York: Academic Press.
Sadock, Jerrold and Arnold Zwicky. 1985. Speech act distinctions in syntax. In Timothy Shopen (ed.), Language typology and syntactic description, vol. 1, 155–96. Cambridge: Cambridge University Press.
Salkie, Raphael. 1988. Review of F. R. Palmer, mood and modality, Journal of Linguistics 24:240–3.
Sapir, Edward. 1922. Takelma. In Franz Boas (ed.), 1–296.
Schank, Roger C. and Robert P. Abelson. 1977. Scripts, plans, goals, and understanding. New York: Academic Press.
Schiffrin, Deborah. 1987. Discourse markers. Studies in Interactional Sociolinguistics 5. Cambridge: Cambridge University Press.

Schlichter, Alice. 1986. The origins and deictic nature of Wintu evidentials. In Wallace Chafe and Johanna Nichols (eds.), 46–59.
Sherzer, Joel F. 1976. An areal-typological study of American Indian languages north of Mexico. North-Holland Linguistic Series 20. Amsterdam: North-Holland.
Shinzato, Rumiko. 1991. Epistemic properties of temporal auxiliaries: A case study from Okinawan, Japanese, and Old Japanese. Linguistics 29:53–77.
Shirai, Yasuhiro. 1990. Putting PUT to use: Prototype and metaphorical extension. Issues in Applied Linguistics 1:78–97.
Silverstein, M. 1974. Dialectal developments in Chinookan tense-aspect systems: An areal-historical analysis. International Journal of American Linguistics, Memoir 29.
Slobin, Dan and Ayhan A. Aksu. 1982. Tense, aspect and modality in the use of the Turkish evidential. In Paul Hopper (ed.), Tense-aspect: Between semantics and pragmatics, 185–200. Amsterdam: John Benjamins.
Slobin, Dan and Karo Zimmer, eds. 1986. Studies in Turkish linguistics. Amsterdam and Philadelphia: John Benjamins.
Soto Ruiz, Clodoaldo. 1976. Gramática quechua: Ayacucho-Chanca. Lima: Ministerio de Educación, Instituto de Estudios Peruanos.
Sparing, Margarethe. 1984. The perception of reality in the volkmärchen of Schleswig-Holstein: A study in interpersonal relationships and world view. Lanham, Md.: University Press of America and The Summer Institute of Linguistics.
Sperber, Dan and Deirdre Wilson. 1986. Relevance: Communication and cognition. Oxford: Basil Blackwell.
Steele, Susan. 1973. The positional tendencies of modal elements and their theoretical implications. Ph.D. dissertation. San Diego: University of California.
Stubbs, Michael. 1983. Discourse analysis: The sociolinguistic analysis of natural language. Chicago: University of Chicago Press.
Swadesh, Morris. 1939. Nootka internal syntax. International Journal of American Linguistics 9:77–102.
Sweetser, Eve. 1982. Root and epistemic modals: Causality in two worlds. Berkeley Linguistics Society 8:484–507.
———. 1987. The definition of lie: An examination of the folk theories underlying a semantic prototype. In Dorothy Holland and Naomi Quinn (eds.), 43–66.
———. 1988. Grammaticalization and semantic bleaching. Berkeley Linguistics Society 14:389–405.

———. 1991. From etymology to pragmatics: metaphorical and cultural aspects of semantic structure. Cambridge: Cambridge University Press.
Talmy, Leonard. 1985. Force dynamics in language and cognition. Cognitive Science 12:49–100.
———. 1991. Fictive motion and change in language and perception. Paper presented at Second Meeting of the International Cognitive Linguistics Association, July 1991, Santa Cruz, California.
Tannen, Deborah, ed. 1982. Georgetown University Round Table on Languages and Linguistics 1981. Washington D.C.: Georgetown University Press.
Taylor, Talbot and Deborah Cameron. 1987. Analyzing conversation: Rules and units in the structure of talk. Oxford: Pergamon.
Thurgood, Graham. 1986. The nature and origins of the Akha evidential system. In Wallace Chafe and Johanna Nichols (eds.), 214–22.
Thompson, Sandra and Anthony Mulac. 1991. A quantitative perspective on the grammaticization of epistemic parentheticals in English. In Elizabeth Traugott and Bernd Heine (eds.), Approaches to grammaticalization, vol. 2, 313–30. Amsterdam: John Benjamins.
Torero, Alfredo. 1964. Los dialectos quechuas. Anales Científicos, 2:446-78. La Universidad Nacional Agraria, La Molina, Peru.
Torres Rubio, Diego de. 1619. Arte de la lengua quichua. Lima: Francisco Lasso.
Traugott, Elizabeth. 1989. On the rise of epistemic meanings in English: An example of subjectification in semantic change. Language 65(1):31–55.
Utley, Francis. 1965. Folk literature: An operational definition. In Alan Dundes (ed.), 7–24.
Verspoor, Marjolyn, Kee Dong Lee, and Eve Sweetser, eds. 1997. Observations on Wanka Quechua conjecture marking and subjection. Lexical and syntactic constructions and the construction of meaning: Proceedings of the bi-annual ICLA meeting in Albuquerque, July 1995, 129-47. Amsterdam and Philadelphia: John Benjamins.
Watson, D. N. 1991. Critical faults and fallacies of questioning. Journal of Pragmatics 15:337–66.
Weber, David. 1986. Information perspective, profile, and patterns in Quechua. In Wallace Chafe and Johanna Nichols (eds.), 137–55.
———. 1989. A grammar of Huallaga (Huánuco) Quechua. Los Angeles: University of California.
Weber, Diana. 1976. Presuposiciones de preguntas en el quechua de Huánuco. Documento de Trabajo 8. Yarinacocha, Peru: Instituto Lingüístico de Verano.

Weber, Robert and Nancy Weber. 1976. Negoción en quechua. Documento de Trabajo 7, 9–57. Yarinacocha, Peru: Instituto Lingüístico de Verano.

Whistler, Kenneth. 1986. Evidentials in Patwin. In Wallace Chafe and Johanna Nichols (eds.), 60–74.

Whorf, Benjamin. 1956. Language, thought and reality. In John B. Carrol (ed.), Selected writings of Benjamin Lee Whorf. Cambridge, Mass.: MIT Press.

Willett, Thomas. 1988. A Cross-linguistic survey of the grammaticization of evidentiality. Studies in Language 12:51–97.

Wise, Mary Ruth. 1986. Preandine Arawakan. In Desmond Derbyshire and Geoffrey Pullum (eds.), 567–642.

Wittgenstein, Ludwig. 1953. Philosophical investigations. New York: Macmillan.

Woodbury, Anthony. 1986. Interactions of tense and evidentiality: A study of Sherpa and English. In Wallace Chafe and Johanna Nichols (eds.), 188–202.

Zadeh, Lotfi. 1965. Fuzzy sets. Information and Control 8:338–53.

Zahn, Charlotte n.d. The reportative suffix in Pastaza Quechua (Inga). ms.